MENTORING IN PHYSICAL EDUCATION AND SPORTS COACHING

Mentoring is a core element of any successful teacher education or coach education programme, with evidence suggesting that teachers and coaches who are mentored early in their careers are more likely to become effective practitioners. Physical education and sports coaching share important pedagogical, practical and cultural terrain, and mentoring has become a vital tool with which to develop confidence, self-reflection and problem-solving abilities in trainee and early career physical education (PE) teachers and sports coaches. This is the first book to introduce key theory and best practice in mentoring, for mentors and mentees, focusing on the particular challenges and opportunities in physical education and sports coaching.

Written by a team of international experts with extensive practical experience of mentoring in PE and coaching, the book clearly explains what mentoring is, how it should work, and how an understanding of socio-cultural factors can form the foundation of good mentoring practice. The book explores practical issues in mentoring in physical education, including pre-service and newly qualified teachers, and in coach education, including mentoring in high-performance sport and the role of national governing bodies (NGBs). Each chapter includes real mentoring stories as well as practical guidance and definitions of key terms, and a pedagogy toolbox brings together the most important themes and techniques for easy reference. This is a hugely useful book for all teacher and coach education degree programmes, for any practising teacher or coach involved in mentoring, and for schools, clubs, sports organisations or NGBs looking to develop mentoring schemes.

Fiona C. Chambers is the Director for Sports Studies and Physical Education in the School of Education at University College Cork, and is a Senior Lecturer in Education (Sports Studies and Physical Education). Her primary research interest is in initial and career-long professional learning for PE teachers and its impact on young people's learning in PE and sport. Fiona has a particular interest in the role of mentor education in developing the pedagogies that PE teachers need to use sport effectively to promote the health and wellbeing of pupils. She is a link convener of the new Sport Pedagogy Network in the European Educational Research Association (EERA), has published extensively in peer-reviewed publications and is a reviewer for *Research Quarterly for Exercise and Sport, Physical Education and Sport Pedagogy, European Physical Education Review,* the *International Journal of Sport Policy and Politics* and the American Educational Research Association.

MENTORING IN PHYSICAL EDUCATION AND SPORTS COACHING

Edited by Fiona C. Chambers

Routledge
Taylor & Francis Group

LONDON AND NEW YORK

First published 2015
by Routledge
2 Park Square, Milton Park, Abingdon, Oxon OX14 4RN

and by Routledge
711 Third Avenue, New York, NY 10017

Routledge is an imprint of the Taylor & Francis Group, an informa business

British Library Cataloguing in Publication Data
A catalogue record for this book is available from the British Library

Library of Congress Cataloging in Publication Data
Chambers, Fiona C.
Mentoring in physical education and sports coaching/Fiona C. Chambers. — 1st
edition.
pages cm
Includes bibliographical references and index.
1. Physical education teacher—Training of. 2. Coaching (Athletics)—Training
of. 3. Mentoring in education. I Title.
GV363.C43 2015
796.07'7—dc23
2014023919

ISBN: 978-0-415-74576-5 (hbk)
ISBN: 978-0-415-74578-9 (pbk)
ISBN: 978-1-315-79768-7 (ebk)

Typeset in Bembo
by Swales & Willis Ltd, Exeter, Devon, UK

Printed and bound by CPI Group (UK) Ltd, Croydon, CR0 4YY

Dedicated to

Pat, Matthew and Georgie
And Maura and Michael

Also, to my 'found' mentors:
Michael Darmody RIP
Jacinta O'Brien RIP
Kathy Armour
Pat Duffy RIP

CONTENTS

CONTRIBUTORS

Professor Kathleen Armour, School of Sport, Exercise and Rehabilitation Sciences, University of Birmingham, UK

Mr Walter E. Bleakley, University of Ulster, Northern Ireland

Professor Deirdre A. Brennan, Ulster Sports Academy, University of Ulster, Northern Ireland

Dr Tania Cassidy, The School of Physical Education, Sport and Exercise Sciences, University of Otago, Dunedin, New Zealand

Dr Fiona C. Chambers, School of Education, University College Cork, Ireland

Professor Donetta Cothran, Department of Kinesiology, Indiana University, USA

Dr Chris Cushion, School of Sport, Exercise and Health Sciences, Loughborough University, UK

Dr Matthew Emmett, California State University, Fresno, California, USA

Dr Hayley Fitzgerald, Carnegie Faculty of Sport and Education, Leeds Metropolitan University, UK

Dr Mark Griffiths, School of Sport, Exercise and Rehabilitation Sciences, University of Birmingham, UK

Dr Simone Hare, School of Human Movement Studies, University of Queensland, Australia

Professor Pilvikki Heikinaro-Johannsson, Department of Sport Sciences, University of Jyväskylä, Finland

Mr Frank A. Herold, School of Sport, Exercise and Rehabilitation Sciences, University of Birmingham, UK

Dr Mirja Hirvensalo, Department of Sport Sciences, University of Jyväskylä, Finland

Professor Pamela Hodges Kulinna, Mary Lou Fulton Teachers College, Arizona State University, USA

Dr Terhi Huovinen, Department of Sport Sciences, University of Jyväskylä, Finland

Ms Ja Youn Kwon, Mary Lou Fulton Teachers College, Arizona State University, USA

Ms Sinéad Luttrell, University College Cork, Ireland

Dr Clifford J. Mallett, School of Human Movement Studies, University of Queensland, St Lucia, Australia

Professor Nate McCaughtry, Division of Kinesiology, Health and Sports Studies, Wayne State University, USA

Dr Louise McCuaig, School of Human Movement Studies, University of Queensland, St Lucia, Australia

Professor Bryan McCullick, Department of Kinesiology, University of Georgia, USA

Mr Paul McFlynn, School of Education, University of Ulster, Northern Ireland

Ms Joan Merrilees, School of Physical Education, Sport and Exercise Sciences, University of Otago, Dunedin, New Zealand

Ms Sue Monsen, School of Human Movement Studies, University of Queensland, St Lucia, Australia

Dr Liam O'Callaghan, Department of Health Sciences, Liverpool Hope University, UK

Dr Sanna Palomäki, Department of Sport Sciences, University of Jyväskylä, Finland

Dr Steven B. Rynne, School of Human Movement Studies, University of Queensland, St Lucia, Australia

Dr Rachel Sandford, School of Sport, Exercise and Health Sciences, Loughborough University, UK

Dr Sally Shaw, School of Physical Education, Sport and Exercise Sciences, University of Otago, Dunedin, New Zealand

Dr Michalis Stylianou, Mary Lou Fulton Teachers College, Arizona State University, USA

Professor Thomas Templin, Department of Health and Kinesiology, Purdue University, USA

Dr Julia Walsh, School of Education, University College Cork, Ireland

INTRODUCTION

Fiona C. Chambers

Vignette

Thirteen years ago, when I was pregnant with my daughter, Georgie, I enrolled in a Bog Oak carving weekend with my Mum. Within twenty minutes of registration, we were asked to go to a room filled with mossy, muddy pieces of bog oak, which had been extracted from the bog, pieces which were 5,000 years old. My piece chose me. I could see the beauty, the line, the majesty, the possibilities of my piece hidden underneath the moss and dirt. I cradled it and brought it with me to the meditation room to reflect on just why this piece had spoken to me. Over the next two days, I began to reveal its beauty, using chisels, rasps and sanders. Our mentor was an elderly gentleman who spoke quietly to us and did not impose. He told us that we were merely stripping away the layers to reveal the final piece and that we could not force our will on it. We were simply unveiling what was already there. The weekend was punctuated with much meditation and reflection about the process of finding the hidden splendour of our piece. And as the weekend drew to a close, a lasting memory was forged on the final morning in our candle-lit meditation room. The room was filled with our splendid individual bog oak pieces, each waxed and rich in colour standing proudly side-by-side, glistening in the flickering candlelight.

For me, this vignette captures two elements, the process of mentor training and the practice of mentoring to reveal the inner strengths and characteristics of the mentee.

The focus of this book: Mentoring as professional practice

Mentoring is a core principle of professional teacher education (McIntyre *et al.* 2005) and coach education (Cassidy *et al.* 2009). Mentoring develops 'the knowledge, skill and professional identity' of future teachers (Grossman *et al.* 2009, p. 273) and coaches (Cassidy *et al.* 2009). This book is a user-friendly *practical and theoretical* guide to the processes involved in effective mentoring. It is written for all those in sport and physical education who seek to use mentoring to support learning. It offers the reader a unique guide to the mentoring process by bringing theories and pedagogical practices of mentoring 'to life' using the voices and experiences of mentors and mentees in physical education and sport contexts.

Mentoring

Mentoring is a wide-ranging concept. It is often defined in relation to styles and types of relationships involved in mentoring, and to variations in perceived benefits of mentoring and mentorship (Patton *et al.* 2005). Mentoring is a profession-building endeavour as mentors and mentees are 'co-learners on a voyage of discovery' (ibid.). Zachary (2000, p. 3) proposes a model where:

> [t]he mentee shares responsibility for the learning setting, priorities, learning and resources and becomes increasingly self-directed. When the learner is not ready to assume that degree of responsibility, the mentor nurtures and develops the mentee's capacity for self-direction from dependence to independence to interdependence over the course of the relationship.

Mentoring and professional learning

The presence of experienced mentors in formative field experiences is a vital component in ensuring meaningful work-based learning for pre-service teachers (McIntyre *et al.* 2005) and coaches (Cassidy *et al.* 2009). There is strong evidence that professional development and training should be centred on teachers' learning, learning how to learn and transforming knowledge into practice for the benefit of their professional and pedagogical growth (Darling-Hammond 2006b; Darling-Hammond 2006a; Darling-Hammond and Rothman 2011). In fact, it has been argued that those teachers who are mentored early in their career are likely to be more effective practitioners (Evertson and Smithey 2000; Humphrey *et al.* 2000). There are a plethora of potential benefits of mentoring for beginning teachers, including reduced feelings of isolation, increased confidence and self-esteem, professional growth, and improved self-reflection and problem-solving capacities (Bullough 2005; Marable and Raimondi 2007; Lindgren 2005; McIntyre and Hagger 1996). In addition, mentees learn to sharpen classroom management expertise, personal time management skills, workloads and behaviour (Lindgren 2005; Malderez *et al.* 2007). More generally, mentors (experts) play an important role in the socialisation and enculturation of pre-service teachers within the community of practice (Wenger 1998), a key professional learning site (Armour *et al.* 2012). Yet, although there is a growing belief in the value of mentoring in teacher education and coach education, questions remain about ways to make the process most effective in action. This book gives readers the opportunity to interrogate mentoring and to learn how to craft a mentoring approach which is meaningful and effective for both mentors and mentees in a physical education or sport coaching context.

How is this book organised?

The text is crafted to reach a variety of readers by explaining the theory of mentoring using the voices and experiences of a range of different mentors and mentees.

Overview of Section 1: Theories of mentoring

In Chapter 1, this section begins with the interrogation of the concept of mentoring. Here, Fiona Chambers, Tom Templin and Bryan McCullick explore practical and theoretical issues in relation to mentoring. They focus particularly on the role of the mentor and the effective mentor relationship characteristics. In Chapter 2, Kathleen Armour explores mentoring and professional development. She describes mentoring and professional responsibility, and highlights potential problems where the mentoring process is not clear to all participants. In Chapter 3, Fiona Chambers, Sinéad Luttrell, Kathleen Armour, Walter Bleakley, Deirdre Brennan and Frank Herold describe the pedagogy of mentoring.

Overview of Section 2: Socio-cultural factors and mentoring

This section allows the reader to step back and to address mentoring from a socio-cultural viewpoint. The section opens with Chapter 4, where Rachel Sandford considers the process of supporting the positive development of disadvantaged/vulnerable youth through mentoring initiatives. In Chapter 5, Liam O'Callaghan shows how physical education, in keeping with the practice of sport more generally, is a domain in which socially constructed notions of 'race' and ethnicity are clearly visible. He shares how this has impacted the experiences of Black and Minority Ethnic (BME) trainee PE teachers. In Chapter 6, Hayley Fitzgerald considers how mentoring can enable Physical Education Teacher Education (PETE) students to work towards inclusion for students with Special Educational Needs (SEN) and disabilities. Liam O'Callaghan returns in Chapter 7, emphasising how physical education is a domain divided along gender lines. He shows how this is visible in numbers of participants, the range of activities included on curricula, and socially constructed notions of masculinity and femininity. Finally, in Chapter 8, Julia Walsh explores the issue of volunteerism in sport, and how the volunteers are the backbone of youth sport. In particular she highlights how volunteers require and expect investment in their professional development though 'embedded' mentoring.

Overview of Section 3: Mentoring and physical education

In this section, the focus is on mentoring in the physical education context. The section opens with Sinéad Luttrell's account in Chapter 9 of how the process of learning to teach, scaffolded by mentor support, is outlined in policy and enacted in practice. This leads to a description in Chapter 10 of the Capability Maturity Model for Mentor Teachers (CM³T) by Fiona Chambers, Sinéad Luttrell, Kathleen Armour, Walter Bleakley, Deirdre Brennan and Frank Herold. CM³T is both (a) a diagnostic tool for mentor training needs and (b) a planning tool for designing bespoke training programmes for mentors at each phase of the Mentor Career Cycle. Fiona leads on from this in Chapter 11 to outline the development of the Telemachus Project, i.e. cultivating school-university partnerships as learning organisations to support the transition of cooperating teachers to a mentoring role in pre-service teacher education. Staying with this theme, in Chapter 12, Pilvikki Heikinaro-Johannsson, Mirja Hirvensalo, Sanna Palomäki and Terhi Huovinen examine the experiences of both mentees/pre-service teachers and physical education teacher educators as they experience the mentoring process. Louise McCuaig, Simone Hare and Sue Monsen, in Chapter 13, look to an alternative mentoring configuration and review one strategy in which a high-performing, fourth-year Health and Physical Education Teacher Education (HPETE) peer-mentor was added to the typical practicum triad. Closing this section, in Chapter 14, Nate McCaughtry, Pamela Hodges Kulinna, Donetta Cothran, Michalis Stylianou and Ja Youn Kwon examine the use of e-mentoring in the professional development of physical education teachers.

Overview of Section 4: Mentoring and sport coaching

The penultimate section shines the spotlight on sport coaching. In Chapter 15, Tania Cassidy, Joan Merrilees and Sally Shaw interrogate how mentoring supports females to 'become' elite performance coaches. In Chapter 16, Chris Cushion outlines how mentoring in coaching remains unstructured, uneven in terms of quality and outcome and uncritical in style, leading to reproduction of culture, power and poor practice. Mark Griffiths, in Chapter 17, corroborates this and describes how mentors are learning facilitators who create transforming environments by assisting the learning process, and in spite of this demanding pedagogical role, mentors are often given little guidance beyond an introductory 'workshop'. In Chapter 18, Clifford Mallett, Matthew Emmett and Steven Rynne outline how despite ill-clarification, the concept of mentoring in sports coaching can generally be conceptualized as 'guidance by a trusted other.' Drawing upon results from an extensive multi-year case study, this chapter aims to identify principles of mentorship effectiveness within the high-performance coaching domain. Julia Walsh and Fiona Chambers draw this section to a close in Chapter 19, emphasising how the quality of sports programmes depends on the quality of coaches who have been trained to be mentors in context.

Overview of Section 5: The Mentor Pedagogy Toolbox: An ecological systems perspective

In Chapter 20, Fiona Chambers synthesises the 'Lessons learned' from each chapter into Chandler *et al.*'s (2011) multi-layer ecological system of mentoring. This consists of three layers: (1) individual mentor characteristics (Ontogenic system); (2) three Microsystems – (a) Mentor-Mentee (dyadic microsystem), (b) Mentor-Mentee within Partnership Organisations (Developmental Network/ Multiple Microsystems) and (c) the formal mentoring programme (Organisational Microsystem); and (3) societal influences (Macrosystem). The Ontogenic, Microsytems and Macrosystem layers combine to form the 'Terroir of Mentoring' schematic, an ecological view of mentoring. This is the Mentor Pedagogy Toolbox.

References

Armour, K., Makopoulou, K. and Chambers, F. C. 2012. Progression in physical education teachers' career-long professional learning: Conceptual and practical concerns. *European Physical Education Review*, 18, 62–77.

Bullough Jr, R. V. 2005. Being and becoming a mentor: School-based teacher educators and teacher educator identity. *Teaching and Teacher Education*, 21, 143–155.

Cassidy, T., Jones, R. and Potrac, P. 2009. *Understanding sports coaching: The social, cultural and pedagogical foundations of coaching practice*. London: Routledge.

Chandler, D. E., Kram, K. E. and Jeffrey, Y. 2011. An ecological systems perspective on mentoring at work: A review and future prospects. *The Academy of Management Annals*, 5, 519–570.

Darling-Hammond, L. 2006a. Constructing 21st century teacher education. *Journal of Teacher Education*, 57, 300–314.

Darling-Hammond, L. 2006b. *Powerful teacher education: Lessons from exemplary programs*. San Francisco: Jossey-Bass.

Darling-Hammond, L. and Rothman, R. 2011. *Teacher and leader effectiveness in high performing education systems*. Washington, DC: Alliance for Excellent Education, and Stanford, CA: Stanford Center for Opportunity Policy in Education.

Evertson, C. M. and Smithey, M. W. 2000. Mentoring effects on protégés' classroom practice: An experimental field study. *Journal of Educational Research*, 93, 294–304.

Grossman, P., Hammerness, K. and McDonald, M. 2009. Redefining teaching, re-imagining teacher education. *Teachers and Teaching: Theory and Practice*, 15, 273–289.

Humphrey, D. C., Adelman, N., Esch, E. E., Riehl, L. M., Shields, P. M. and Tiffany, J. 2000. *Preparing and supporting new teachers: A literature review*. Menlo Park, CA: SRI International.

Lindgren, U. 2005. Experiences of beginning teachers in a school-based mentoring programme in Sweden. *Educational Studies*, 31, 251–263.

Malderez, A., Hobson, A. J., Tracey, L. and Kerr, K. 2007. Becoming a student teacher: core features of the experience. *European Journal of Teacher Education*, 30(3), 225–248.

Marable, M. and Raimondi, S. 2007. Teachers' perceptions of what was most (and least) supportive during their first year of teaching. *Mentoring and Tutoring: Partnership in Learning*, 15, 25–37.

McIntyre, D. and Hagger, H. 1996. *Mentors in schools: Developing the profession of teaching*. London: David Fulton Publishers.

McIntyre, D., Hagger, H. and Wilkin, M. 2005. *Mentoring: Perspectives on school-based teacher education*. London: Routledge Falmer.

Patton, K., Griffin, L. L., Sheehy, D., Arnold, R., Gallo, A., Pagnano, K., Dodd, P., Henniger, M. L. and James, A. 2005. Navigating the mentoring process in a research-based teacher development project: A situated learning perspective. *Journal of Teaching in Physical Education*, 24, 302–325.

Wenger, E. 1998. *Communities of practice: Learning, meaning and identity*. Cambridge, UK: Cambridge University Press.

Zachary, L. J. 2000. *The mentor's guide: Facilitating effective learning relationships*. San Francisco: Jossey-Bass.

SECTION 1
Theories of mentoring

1

MENTORING

A primer

*Fiona C. Chambers, Thomas Templin
and Bryan McCullick*

> Ward "Piggy" Lambert never seemed to see limitations . . . only possibilities. With him, I gained one of the most important mentors of my career. From Coach Lambert, I learned the philosophies that were to become my trademark both on and off the court: conditioning, skill, and team spirit. He demonstrated the importance of unity and cohesion for making a team, and this was a lesson I never forgot. He modeled the importance of decisive action and taking risks, but he also cautioned . . . not to be reckless. He showed . . . responsibility, compassion, and (perhaps above all else) how to bring your personal principles into your career . . . . His example gave me both the immediate counsel I craved and the confidence to trust my own instincts. As a mentor, he was a giant.
>
> *Wooden 2009, pp. 49–50*

As you might have guessed, this vignette is not derived from data collected during empirical studies of effective mentors' qualities. In fact, the story is taken from a popular book written by a famous coach and teacher, John Wooden. Wooden was the legendary University of California, Los Angeles (UCLA) men's basketball coach and he wrote this piece to describe his own mentor, i.e. his college basketball coach. As it turns out, Wooden (2009) had several people he considered mentors for and at different parts of his life. His description, however, of his coaching mentor paints a picture that probably resonates with many of us. Quite eloquently, Wooden describes Ward "Piggy" Lambert's personal characteristics and mentoring actions that made him such a powerful influence on Wooden's coaching career.

Oftentimes, theory and research findings are believed to be at odds with what many consider the 'real world'. With a combined total of sixty-five years of both mentoring pre-service teachers and working with practicing teachers, the authors have heard arguments from both sides: 'Dr Templin, what you are teaching us is good . . . in theory', an undergraduate has been known to say, or at a conference we'll hear a researcher intone, 'Teachers just don't understand research, so that is why they don't put stock in it'.

We are not worried about which side is 'right', we just believe that when it comes to identifying the qualities of effective mentors, science and the real world align quite nicely. The combined knowledge from (a) mentoring literature, (b) first-hand accounts of mentoring relationships and (c) the biographical information from recognized teachers of sport and physical activity show that the qualities of effective mentors align. The language might differ, but the ideas and concepts expressed are in essence comparable.

In this chapter, we want to explore mentoring so as to 'set the table' for the rest of the book. Specifically, the three-fold purpose of this chapter is to (i) provide a background to and definition of mentoring, (ii) identify practical and theoretical issues surrounding the construct of mentoring and (iii) discuss the place of mentoring in teacher and coach development. In the end, this chapter should provide a nice segue into the remaining chapters in this text that present how mentoring occurs in various contexts, and culminate in the production of a mentoring schematic of lessons learned from each of the remaining chapters.

Background and definition of mentoring

The term 'mentor' is first mentioned in Homer's *The Odyssey*. In this mythological tale, Mentor (or Mentês), the son of Alcumus, an Ithacan noble and trusted friend of Odysseus, was charged with looking after the welfare and education of Odysseus' son, Telemachus, when Odysseus left to fight in the Trojan War. The French archbishop, theologian and writer François Fénelon wrote of how Athena, goddess of war, handicraft and wisdom, assumed the guise of Mentor when she accompanied Telemachus in search of his father. *Les aventures de Télémaque*, published in 1699, was written to educate the grandson of Louis XIV and includes the first recorded modern mention of mentoring (*Encyclopaedia Britannica* 2008). Interestingly, this definition of mentoring has endured in the midst of much debate on the subject. Theorists have agreed on the function and focus of mentoring.

Currently, literature on mentoring offers a broad view of the construct of mentoring and defines it vis-à-vis the mentoring relationship and how the mentor behaves within that relationship. This commentary is specifically related to the perceived benefits of mentoring (Patton *et al.* 2005). Turning to the etymology of the noun *mentor*, investigations reveal that it emanates from the noun *mentos* meaning intent, purpose, spirit or passion; wise advisor; 'man-tar' one who thinks; and 'mon-i-tor' one who admonishes (*Online Etymology Dictionary* 2007). The dictionary supports this pastoral and professional description, describing the mentor as 'a wise and trusted guide and advisor'; 'a wise and trusted counselor or teacher'; an 'experienced advisor and supporter'; 'a guide, a wise and faithful counselor'; and 'a person who gives another person help and advice over a period of time and often also teaches them how to do their job'. Kram (1985) indicates that the mentor 'supports, guides, and counsels a young adult as he or she accomplishes mastery of the adult world or the world of work' (p. 2). This is quite a hierarchical view of the mentor-mentee relationship, with the mentor in charge and the mentee in a more passive and compliant role. In other literature, however, a picture of a more symbiotic mentor-mentee relationship emerges. Ayers and Griffin (2005) speak of a 'reciprocal dimension of mentoring relationships [that] can help us better understand the mentoring dynamic as the co-construction of new knowledge and understanding for both mentors and protégés' (p. 369).

Within this perception of the mentoring liaison, the mentor designs a bespoke learning experience for the mentee, offering different types of support as the mentee moves through his or her journey. To do this, Kram (1985) asserts that the mentor has a range of psychosocial functions, including role-modeling, counseling, friendship, acceptance and confirmation. These aspects of the relationship enhance a sense of competence, clarity of identity and effectiveness in a professional role. Through this process, the mentee role evolves from passive receiver to active learner, where knowledge is no longer acquired from the mentor, but is replaced by self-directed knowledge and critical reflection. In this way, the role of mentor has the potential to become mutually beneficial in terms of professional growth. A considerable list of benefits accrue to both mentor and mentee. Turning specifically to the mentee, McIntyre *et al.* (1994) refer to the main benefits of mentoring as being reduced feelings of isolation, increased confidence and self-esteem, professional growth, and improved self-reflection and problem-solving capacities. In reality, both parties profit, as participating in mentoring can serve as a stimulus for reflection, a means of engaging in professional dialogue and a validation of good practice. 'Serving as a mentor pushes one not only to model but also to be accountable for that modeling. Identifying the rationale requires reflection-on-action for validation' (Weasmer and Woods 2003, p. 69; Jordan *et al.* 2008). According to Jordan *et al.* (2008, p. 202), reflection can be on practice, in practice and for practice and is rooted in Schon's (1987) framework of reflective practice. Such reflection is prompted by the mentee-mentor relationship in two ways:

> As host teachers address their classes, aware that their student teachers are watching, their reflection-in-action presses them to strive toward good teaching decisions, as they visualize what the student teachers witness. Likewise, the student teacher's presence stimulates the host teacher toward reflection-on-action in order to later explain his or her classroom behaviours.
>
> *Weasmer and Woods 2003, p. 74*

In sum, Healy and Welchert (1990) state that 'mentoring is seen as a reciprocal relationship in a work environment between an advanced career incumbent (mentor) and a beginner (protégé) aimed at promoting the career development of both' (p. 17).

Practical and theoretical issues in mentoring

Perhaps what is most important when introducing the construct of mentoring is to identify the characteristics of (a) an ideal mentor and (b) the ultimate mentoring relationship. The literature abounds with such information. While we do not (and could not) cover every possible finding or position on these topics, we do believe it essential for this literature to be summarised before moving on to the other chapters.

Characteristics of ideal mentors

As suggested in the earlier discussion, having a mentee-centred approach to mentorship requires that the mentor possess certain characteristics. Numerous sources (Allen and Eby 2010; Ensher and Murphy 2005; Kram 1985; Zachary and Fischler 2009; Zachary 2005; Merriman 1983; Ragins and Kram 2007) provide various paradigms of effective mentoring and the promotion of adult development. In relation to teacher development, Shulman and Sato (2006) and Feiman-Nemser (1996) provide insights into mentoring teachers with the goal of developing 'highly qualified teachers' and the nuances of teacher socialization during this process. Within physical education and sport, various studies or reviews (Bloom *et al.* 1998; Cushion 2006; Richards and Templin 2011; Galvin 2004; Marshall 2001; Rikard and Banville 2010; Weaver and Chelladurai 1999; Wright and Smith 2000; Jones *et al.* 2009) have addressed the elements of effective mentoring of teachers and sport coaches alike.

Initially, one must understand that mentoring occurs within a framework of phases (Kram 1985), which are non-linear processes of mentoring:

- Initiation – The mentee and mentor establish roles and responsibilities and setting relationship parameters.
- Cultivation – Both mentee and mentor build knowledge, skills and dispositions in a collegial manner thus promoting an emotional bond.
- Separation – The mentee shapes his or her own identity and pathways to successful performance.
- Redefinition – The mentee develops autonomous identity within a collegial mentor-mentee relationship.

Throughout these phases, effective mentors (a) possess particular social traits, (b) demonstrate significant levels of emotional intelligence (Cox 2000), (c) are intentional role models (Gilbert 1985) and (d) are well known as scholars and professionals (Manathunga 2007). Moreover, it is argued by Kram (1985) that the most successful mentors are those who volunteer to mentor and who see a benefit in kind, i.e. to enhance their own career development. Therefore, the mentoring act can be deemed both altruistic and self-promoting as the mentor-mentee relationship is often a vehicle for achieving midlife 'generativity' (Erikson 1963). The mentor's task is 'to open up a hospitable space allowing the student to be herself, because she is received graciously' (O'Reilley 1998, p. 8) and within this 'safe space' the paradox of mentorship can flourish. Here:

> An experience of transcendence for the mentor and transformation for the mentee . . . or change in perspective . . . [is] iconoclastic in nature so as to throw the [mentee] off his or her comfortable and customary perch . . . making the familiar unfamiliar [forcing] a re-examination of the known world.
>
> *Yamamoto 1988, p. 187*

Such a perspective reveals the complex nature of the mentor-mentee relationship, where the mentee is held accountable in examining, reflecting upon, and acting within new roles and events in their career or life. In reality, an effective mentor-mentee relationship is not always a 'one-way street' or a 'top-down' set of interactions whereby the mentee is indentured. Rather, the relationship is built on the premise that the mentee will develop a sense of agency and ultimately separate from and redefine the relationship.

In summary, whether one serves as mentor from a hospitable or dissonant standpoint (or indeed, a combination of the two perspectives), the mentor should display a host of emotional and behavioural characteristics and elements that facilitate the mentee's progress as a developing professional. Importantly, the mentor must acknowledge that mentees come from different places and backgrounds and that this will shape the relationship. Regardless of the life history of an individual, these characteristics should instill a unique hope and vision for the future for each mentee (Parks 2000). Figure 1.1 presents a list of characteristics aligned to effective mentoring and effective mentor-mentee relationships.

Characteristics of effective mentoring relationships

There is little question that effective mentoring relationships can be mutually beneficial for both the mentors and protégés. However, for mentoring relationships to be valuable, some crucial features must exist. Research has noted that 'good' mentoring relationships are somewhat reliant on the context, but it has also identified a common set of features that serve as essential markers of productive mentoring relationships, regardless of the environments in which they occur.

This is especially true for physical education (PE) teachers and coaches. Studies in other professions, such as nursing and business, highlight the potential benefits of effective mentoring relationships. While effective mentoring relationships are defined by a complex interaction of variables and there are many ways to conceptualize and create mentoring relationships, the literature consistently identifies beneficial mentoring relationships as having critical elements that can be characterized as a structure with indispensable features, and a probability of rewards for both parties.

Mentoring relationships may take on many different forms, and depending on the context, what works in one mentoring relationship may not work in another.

Mentor as...

Teacher/Role Model/Resource – displaying skills, knowledge, and dispositions linked to effective teaching that the mentee may emulate.

Motivator/Communicator/Counselor/Confidant – creating of emotional bond that serves as inspiration and encouragement while based on trust, open communication and nurturing.

Evaluator – willing and able to provide feedback based on formal and informal evaluation.

Collaborator/Colleague – addressing planning, performance, and evaluation of teaching in a cooperative and reciprocal manner.

Negotiator/Boundary Setter – establishing parameters of the relationship so that it may be mutually beneficial.

Liberator – facilitating separation and redefinition of relationship whereby the mentee establishes own pathways to success grounded in the mentoring relationship.

Mentor as being...

Accessible – being available to the mentee for ongoing development. There are no time gaps in the relationship, but a continuous partnership.

Accountable – for the performance of roles whereby the relationship grows and positive outcomes are realized.

FIGURE 1.1 Roles and characteristics of effective mentors and effective mentor–mentee relationships

Kram 1985; Zachary 2012

However, research studies on mentoring relationships indicate that there appear to be four indispensable structural features of successful mentoring relationships: thorough mentor training, balanced mentor and protégé matching, individualization of protégé needs and clear rewards for both mentor and protégé.

The job of a mentor must be learned through formal training (Heirdsfield *et al.* 2008). Formal training allows a mentor to learn the necessary knowledge and skills for mentoring. This knowledge and skill set aids mentors in creating a framework for working with protégés and helps them gain confidence in their own abilities in their new role. Upon completion of a mentor training programme, mentors should (a) possess a firm grasp of the mentoring process; (b) be able to utilize reflective skills to better understand their own strengths and weaknesses; (c) establish the goals of the mentoring relationship and know how to set individual goals with their protégé; and (d) have interviewing skills that enable deeper conversation with their protégé. Also, importantly, if mentors do not engage in the correct training, they become simply 'well meaning amateurs' (Cavanagh 2006, p. 381). Within the mentoring dyad (mentor and mentee), mentors who are trained to use effective mentor pedagogies promote transformative learning through Daloz' (1986) model of supporting and challenging the mentee. This approach advances the holistic development of the adult learner, as both person and professional, through 'the dyad actively examining dilemmas' (Dominguez and Hager 2013, p. 176).

Mentor training, alone, does not guarantee a successful mentoring relationship. Efforts must be made to carefully match the mentor and the protégé for suitability. Put succinctly, the importance of ensuring that the mentor *both* is suitable, i.e. possesses the right disposition for the role, *and* 'participate(s) in appropriate and informed mentor training and development opportunities' (Hobson and Malderez 2013, p. 13; Chambers *et al.* 2012) cannot be underestimated.

Evidence indicates the most successful mentoring relationships are comprised of mentors and protégés who are matched on the basis of similar interests or demographics (Fowler 2004). Whether it is age, gender, or a major field of study, mentors need to have commonalities with their protégés, which can serve as a 'jumping off point' for their relationship and assist in the establishment of a rapport. Matching mentor to protégé allows for a certain level of comfort knowing that the person you are working with shares specific characteristics.

While the goals of some mentoring relationships are formally set forth by those coordinating the mentoring programme, the focus should be aligned with the protégé's needs as much as possible (Onchwari and Keengwe 2008). In fact, within mentoring programmes, relationships which are designed to satisfy mentees' needs and goals increase their probability of success by providing the right type of mentoring at the right time, by matching mentees with appropriate mentors and by helping mentees to learn with a method that best suits them (Armstrong *et al.* 2002). It is important to remember that mentoring is not solely 'about the relationships, it's about the quality of the conversations' (Cavanagh 2006, p. 318) between mentor and mentee.

It is likely the protégé may already have an idea of what specific help he or she desires from a mentor or, that a mentor could have an understanding of what a protégé may need because of previous experiences as a mentor. It is important for the mentor to find a balance between the goals of the mentor relationship, as prescribed by the administration, and expectations that the protégé has for the relationship. If a mentor fails to understand the expectations of the protégé, it can lead to frustration and cause problems in the relationship. Further, it can lead to lack of communication and even distrust, possibly distracting from the ultimate goal of the mentoring relationship, i.e. helping the protégé to develop as a teacher or coach.

Conclusion

Mentors, mentees, and organizations may be transformed through the design of evidence-based and theoretically informed mentoring programmes in pursuit of maximizing the human potential of faculty, students and the communities within which they conduct their work (Dominguez and Hager 2013, p. 185). Theoretical frameworks provide *pathways of knowledge* for researchers to build upon that can be *advanced using verifiable practices* (ibid.). This chapter provides a theoretical 'backbone' to how mentoring is construed in this text.

And now, we lead to a comprehensive section on the *theories of mentoring*, exploring mentoring and professional development, and the pedagogy of mentoring. The blinkers will then move outward to interrogate *socio-cultural factors and mentoring*, specifically analyzing mentoring and youth, 'race', special educational needs and disability, gender and volunteerism. We will then consider specific mentoring contexts. From here, we will turn to the *physical education–teacher education context* and grapple with effective models of mentoring, how to train mentors across the career span, mentoring pre-service teachers, group mentoring, mentoring newly qualified teachers, peer-mentoring and e-mentoring. In the final section, we will consider the *coaching context* in depth and will investigate national governing bodies: sport policy, practice and mentoring, mentoring for success in sport coaching, training coaches as mentors, mentoring high-performance athletes and designing sustainable models of mentoring for sports clubs (the LACE model). The book closes with a synthesis of the 'Lessons learned . . . what could we add to the Mentor Pedagogy Toolbox' sections from each chapter. These entries are collated using Chandler *et al.*'s (2011, p. 523) ecological systems perspective of mentoring framed within the newly devised *Terroir of Mentoring* schematic.

Key terms: effective mentoring, role of effective mentor, characteristics of effective mentor.

References

Allen, T. D. and Eby, L. T. 2010. *The Blackwell Handbook of Mentoring: A Multiple Perspectives Approach.* Chichester, UK: John Wiley & Sons.

Armstrong, S., Allinson, C. and Hayes, J. 2002. Formal mentoring systems: An examination of the effects of mentor/protégé cognitive styles on the mentoring process. *Journal of Management Studies,* 39, 1111–1137.

Ayers, S. and Griffin, L. L. 2005. PETE Mentoring as a Mosaic. *Journal of Teaching in Physical Education,* 24, 368–378.

Bloom, G. A., Durand-Bush, N., Schinke, R. J. and Salmela, J. H. 1998. The importance of mentoring in the development of coaches and athletes. *International Journal of Sport Psychology,* 29, 267–281.

Cavanagh, M. 2006. Coaching from a systemic perspective: A complex adaptive conversation. In D. R. Stober and A. M. Grant (Eds.) *Evidence Based Coaching Handbook: Putting Best Practices to Work for Your Clients.* Hoboken, New Jersey: John Wiley & Sons.

Chambers, F. C., Armour, K., Luttrell, S., Bleakley, E. W., Brennan, D. A. and Herold, F. A. 2012. Mentoring as a profession-building process in physical education teacher education. *Irish Educational Studies,* 31, 345–362.

Chandler, D. E., Kram, K. E. and Yip, J. 2011. An ecological systems perspective on mentoring at work: A review and future prospects. *The Academy of Management Annals,* 5, 519–570.

Cox, E. R. J. 2000. The call to mentor. *Career Development International,* 5, 202–210.

Cushion, C. J. 2006. Mentoring: Harnessing the power of experience. In R. L. Jones (Ed.), *The Sports Coach as Educator: Re-conceptualising Sports Coaching.* London: Routledge, pp. 128–144.

Daloz, L. A. 1986. *Effective Teaching and Mentoring: Realizing the Transformational Power of Adult Learning Experiences.* San Francisco, CA: Jossey-Bass.

Dominguez, N. and Hager, M. 2013. Mentoring frameworks: Synthesis and critique. *International Journal of Mentoring and Coaching in Education*, 2, 171–188.

Encyclopaedia Britannica, 2008. *s.v.* 'Fénelon'. Chicago, Illinois: Encyclopaedia Britannica.

Ensher, E. A. and Murphy, S. E. 2005. *Power Mentoring: How Successful Mentors and Protégés Get the Most Out of Their Relationships*. San Francisco, CA: Jossey-Bass.

Erikson, E. H. 1963. *Childhood and Society*. New York: Norton.

Feiman-Nemser, S. 1996. *Teacher Mentoring: A Critical Review. ERIC Digest, ED397060. Washington, DC: ERIC Clearinghouse on Teaching and Teacher Education.*

Fowler J. 2004. The tiered mentoring program: Linking students with peers and professionals. *HERDSA News*, April 2004.

Galvin, B. 2004. *A Guide to Mentoring Sports Coaches*. Leeds: Coachwise Business Solutions/ The National Coaching Foundation.

Gilbert, L. A. 1985. Dimensions of same-gender student-faculty role-model relationships. *Sex Roles*, 12, 111–123.

Healy, C. C. and Welchert, A. J. 1990. Mentoring relations: A definition to advance research and practice. *Educational Researcher*, 19, 17–21.

Heirdsfield, A. M., Walker, S., Walsh, K. and Wilss, L. 2008. Peer mentoring for first-year teacher education students: The mentors' experience. *Mentoring and Tutoring*, 16, 109–124.

Hobson, A. J. and Malderez, A. 2013. Judgementoring and other threats to realizing the potential of schoolbased mentoring in teacher education. *International Journal of Mentoring and Coaching in Education*, 2, 89–108.

Jones, R. L., Harris, R. and Miles, A. 2009. Mentoring in sports coaching: A review of the literature. *Physical Education and Sport Pedagogy*, 14, 267–284.

Jordan, A., Carlile, O. and Stack, A. 2008. *Approaches to Learning: A Guide for Teachers*. Oxford: Open University Press.

Kram, K. E. 1985. *Mentoring at Work: Developmental Relationships in Organizational Life*. Glenview, IL: Scott, Foresman.

Manathunga, C. 2007. Supervision as mentoring: The role of power and boundary crossing. *Studies in Continuing Education*, 29, 207–221.

Marshall, D. 2001. Mentoring as a development tool for women coaches. *Canadian Journal for Women in Coaching*, 2, 1496–1539.

McIntyre, D., Hagger, H. and Wilkin, M. 1994. *Mentoring: Perspectives on School-Based Teacher Education*. London: Routledge-Falmer.

Merriman, S. 1983. Mentors and protégés: A critical review of the literature. *Adult Education Quarterly*, 33, 161–173.

Onchwari, G. and Keengwe, J. 2008. The impact of a mentor-coaching model on teacher professional development. *Early Childhood Education Journal*, 36(1), 19–24.

Online Etymology Dictionary. *s.v.* 'mentor'. Accessed at http://www.etymonline.com (accessed on 29 March 2005).

O'Reilley, M. R. 1998. *Radical Presence: Teaching as Contemplative Practice*. Portsmouth, NH: Boynton/Cook, Heinemann.

Parks, S. D. 2000. *Big Questions, Worthy Dreams: Mentoring Young Adults in Their Search for Meaning, Purpose, and Faith*. San Francisco, CA: Jossey-Bass.

Patton, K., Griffin, L. L., Sheehy, D., Arnold, R., Gallo, A. M., Pagnano, K., Dodds, P., Henninger, M. L. and James, A. 2005. Navigating the mentoring process in a research-based teacher development project: A situated learning perspective. *Journal of Teaching in Physical Education*, 24, 302–325.

Ragins, B. R. and Kram, K. E. 2007. *The Handbook of Mentoring at Work: Theory, Research, and Practice*. Thousand Oaks, CA: Sage Publications.

Richards, K. A. and Templin, T. J. 2011. The influence of a state mandated induction assistance program on the socialization of a beginning physical education teacher. *Journal of Teaching in Physical Education,* 30, 340–357.

Rikard, G. L. and Banville, D. 2010. Effective mentoring: Critical to the professional development of first year physical educators. *Journal of Teaching in Physical Education,* 29, 245–261.

Schon, D. A. 1987. *Educating the Reflective Practitioner: Toward a New Design for Teaching and Learning in the Professions.* San Francisco, CA: Jossey-Bass.

Shulman, J. H. and Sato, M. (Eds.) 2006. *Mentoring Teachers Toward Excellence: Supporting and Developing Highly Qualified Teachers.* San Francisco, CA: Jossey-Bass Publishers.

Weasmer, J. and Woods, A. M. 2003. Mentoring: Professional development through reflection. *The Teacher Educator,* 39, 64–77.

Weaver, M. A. and Chelladurai, P. 1999. A mentoring model for management in sport and physical education. *Quest,* 51, 24–38.

Wooden, J. 2009. *A Game Plan for Life: The Power of Mentoring.* New York: Bloomsbury.

Wright, S. C. and Smith, D. E. 2000. A case for formalized mentoring. *Quest,* 52, 200–213.

Yamamoto, K. 1988. To see life grow: The meaning of mentorship. *Theory into Practice,* 27, 183–189.

Zachary, L. J. 2005. *Creating a Mentoring Culture: The Organization's Guide.* San Francisco, CA: Jossey-Bass.

Zachary, L. J. 2011. *The Mentor's Guide: Facilitating Effective Learning Relationships.* San Francisco, CA: Jossey-Bass.

Zachary, L. J. and Fischler, L. A. 2009. *The Mentee's Guide: Making Mentoring Work for You.* San Francisco, CA: Jossey-Bass.

Resources

Wooden, J. 2009. *A Game Plan for Life: The Power of Mentoring.* New York: Bloomsbury.

Zachary, L. J. 2005. *Creating a Mentoring Culture: The Organization's Guide.* San Francisco, CA: Jossey-Bass.

Zachary, L. J. 2011. *The Mentor's Guide: Facilitating Effective Learning Relationships.* San Francisco, CA: Jossey-Bass.

Zachary, L. J. and Fischler, L. A. 2009. *The Mentee's Guide: Making Mentoring Work for You.* San Francisco, CA: Jossey-Bass.

2

'MENTORING' AND PROFESSIONAL DEVELOPMENT

Kathleen Armour

Overview

This chapter considers mentoring both as a professional learning tool and as a professional responsibility. As has been widely argued elsewhere, professions are characterised by access to and guardianship of a specialised body of knowledge, which they deploy to serve their clients (Day and Townsend 2009; Day and Sachs 2004). This explains why all definitions of a *profession* identify continuous career-long learning as a defining characteristic (e.g. Brunetti 1998). In other words, *not* to engage in professional development would render a teacher *unprofessional*. This chapter explores the potential value of mentoring in professional learning in teaching and coaching, and also the potential for problems where the nature and purpose of the activity are not wholly clear to all participants.

Mentoring as a form of professional development offers numerous advantages. It has long been argued that traditional systems of professional development for teachers are inadequate (Wayne *et al.* 2008) because they are too distant from the realities of practice (Timperley 2008). It is interesting to note, therefore, that engaging in *in situ* mentoring, where teachers take a degree of responsibility for the professional development of their colleagues (new and experienced), appears to overcome many of the criticisms of traditional professional development. Yet, mentoring should not be regarded as a rather simplistic and inexpensive professional development panacea. In particular, for any mentoring programme to be successful, it is important that all parties have the time and opportunity to develop a shared understanding of the ways in which a specific mentoring programme has been conceptualised. A composite vignette illustrates this point, and the analysis section that follows explores the implications.

Vignettes

Examples are drawn from three research projects that used similar research methods to study mentoring programmes in different contexts. All three projects provided strong evidence to suggest that clarifying the way in which the term *mentoring* is being used, and setting clear and shared expectations around the process, are necessary steps towards establishing successful mentoring activities.

Methods

The three projects were programme evaluations of specific mentoring initiatives, and they used a similar range of qualitative methods. The demands of programme evaluation in large-scale social programmes are well documented (Rossi *et al.* 2004), and it has been argued that such research in educational contexts should be 'methodologically ecumenical' (House 2005, p. 1071). As House notes:

> Social causation is more complex than regularity theory suggests. Even with the same program, there are different teachers at different sites who produce different results. We might try to control for the teachers, but there are so many variables that might influence the outcomes, the researchers cannot control for all of them.

In the projects described in this chapter, qualitative research methods allowed the researchers to investigate the issues in authentic contexts (Stake 2005), in particular by allocating research time and resources to analysing complex case studies. Detailed case protocols were established in each project to ensure a common approach across cases, and the main methods used were individual interviews, focus groups, observations and document analysis. The following data were obtained from face-to-face, individual semi-structured interviews. In all three projects, data were analysed systematically using a constructivist, grounded-theory framework (Charmaz 2006) to identify recurring themes around the research questions. Illustrations of this process can be found in the original sources.

Project one: Mentoring in a coach education programme (Armour et al. 2012)

Background: In a new initiative, a national governing body of sport in the UK appointed a small group of professional coach educators (PCEs) to act as mentors in local areas to support the development of youth coaches *in situ* in their clubs. The initiative was broadly welcomed by all participants, but differing perceptions of the role of the PCEs led to frustrations and restrictions.

Data extracts: The following data extracts are taken from an unpublished research report prepared for the sponsors. From the club's perspective, the role of the PCE was to act as an extra and convenient pair of hands to deliver official governing-body youth-coaching awards. The club was primarily interested in numbers, i.e. getting as many coaches through the awards as possible in the shortest amount of time. For example, when asked about his understanding of the role of the PCEs, one club director said:

> Yeah it's basically working with our coordinator at nines to fourteens, concentrating on getting coaches through the qualification.
>
> *Club Director, 2012*

> I think it's him (PCE) sitting down with me and deciding what I need and at the moment qualifications was number one and we sat down and we had a meeting and qualifications was the key thing that I wanted to get addressed.
>
> *Club Director, 2012*

The PCE, however, had been tasked by the governing body with a much wider role, and this had been communicated to the clubs. For example, one PCE explained that he was clear about his role: to support coach education and facilitate coach development through mentoring, practice-modeling and helping coaches to become more reflective:

> So we had an idea around coach development . . . do the awards and then we go in to their work place . . . video them, and then processes of self reflect, and a personal development plan from that.
>
> *PCE, 2012*

The PCE envisaged a role in which he would act as a 'mirror' to help the coaches to become critically aware about elements of their existing practices and impact on young players. Yet, the divergence in understandings about the purpose and value of the PCE role limited the mentoring activities that could be undertaken in this club:

> So I organised a mentoring course for the club directors and their deputies, two per club. We held the course at 'X'. The Director of that club pops his head in and says he'll be back in half an hour, quick phone call. Never saw him again.
>
> *PCE, 2012*

Project two: Adult mentors in a Positive Youth Development programme (Sandford et al. 2010)

Background: In a programme funded by a corporate sponsor, outdoor and adventurous physical activity was used as a vehicle for enhancing young people's personal and social development. The participants were adolescents who were defined by their teachers as being disaffected or disengaged from one or more aspects of school life. The programme also included the involvement of adult volunteers (from the corporate sponsor) as learning mentors for the young people. The evaluation ran for four years.

Data extracts: The aim of including adult mentors was, through a form of engagement mentoring (Colley 2003), to increase young people's academic aspirations/achievement and reduce deviant behaviour. At the same time, there was an expectation that the benefits of the mentoring process would be two-way, with additional gains for the adult mentors (Eby and Lockwood 2005). Certainly the corporate sponsors felt this latter aspiration had been achieved:

> I think that the amount that our staff have got out of this over the years has been phenomenal and that, for us, is a very positive outcome. It's not just that people have done it, but how that has impacted some people, as an individual and also in their professional development.
>
> *Corporate Sponsor: Sandford et al. 2010, p. 143*

From the point of view of the mentors, there were also some notable successes:

> [It's been] emotionally draining, physically demanding, VERY rewarding – both in learning about leadership, about myself and about putting something back.
>
> *Mentor: Sandford et al. 2010, p. 145*

There were, however, many problems with the mentoring process over the course of the programme. There was a lack of clarity about the role of a 'mentor' and also the mechanisms to enable them to fulfil their role with the young people during and after the specific programme activities. These two extracts illustrate the dimensions of this issue and the frustration that resulted:

> No one really knew what was expected of us (at the activity weeks), when we were supposed to be somewhere, where we were supposed to be, what we were supposed to be doing, and that was quite mentally draining.
>
> *Mentor: Sandford et al. 2010, p. 145*

> I think it was quite confusing for the instructors, because the first question that mine said to me was "so why are you here? What's your role? And you needn't think you're going to interfere with anything I'm going to do".
>
> *Mentor: Sandford et al. 2010, p. 146*

Project three: Athlete mentors in schools (Armour and Duncombe 2011)

Background: This programme was based on the belief that successful sports stars who have striven to achieve success over a long period of time could offer personal guidance to young people. 'Athlete mentors', all of whom had achieved high levels of success in their sport, were recruited to work with groups of pupils in schools. The young participants were selected by their teachers because they were disaffected or disengaged from education. The intention was that the athlete mentors would visit each school three times, and that they would follow a structured series of engagement and 'inspirational' activities with pupils.

Data extracts: The programme was generally well received by schools and the young people were thrilled to meet sporting celebrities. Yet, the potential impact of the programme was restricted because the athletes found it difficult to complete the required number of visits and there was confusion between the concepts of 'mentor' and 'role model'. MacCallum and Beltman (2002, p. 34) describe a mentoring relationship as a 'one-to-one, long-term, supportive relationship between a more experienced, usually older person and a younger, less experienced or knowledgeable person'. On the other hand, Payne *et al.* (2002, p. 4) define a role model as someone worthy of imitation, 'an individual who inspires individuals or groups of people, through personal contact and relationship'. These two roles are quite different, so whereas the schools were led to expect an athlete *mentor*, what they tended to get was a rather more distant *role model*. The teachers commented:

- More visits from the athlete mentors were required, and they should be sustained over time
- The athletes needed to be better matched to pupils (class, gender etc.)
- The pupils were promised three visits, but this was not always possible for the athletes

The teachers were very keen for their schools to participate in the programme, but few had planned to capitalise on the athlete visits, for example, by providing extension activities. Instead, the teachers appeared to expect some (magical?) benefits to accrue for pupils because they had been 'inspired' by the athletes. The misconceptions in this project, therefore, ranged from conceptual to organisational.

Analysis . . . What does this mean for professional learning?

At one level, it is difficult to argue against the notion of mentoring as a means of offering tailored and in-context professional learning support. Zachary (2000, p. 167) pointed out that '[m]entoring programs enjoy sustainability over time when mentoring is embedded in an organisational cultural that values continuous learning'. Moreover, Conway *et al.* (2009, p. 118) highlights the importance of multi-directional mentoring and points out that:

> [i]nternationally, the development of mentoring in schools in conjunction with university-school partnerships has become a key feature of re-designed teacher education over the last decade.

Yet, in practice, as was illustrated in the vignettes, mentoring can be ineffective because neither mentor nor mentee fully understands what is required. In these circumstances, it is unsurprising to find that mentoring programmes are somewhat disappointing for all parties.

An analysis of dictionary definitions of mentoring reveals that a 'mentor' is commonly understood as an experienced adviser/supporter, and an older, more experienced person who advises and guides a younger, less experienced person. The term *trainer* is also linked to the notion of a mentor. It is easy to see, therefore, why mentoring appears to be such a powerful professional learning (or perhaps more accurately, management) tool. Yet mentoring, as defined here, is also underpinned by some interesting assumptions that could be challenged. These include the assumption that the older/more experienced person should 'mentor' the younger and less experienced; that 'training' and 'guiding' can be accepted uncritically; and that the older/more experienced person will 'guide' in the 'right' ways. It seems likely that mentoring is a rather more complex and dynamic process than these definitions suggest.

The theories of learning that underpin mentoring programmes are worthy of some analysis. Using the definitions of mentoring described here, for example, two points stand out. Firstly, mentoring undoubtedly has the capacity to address some of the common critiques of traditional continuing professional development (CPD) by offering *in situ* and sustained professional and personal support that is tailored to the needs of the individual. On the other hand, looking back at the vignettes, it might be argued that the implicit theory of learning embodied in them is what might be termed 'moral idealism'. Thus, a 'mentor' was identified – or self identified – who appeared to be able to offer strategic guidance to a mentee who was understood as being deficient in some respect. The stated goals of mentoring are usually pro-social and pro-management/organisation, so in the neo-liberal, performative culture that increasingly characterises schools (Evans 2012), the 'guiding' process is usually offered within clearly defined performance-management and accountability structures. In other words, in these kinds of programmes, both the direction of travel for the mentoring activity, and the destination, are pre-determined.

Despite claims that multi-directional mentoring is the ideal (Conway *et al.* 2009), the most common model is uni-directional mentoring from the experienced to the novice and in an organisational direction. Yet, as Berry (2012, p. 397) found, even in extreme managerialist school cultures, teachers are able to exercise their agency and resist performativity pressures by retaining a strong belief in education as a broader humanist project:

> Teachers acknowledge . . . the prevalence of performativity and survivalism yet often retain loyalty to the concept of education as a liberal humanist project . . . they manage to cling to a notion of teaching that transcends the demands of the pursuit of measurable standards.

In this context, a recent paper by Daniels (2012) is interesting. Daniels offers some insight into the process whereby teachers might subvert a managerial approach to mentoring. Drawing on the work of Vygotsky and Bernstein to generate a rich and dynamic understanding of learning, he highlights Bernstein's key *recontextualising principle* in pedagogic discourse, which 'selectively appropriates, relocates, refocuses and relates other discourses to constitute its own order' (p. 6). Daniels argues that:

[i]n order to understand pedagogic discourse as a social and historical construction, attention must be directed to the regulation of its structure, the social relations of its production and the various modes of its recontextualising as a practice.

ibid.

The links to mentoring are obvious. It can be anticipated that in any mentoring-mentee exchange, both parties are likely to be engaging in an ongoing process (a 'dance') of recontextualisation. To make the assumption, therefore, that mentoring will always – or even sometimes – result in clear outcomes that match pro-social and management/organisation goals seems naïve at best. Added to that is the idealism underpinning efforts to 'assign a mentor'. This is a process in which many organisations engage, including schools and universities, and it assumes that the organisation can select appropriate and influential (pro-social) mentors. Yet, a moment's reflection on our personal experiences of mentoring may suggest that the outcome is likely to be somewhat more random. Powerful mentors are more likely to be 'found' by the individual than 'assigned' by the organisation. Moreover, to complicate things further, 'found' mentors are more likely to be those who support – rather than challenge – a mentee's existing philosophies and practices.

Lessons learned . . . What could we add to the Mentor Pedagogy Toolbox?

What we might conclude, therefore, is that mentoring can play a part in CPD, but although it is both convenient and relatively inexpensive, it is unlikely to be a panacea. A highly performative and risk-averse school culture will undoubtedly impact upon a mentee's understanding of acceptable levels of challenge and critique in a formal mentoring relationship. Informal mentors, on the other hand, can be perceived as offering safety and support, and are likely to be powerful even (especially?) where they espouse anti-organisational goals.

The key lessons to be learned from the vignettes and the analysis are the following:

- Mentoring is a complex social activity that takes place in a complex social context, key features of which will influence the scope of potential learning;
- In mentoring programmes, all parties are likely to interpret the activity differently;
- In mentoring dyads, both parties will seek to recontextualise the mentoring activity and simultaneously reconstruct themselves;
- 'Assigning' effective formal mentors is a challenging task;
- Informal/found mentors are likely to be very powerful and may act to support a mentee by reinforcing current beliefs and prior assumptions; and
- Highly performative cultures influence the potential range and impact of mentoring programmes.

I have argued elsewhere (Armour *et al.* 2013) that if the aspiration is to encourage and support teachers to learn and develop across their careers, perhaps we should abandon the term *teacher*, instead conceptualising teachers as 'lead learners'. Pedder *et al.* (2005, p. 237) argue that classrooms and schools 'need to become crucibles of learning for teachers as much as for their students' and they describe learning *with* colleagues as 'indispensable' in the quest to raise the quality of educational provision. It could be argued that learning *with* professional learning colleagues, in the interests of pupils, fits the ideal of an education profession. Perhaps it also signals that the term *mentoring* in the contexts of teaching (and, indeed, coaching) needs to be redefined to reflect the position of these practitioners as lead learners (Armour *et al.* 2013).

Key terms: professional responsibility, coach education, positive youth development, theories of learning, mentoring and professional learning, performativity, formal and informal mentoring, recontextualisation, learning as becoming, learning professions.

References

Armour, K. M., Chambers, F. C. and Makopoulou, K. 2013. Conceptualising teaching as learning: The challenge for teacher education. In S. Capel and M. Whitehead (Eds.) *Debates in Physical Education*. London: Routledge, pp. 205–219.

Armour, K. M. and Duncombe, R. 2011. Changing lives? Critical evaluation of a school-based athlete role model intervention. *Sport, Education and Society*, 17(3), 381–403.

Armour, K. M., Griffiths, M. and Cushion, C. C. 2012. Professional Coach Educators (PCE): External Evaluation of the Pilot Scheme by the University of Birmingham and Loughborough University, UK. Unpublished report, January.

Berry, J. 2012. Teachers' professional autonomy in England: Are neo-liberal approaches incontestable? *Forum*, 54(3), 397–410.

Brunetti, G. J. 1998. Teacher education: A look at its future. *Teacher Education Quarterly*, Fall, 59–64.

Charmaz, K. 2006. *Constructing Grounded Theory: A Practical Guide Through Qualitative Analysis*. London: Sage Publications.

Colley, H. 2003. *Mentoring for Social Inclusion: A Critical Approach to Nurturing Mentor Relationships*. London: Routledge Falmer.

Conway, P. F., Murphy, R., Rath, A., and Hall, K. 2009. *Learning to Teach and Its Implications for the Continuum of Teacher Education: A Nine-Country Cross-National Study*. Maynooth: Teaching Council of Ireland.

Daniels, H. 2012. Institutional culture, social interaction and learning. *Learning, Culture and Social Interaction*, 1, 2–11.

Day, C. and Sachs, J. 2004. Professionalism, performativity and empowerment: Discourses in the politics, policies and purposes of continuing professional development. In C. Day and Judyth Sachs (Eds.) *International Handbook on the Continuing Professional Development of Teachers*. Milton Keynes, UK: Open University Press, pp. 3–32.

Day, C. and Townsend, A. 2009. Practitioner action research: Building and sustaining success through networked learning communities. In Noffke, S. and Somekh, B. (Eds.) *The Sage Handbook of Educational Action Research*. Sage, pp. 178–189.

Eby, L. T., and Lockwood, A. 2005. Protégés' and mentors' reactions to participating in formal mentoring programs: A qualitative investigation. *Journal of Vocational Behavior*, 67(3), 441–458.

Evans, J. 2012. Ideational border crossings: Rethinking the politics of knowledge within and across disciplines. *Discourse: Studies in the Cultural Politics of Education,* 35(1), 45–60.

House, E. 2005. Qualitative evaluation and changing social policy. In N. K. Denzin and Y. S. Lincoln (Eds.) *The Sage Handbook of Qualitative Research* (3rd edition). London: Sage Publications, pp. 1069–1082.

MacCallum, J. and Beltman, S. 2002. *Role Models for Young People: What Makes an Effective Role Model Program?* Tasmania: National Youth Affairs Research Scheme.

Payne, W., Reynolds, M., Brown, S. and Fleming, A. 2002. *Sports Role Models and Their Impact on Participation in Physical Activity: A Literature Review.* Victoria, Australia: University of Ballarat.

Pedder, D., James, M., and Macbeath, J. 2005. How teachers value and practise professional learning. *Research Papers in Education,* 20(3), 209–243.

Rossi, P. H., Lipsey, M. W. and Freeman, H. E. 2004. *Evaluation. A Systematic Approach* (7th edition). London: Sage Publications.

Sandford, R., Armour, K. M., and Stanton, D. J. 2010. Volunteer mentors as informal educators in a youth physical activity program. *Mentoring and Tutoring: Partnership in Learning,* 18(2), 135–153.

Stake, R. E. 2005. Qualitative case studies. In N. K. Denzin and Y. S. Lincoln (3rd edition) *The SAGE Handbook of Qualitative Research.* California: Sage Publications, pp. 443–466.

Timperley, H. 2008. *Teacher Professional Learning and Development.* UNESCO/International Academy of Education. Available from http://www.ibe.unesco.org/fileadmin/user_upload/Publications/Educational_Practices/EdPractices_18.pdf (accessed 26th March, 2014).

Wayne, A. J., Suk Yoon, K., Zhu, P., Cronen, S., and Garet, M. S. 2008. Experimenting with teacher professional development: Motives and methods. *Educational Researcher,* 37(8), 469–479.

Zachary, L. J. 2000. *The Mentor's Guide: Facilitating Effective Learning Relationships.* San Francisco, California: Jossey-Bass.

Resources

Armour, K. M., Chambers, F. C. and Makopoulou, K. 2013. Conceptualising teaching as learning: The challenge for teacher education. In S. Capel and M. Whitehead (Eds.) *Debates in Physical Education.* London: Routledge, pp. 205–219.

Garvey, B., and Alred, G. 2000. Educating mentors. *Mentoring and Tutoring: Partnership in Learning,* 8(2), 113–126.

3

THE PEDAGOGY OF MENTORING

Process and practice

*Fiona C. Chambers, Sinéad Luttrell,
Kathleen Armour, Walter E. Bleakley,
Deirdre A. Brennan and Frank A. Herold*

Overview

The pedagogy of mentoring describes how mentees learn and the pedagogical knowledge and skills that mentor teachers need to support them to learn effectively (Chambers *et al.* 2012, p. 347). The central goal in mentoring pedagogy is to encourage mentees to become autonomous learners (James *et al.* 2006). A strategic aspect to consider when planning mentor pedagogical approaches is the location of the mentee in Frances Fuller's concerns-based model (1969). In her concerns-based theory, the pre-service teacher or novice coach moves through three stages. In the first stage, the concern is for self, i.e. surviving the teaching/coaching experience, feeling incompetent and worrying about peer acceptance. In the second stage, the pre-service teacher/novice coach moves to being concerned about the teaching/coaching task, in particular managing and instructing pupils/athletes. Finally, in the third stage, the blinkers move further outward and the concern shifts to the impact of teaching and coaching on the pupils/athletes. In this final stage, the pre-service teacher/coach begins to consider differentiated tasks and develops a clear focus on pupil/athlete learning and how to enhance this process. Glickman *et al.* (2001) outline three styles of mentoring which may help a mentee move through the layers of Fuller's Concerns Model. These are directive, non-directive and collaborative. An accomplished mentor will transition between each style with confidence, responding to the levels of abstract thinking, expertise and commitment to teaching displayed by the pre-service teacher (Furlong and Maynard 1995). For example, a directive style is required if a mentee is operating at a low level in each of these aspects, whereas a mentee who is at a mid-level may benefit from a more collaborative approach. Mentees who are functioning at a high level across these three areas will require a more non-directive approach, where the mentor nudges the mentee through probing questions, posing problems, and so on.

When interrogating the strength of the mentor-mentee interaction using Furlong and Maynard's mentoring styles model, the work of Daloz (1986) is helpful. The potency of this interaction is dependent on the nature of mentor support and challenge. It champions the concept of mentor as critical friend (Kwan and Lopez-Real 2005) offering support and challenge, as necessary. This view is corroborated by Smith (2007), who defines mentoring as 'a particular mode of learning wherein the mentor not only supports the mentee, but also challenges them productively so that progress is made' (p. 277). Daloz' (1986) model emanates from the work of both Dewey (1938, 1910) and Piaget (1970) and centres on transformative learning (Zeichner 2010), which leans on constructivist theories of learning, and involves the development of the adult learner as both person and professional. It is a holistic view and incorporates the development of the intuitive processes of the mentee through the disruption of old patterns of meaning, leading to a fresh view of the self in the world (Dirkx 1998). This aligns with Fairbanks et al.'s (2000, p. 103) definition of mentoring in teacher education as 'complex social interactions that mentor teachers and student teachers construct and negotiate for a variety of professional purposes and in response to the contextual factors they encounter'. This leads to a more nuanced description of the pedagogy of mentoring which, according to Lai (2005), has three dimensions, i.e. relational (relationship between mentor-mentee), developmental (personal and professional development of mentee) and contextual (cultural and situational issues in the mentoring setting).

Vignette

Background

This vignette describes a cross-border study that investigated the process and practice of mentoring in physical education–teacher education in three case-study sites (Birchfield University [Republic of Ireland], Rivermount University [Northern Ireland] and Larkhill University [England]) between April 2010 and March 2011. It was funded by the Standing Conference on Teacher Education North and South (SCoTENS) and was guided by key research questions, one of which asked: 'What is known about the characteristics of "effective mentoring" in work-based learning?'

Methods

At each of the research sites the participants comprised two researchers and a cohort of mentor teachers (see Table 3.1). Mentor teachers volunteered to be part of the study. All participants signed the consent letters and pseudonyms were used throughout. A range of data collection methods were used (desk study, document analysis, open profile questionnaire, online discussion forum and a collaborative one-day seminar). Data were analysed thematically around the research questions, with some grounded theory (Strauss and Corbin 1998).

TABLE 3.1

	Mentor	Mentoring Experience	University Tutor (UT)
Site 1: Birchfield University *Republic of Ireland*	Conor Nora Tracy Aoife Laoise	1 year 6 years 10 years 20 years 32 years	Abigail Lucy
	Mentor	Mentoring Experience	University Tutor (UT)
Site 2: Rivermount University *Northern Ireland*	Matthew Georgie	10 years 20 years	Edward Caroline
	Mentor	Mentoring Experience	University Tutor (UT)
Site 3: Larkhill University *England*	William Sarah Andrew	10 years 20 years 30 years	Simon Evelyn

Findings

From this process, a Position Statement on Effective Physical Education Teacher Education (PETE) Mentoring was generated comprising five key themes, two of which are reported here.

Theme A: The mentor should provide support and guidance to the pre-service PE teacher both professionally and personally.

A clear data thread is evident in this study showing mentor teachers embracing a holistic view of the mentor role. In the first example, Georgie, mentor, explains that the purpose of the mentor is:

> [t]o support and guide them on their professional development and not only professionally but maybe personally because there may be some other issues like time management or conflict or preparation that you may have to support them with as well. Primarily the role is support and guidance.
>
> *Georgie, mentor, Rivermount University, Northern Ireland, online seminar, 9th March 2011*

In the second example, Laoise, mentor, outlines the nature of the support offered to mentees during this process, i.e. that it should be:

[a]ll positive . . . keep feeding them the positive information and develop that confidence really . . . in order for those competencies to then grow and develop.

Laoise, mentor, Birchfield University, ROI,
online seminar, 9th March 2011

In the third example, Nora, mentor, builds on this notion, outlining the benefits to such a positive approach:

Confidence is key because they can find themselves getting wiped out throughout the year just poured with teaching and lesson plans and all that sort of stuff. The mentor must develop an approachable attitude but also be capable of providing criticism, advice and encouragement.

Nora, mentor, Birchfield University, ROI, online seminar, 9th March 2011

Simon, UT, further advocates that a high-quality professional dialogue between mentor and mentee is paramount, stating that this approach helps to:

[d]evelop trainee teachers into critical practitioners, into reflective practitioners and empower them to actually develop into those. So, to develop into people who are reflective of their own practice and into people who are also prepared to take new things on board as they're finding their feet.

Simon, UT, Larkhill University, England,
online seminar, 9th March 2011

Theme B: The mentor teacher should ensure a safe learning space for the pre-service PE teacher where he or she is free to take risks and explore praxis in a variety of contexts.

Data excerpts highlight the variety of sites in which praxis (or theory-informed practice) is emphasized within teacher education and the role of the mentor in this work. In the first example, Andrew, mentor teacher, asserts:

The core purpose of mentoring for me is supporting the trainee in making the link between perhaps a theoretical and performance background into the teaching environment.

Andrew, mentor, Larkhill University, England,
online seminar, 9th March 2011

In the second example, Aoife agrees, but proclaims that the university and school have different but symbiotic roles in preparing pre-service teachers:

The university focuses more on the theory and the school allows the opportunity for the practical application of that theory to take place in a very secure and safe environment for the trainee.

Aoife, mentor, Birchfield University, ROI,
online seminar, 9th March 2011

In the third example, Simon, UT, insists that the school setting offers a praxis-centred site with risk-seeking opportunities to:

> [t]ry and see what happens. Take that risk and try out different things. You can see what happens and how the pupils actually respond to that. It doesn't matter if the lesson goes belly up.
>
> *Simon, UT, Larkhill University, England,*
> *online seminar, 9th March 2011*

Data sets also reveal the nature of the learning experiences on teaching practice (TP) in schools. In the first example, Abigail extends Simon's observation, suggesting that when mentoring is effective, it is 'a very nice mechanism of leading them gently in to it and there is a bit of a safety net and it's okay if things go wrong' (Abigail, University Tutor (UT), Birchfield University, ROI, online seminar, 9th March 2011). In the second example, Edward, UT, concurs with Abigail and describes how the mentor creates a 'safe learning environment . . . and can comfort them if things go wrong' (Edward, UT, Rivermount University, Northern Ireland, online seminar, 9th March 2011).

Analysis

A mentor is a critical friend (Brooks and Sikes 1997) who shapes the person-pedagogue (Armour and Fernandez-Balboa 2001). In other words, the mentor is charged with building the mentee's agency as a learner to avoid 'learning helplessness' (Maier and Seligman 1976). Agency is developed when mentors freely share their views on progress with the mentee. Through meaningful reflection in action and on action (Schon 1983), such interactions lead to mentee 'learnacy' (Claxton 2004), which is the ability and willingness to manage and shape learning progress to a point when this can be done independently without reliance on a mentor.

In order to be an effective 'critical friend', mentor teachers must have key attributes and must be suitable for this role, i.e. having the 'right' disposition and expertise (Chambers *et al.* 2012). Mentors should be both willing and able to mentor. In instances where mentors are not suitable and are untrained, their work can have a significant detrimental effect on the mentee and 'can actually stunt beginner teachers' professional learning and growth' (Hobson and Malderez 2013, p. 92). A more forensic view of suitability reveals that the mentors not only (a) possess particular interpersonal traits with high levels of emotional intelligence and (b) are intentional role models (Gilbert 1985), but (c) are also highly respected scholars and professionals (Manathunga 2007). A *suitable* mentor with training can deliver a smorgasbord of mentor career functions, e.g. as sponsorship, exposure and visibility, providing challenges, protection and training in ethical procedures. However, the reality is there are often very loose methods of mentor selection based on availability rather than suitability (Ingersoll and Smith 2004; Fletcher 2000). This leads to mentors who lack the skills and knowledge required for the role. Another problem is that many mentors are not trained for the role and, even where they are, training programmes are of inconsistent quality (Abell et al. 1995).

The mentor offers psychological support to the mentee 'providing the mentee with a safe place to release emotions' or 'let off steam' (Malderez and Bodsczky 1999; Malderez and Wedell 2007). This psychosocial function will also involve developing mentee self-efficacy through building competence and confidence. Grossman, Hammerness and McDonald (2009) posit that mentoring is a central pillar of professional teacher education. It has the power to develop knowledge, skill and professional identity (ibid., p. 273). Having created a bubble of safety for the mentee, the mentor will develop both their professional and pedagogical identity through Lai's (2005) three-dimensional mentoring model – relational, developmental and contextual. Through this construct, mentors have a pivotal role as identity agents, i.e. they can be purposeful co-constructors of mentees' identities when they use a transformative pedagogical approach that involves fostering collaborative learning and empowering mentees to think creatively and critically. Specifically, Wan et al. (2010, p. 287) proffer this view on the role of mentors:

> To reinforce the skills of building rapport and trust with their students, pre-service teachers should be assisted by experiencing slightly risky pedagogies, for example, in pursuing more self-directed learning.

In this study, the willingness to encourage to engage in risky pedagogies and self-directed learning depended on the disposition and expertise of the mentor, i.e. the position of the mentor in his or her professional life or 'phase in professional life' (Sikes 1992). Huberman (1989), in his study of Swiss teachers, charted the professional life cycle of teachers and discovered that teachers' dispositions changed as they moved through their professional life cycles (see Figure 3.1). Three mentors are mapped onto this professional career cycle:

Mentor teacher at career entry phase. *Conor, mentor teacher, Birchfield University, Republic of Ireland (1 year experience).*

Conor was immersed in surviving his initial mentoring experiences, and as a teacher in induction phase, was also trying to negotiate his early career teaching experience. He was experiencing 'reality shock' (Veenman 1984) both as a mentor and as a teacher. Odell (1990) avers that teachers in this phase need to be mentored closely themselves to overcome difficulties encountered as a beginning teacher. This was not an ideal situation. In his capacity as mentor, he was continually discovering new territory (McCormick and Barnett 2006). Conor was therefore located in the first layer of Fuller's concerns-based model, being 'concerned about self' as mentor (Fuller 1969). He was therefore limited to offering high mentor support/low mentee risk (Daloz 1986) pedagogical strategies which involved modelling and directive practice (Glickman et al. 2001) at, perhaps, a foundation level of Bloom's (1956) taxonomy of learning domains.

Mentor teacher at experimentation/activism phase. *Matthew, mentor teacher, Rivermount University, Northern Ireland (10 years experience).*

He has not been formally trained for this role and is on the boundary of two of Fuller's levels (1969), i.e. the concerns about tasks and about pre-service teacher learning levels. He reported using a collaborative learning style (Glickman *et al.* 2001) with mentees, and encouraged pre-service teacher learning at the intermediate levels of Bloom's taxonomy (1956).

Mentor teacher at serenity/relational distance phase. *Andrew, mentor teacher, Larkhill University, England (30 years experience).*

As a trained mentor, Andrew is 'fully concerned with impact on pre-service teacher learning' in Fuller's (1969) Concerns model. Therefore, he was able to offer a range of mentor pedagogical strategies using low mentor support/high mentee risk (Daloz 1986). He enabled the mentee to negotiate risky and unpredictable situations through a non-directive mentoring style. This catapulted the mentee to the highest levels of learning in Bloom's taxonomy (1956).

The analysis led to the development of a 'continuum of factors influencing mentor pedagogy' (see Figure 3.1) (Chambers *et al.* 2012):

> This continuum shows an intersection of five theoretical frameworks which together describe the factors which influenced the mentoring pedagogies used by the mentors in this study. The assertion is that a mentor's (1) teaching expertise and disposition (Huberman 1989) together with his/her (2) mentoring expertise and (3) position in the Concerns Model (Fuller *1969*) may influence (4) the pedagogies employed by the mentor within the 'Model of Support and Challenge' (Daloz 1986) e.g. mentoring styles (Glickman, Gordon, and Ross-Gordon 2001) to (5) support pre-service teacher (p. 358) learning across Bloom's taxonomy of learning domains (Bloom *et al.* 1956).

Each mentor can be placed on a continuum of mentor pedagogies according to the following criteria in Figure 3.1:

Lessons learned . . . What could we add to the Mentor Pedagogy Toolbox?

- The mentor needs to *both* be suitable, i.e. possess the right disposition for the role, *and* 'participate in appropriate and informed mentor training and development opportunities' (Hobson and Malderez 2013, p. 13).
- Effective mentor pedagogies promote transformative learning (Mezirow and Taylor 2009) through Daloz' (1986) model of supporting and challenging the mentee, which advances the holistic development of the adult learner as both person and professional.
- Effective mentor pedagogies need to address the three dimensions of the mentoring process: relational (relationship between mentor-mentee), developmental (personal and professional development of mentee) and contextual

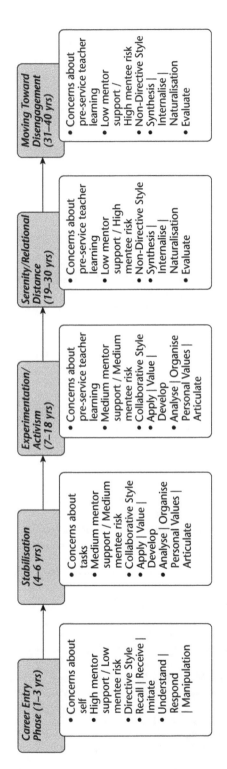

FIGURE 3.1 Continuum of factors influencing quality of mentor pedagogy

Chambers et al. 2012

(cultural and situational issues in the mentoring setting) (Lai 2005). The foci of these pedagogies include showing empathy and trust, fostering positivity, being protective, being supportive, building rapport, applying mentoring styles, delivering criticism, managing the co-existence of personal and professional relationships, and possessing subject knowledge.

Key terms: pedagogy of mentoring, pedagogical knowledge and skills, continuum.

References

Abell, S. K., Dillon, D. R., Hopkins, C. J., McInerney, W. D. and O'Brien, D. G. 1995. 'Somebody to count on': Mentor/intern relationships in a beginning teacher internship program. *Teaching and Teacher Education*, 11, 173–188.

Armour, K. M. and Fernandez-Balboa, J. M. 2001. Connections, pedagogy and professional learning. *Teaching and Teacher Education,* 12, 103–118.

Bloom, B. S., (Eds.) Engelhart, M. D., Furst, E. J., Hill, W. H. and Krathwohl, D. R. 1956. *Taxonomy of Educational Objectives: The Classification of Educational Goals; Handbook I: The Cognitive Domain.* New York: Longmans, Green.

Brooks, V., and Sikes, P. 1997. *The Good Mentor Guide: Initial Teacher Education in Secondary Schools.* Buckingham: Open University Press.

Chambers, F. C., Armour, K., Luttrell, S., Bleakley, E. W., Brennan, D. A. and Herold, F. A. 2012. Mentoring as a profession-building process in physical education teacher education. *Irish Educational Studies,* 31, 345–362.

Claxton, G., 2004. Learning is learnable (and we ought to teach it). In John Cassell (Ed.) *Ten Years On: The National Commission for Education Report.*

Daloz, L. A. 1986. *Effective Teaching and Mentoring: Realizing the Transformational Power of Adult Learning Experiences.* San Francisco, CA: Jossey-Bass.

Dewey, J. 1910. *How We Think.* Boston: D.C. Heath & Co.

Dewey, J. 1938. *Experience and Education.* New York: Collier Books.

Dirkx, J. M. 1998. Transformative learning theory in the practice of adult education: An overview. *PAACE Journal of Lifelong Learning,* 7, 1–14.

Fairbanks, C. M., Freedman, D. and Kahn, C. 2000. The role of effective mentors in learning to teach. *Journal of Teacher Education,* 51, 102–112.

Fletcher, S. 2000. *Mentoring in Schools: A Handbook of Good Practice.* London: Routledge.

Fuller, F. 1969. Concerns of teachers: A developmental conceptualization. *American Educational Research Journal,* 6, 207–226.

Furlong, J. and Maynard, T. 1995. *Mentoring Student Teachers: The Growth of Professional Knowledge.* London: Routledge.

Gilbert, L. A. 1985. Dimensions of same-gender student-faculty role-model relationships. *Sex Roles,* 12, 111–123.

Glickman, C. D., Gordon, S. P. and Ross-Gordon, J. M. 2001. *SuperVision and Instructional Leadership: A Developmental Approach.* Needham Heights, Massachusetts: Allyn and Bacon.

Grossman, P., Hammerness, K. and McDonald, M. 2009. Redefining teaching, re-imagining teacher education. *Teachers and Teaching: Theory and Practice,* 15, 273–289.

Hobson, A. J. and Malderez, A. 2013. Judgementoring and other threats to realizing the potential of schoolbased mentoring in teacher education. *International Journal of Mentoring and Coaching in Education,* 2, 89–108.

Huberman, M. 1989. The professional life cycle of teachers. *Teachers College Record,* 91, 31–57.

Ingersoll, R. M. and Smith, T. M. 2004. Do teacher induction and mentoring matter? *NASSP Bulletin,* 88, 28–40.

James, M., Black, P., McCormick, R., Pedder, D. and Wiliam, D. 2006. Learning how to learn, in classrooms, schools and networks: Aims, design and analysis. *Research Papers in Education,* 21, 119–132.

Kwan, T. and Lopez-Real, F. 2005. Mentors' perceptions of their roles in mentoring student teachers. *Asia-Pacific Journal of Teacher Education,* 33, 275–287.

Lai, E. 2005. *Mentoring for In-service Teachers in a Distance Teacher Education Programme: Views of Mentors, Mentees and University Teachers.* Paper presented at the Australian Association for Research in Education International Education Research Conference. Parramatta.

Maier, S. F. and Seligman, M. E. P. 1976. Learned helplessness: Theory and evidence. *Journal of Experimental Psychology: General,* 105, 3–46.

Malderez, A. and Bodsczky, C. 1999. *Mentor Courses: A Resource Book for Trainer-Trainers.* Cambridge: Cambridge University Press.

Malderez, A. and Wedell, M. 2007. *Teaching Teachers: Processes and Practices.* London: Continuum.

Manathunga, C. 2007. Supervision as mentoring: The role of power and boundary crossing. *Studies in Continuing Education,* 29, 207–221.

McCormick, J. and Barnett, K. 2006. *Relationships Between Teacher Career Stages/States and Locus of Control: A Multilevel Analysis.* A paper presented at the Annual Conference of the Australian Association for Research in Education. Adelaide.

Mezirow, J. and Taylor, E. W. 2009. *Transformative Learning in Practice: Insights from Community, Workplace, and Higher Education.* San Francisco, CA: Jossey-Bass.

Odell, S. J. 1990. Support for new teachers. In M. Bey and C. T. Holmes (Eds.), *Mentoring: Developing Successful New Teachers.* Reston, VA: Association of Teacher Educators.

Piaget, J. 1970. *Science of Education and the Psychology of the Child.* London: Longman Group.

Schon, D. A. 1983. *The Reflective Practitioner: How Professionals Think in Action.* New York: Basic Books.

Sikes, P. 1985. The life cycle of the teacher. In S. Ball and I. Goodson (Eds.) *Teachers' Lives and Careers.* Lewes, Falmer, pp. 27–60.

Smith, A. 2007. Mentoring for experienced school principals: Professional learning in a safe place. *Mentoring and Tutoring: Partnership in Learning,* 15, 277–291.

Strauss, A. and Corbin, J. 1998. *Basics of Qualitative Research: Techniques and Procedures for Developing Grounded Theory.* London: Sage Publications.

Veenman, S. 1984. Perceived problems of beginning teachers. *Review of Educational Research,* 54, 143–178.

Wan, N., Nicholas, H. and Williams, A. 2010. School experience influences on pre-service teachers' evolving beliefs about effective teaching. *Teaching and Teacher Education,* 26, 278–289.

Zeichner, K. 2010. Rethinking the connections between campus courses and field experiences in college- and university-based teacher education. *Journal of Teacher Education,* 61, 89–99.

Resources

Evans, M. (Ed.) 2012. *Teacher Education and Pedagogy: Theory, Policy and Practice.* Cambridge: Cambridge University Press.

SECTION 2
Sociocultural factors and mentoring

4

MENTORING YOUTH

Rachel Sandford

Overview

This chapter explores the concept of youth mentoring and considers the process of supporting the positive development of disadvantaged and vulnerable youth through mentoring initiatives. Drawing upon data from the evaluation of one particular physical activity programme, the discussion illustrates the purpose, structure and experience of the mentoring process. Specifically, it outlines the rationale for using mentors within such programmes, highlights key findings regarding programme impact (from the perspective of mentors, mentees and teachers) and identifies elements of good practice that can aid the delivery of future initiatives in this area.

Vignette

This HSBC/OB[1] (Outward Bound) project focused on the use of outdoor/adventurous physical activities as a vehicle to facilitate young people's development. Working with five schools from a disadvantaged area of London, the project aimed to enhance positive community relations as well as support pupils' (re)engagement with education. A central element of the project was the inclusion of HSBC employees as volunteer mentors, who were trained to work with pupils both within the residential outdoor/adventurous activity sessions and in school-based follow-up activities. Within this training, mentors covered issues relating to youth culture, child protection and managing challenging behaviour. They were also introduced to the concept of 'informal education' (whereby learning is perceived to be a collaborative process and commonplace contexts/conversations are viewed as opportunities to 'draw out' educational messages) as a learning strategy.[2]

Through group discussions and role-play, mentors were given practical advice on building and maintaining positive relationships with young people, and the ways in which they could enhance and support pupil learning. As the project progressed, new mentors also gained valuable knowledge from experienced colleagues who had been involved with previous cohorts.

During the lifetime of the project, approximately 750 young people (13–14 years) participated in project activities, supported by 7 regular members of school staff and 57 different mentors. The mentors were each allocated to a specific group for the residential sessions[3], but were thereafter just linked with one project school. Data on mentors' perceptions and experiences of the project were generated through observations of the activity sessions, informal conversations, interviews, focus groups and reflective journals. The aim here was to determine their thoughts about the mentoring process (e.g. what they felt they had brought to and gained from it) and discuss any key issues or concerns. In addition, data on the role, value and effectiveness of mentors were generated from others (e.g. teachers, pupils and project management staff) via various methods (interviews, focus groups, journals and surveys). Data were collated and analysed systematically by coding in stages, in order to generate and verify key themes. The extended nature of the project also allowed for an integrated process of data analysis and collection, allowing key issues, concerns or learning points to be fed back into the mentor training programme. Some key findings that relate to the mentoring element of the project are highlighted in the following fictional narratives, which blend multiple voices to give summative accounts of mentors', mentees' and teachers' views. These narratives suggest that there are potential benefits to be gained (for mentors, mentees and schools) from the mentoring process, but also hint at the various social and contextual factors that can influence the nature and degree of impact (Sandford *et al.* 2010; Armour and Sandford 2013).

> I was after a bit of a challenge and mentoring seemed a good opportunity. I thought I could be a positive influence for some young people, perhaps teach them new skills, and widen their horizons. For me, it was about trying to support positive development. Some mentors felt they were 'neutral' adults, but I saw myself more as a supporter, an educator. I'm not sure I had a clear understanding of that going into the project though! No-one really knew what was expected of us to start with or what we were supposed to be doing. Keeping in touch beyond the activities was one of the hardest things about mentoring. How could we physically keep in contact so that we didn't lose what we'd already built? It was really difficult doing that through the school, to be honest. I think that's why so many mentors lost interest. It was why the on-going training was important too, though, and why those who kept up with that, who really bought into it, stayed involved more. It certainly allowed me to develop my understanding, so now I have a better sense of what it means to 'mentor'. It's to encourage people and make them work as a little sort of unit together. It is to be there almost in the background,

but sometimes you are not in the background you are at the front guiding people; it is completely dynamic. I thought the mentoring was brilliant. I thoroughly enjoyed it and got a lot out of it from a personal point of view. It changed my perspective of young people. It was emotionally draining and physically demanding, but very rewarding.

Nick, mentor

It was good meeting new people. Some of the mentors were really funny and helped you learn things. Sometimes they gave you advice about things and got you to think about the future. It was nice to speak with different grown-ups too; they weren't all bossy like teachers or parents! I liked a lot of the mentors, but some of my friends didn't know who they were. We were asked in an interview what we had thought of the mentors and someone said 'what's a mentor?'! Some people weren't interested in the mentors – and some mentors didn't seem that interested in us – but I got on really well with one mentor, John, so I was glad when my teacher said she'd help us keep in touch outside of school. He helped me focus on my school work and got me some work experience.

Ryan, mentee

I think the mentors made a valuable contribution to the project. They were often proactive, helpful and around if pupils needed help with something. It was good to have someone from outside school to share the workload and support pupils' learning. I particularly liked the way they reinforced the instructors' teaching points and encouraged pupils to transfer learning to school or home. It was difficult to start with, though, because we weren't always sure what they were supposed to be doing and what long term role they were going to play. Some of them disappeared after the activity sessions, but others were really keen. The best mentors stuck around; they helped instigate involvement in other projects, arranged work experience and built up good relationships with HSBC. They were the ones who had most impact.

Jayne, teacher

Analysis

The concept of youth mentoring has become increasingly fashionable within the field of education, and this has led to significant growth in structured mentoring initiatives (DuBois and Karcher 2005). Addressing problems of social exclusion and disaffection has become a key target for many such programmes within the UK, Europe and beyond, grounded in research which suggests that a learning relationship with an adult other than a parent (or teacher) can lead to positive outcomes for vulnerable young people (Bennetts 2003). Indeed, as Newburn and Shiner (2006, p. 24) point out, many contemporary initiatives are 'underpinned by the view that some of the problems of inadequate socialization, personal dysfunction and disaffection can be offset by the support of a mentor'. Colley (2003) describes this kind of remedial approach as 'engagement mentoring' and argues that the goals of such initiatives can be seen to include increasing academic success, lowering deviant behaviour, increasing self-esteem and improving employability. These certainly resonate with some of the key aims of the HSBC/OB project outlined previously (specifically 'to facilitate young people's personal, social and educational development' and 'support pupils' (re)engagement with education'), and provide additional justification for the use of informal education (IE) as a learning strategy for mentors within this project. In this way, there are also perceptible links to some of the literature on positive youth development and resiliency, particularly in the sense that positive mentoring relationships can facilitate the development of key life skills, which can represent significant 'social capital' and function as a means of protection against difficult life circumstances (Lerner et al. 2005). Such views help to reinforce the assertion, also prevalent within the physical education literature, that it is the social processes experienced and not the activity undertaken per se that lead to positive outcomes for young people (e.g. Sandford et al. 2008).

The previous narratives lend credence to the notion that there are benefits for all in the mentoring process. These benefits were personal, social, educational and contextual and not all were anticipated or planned for. This highlights something of the fluidity of mentoring relationships, but also raises a question about clarity of purpose with regard to mentors' roles and expectations. Mentors who grasped the notion of what the project was trying to achieve (mentors like Nick) were perceived to engage more effectively and, consequently, were identified as those who 'had most impact' (Jayne). As noted previously, there was an initial lack of clarity regarding the nature and scope of the mentor role in the HSBC/OB project: i.e. were mentors neutral adults, role models or educators? This led to 'confusion' among mentors and teachers and even resulted in a lack of comprehension among some young people. The mentor role did become clearer through the life of the project, however, thanks in part to the iterative nature of the evaluation, allowing lessons to be learnt from the initial mentors' experiences and for these to be fed directly back in to subsequent mentor training. This kind of 'feedback system' would certainly appear to be an important feature of effective programme design.

Another issue to highlight from the narratives is the importance of mentor selection. As Nick suggests, mentors must 'buy into' the process and be genuinely interested in working with young people. Those who do not commit in this way could potentially 'lose interest' and 'disappear' thus limiting the impact of the process. Ryan would appear to concur, but also notes that this is a two-way process and that young people, too, need to actively engage with the mentoring process ('Some pupils just weren't interested in the mentors – and some mentors didn't seem that interested in us'). Studies have shown that the nature of the mentoring relationship is all important (e.g. Rhodes et al. 2002). Young people value mentors who are personable, and it has been argued that successful mentoring relationships are often underpinned by qualities of trust, reciprocity and shared experience (Philip et al. 2004). Some such mentoring experiences were evident in the

HSBC/OB project ('some of the mentors were really funny and helped you learn things'), but the arbitrary allocation of mentors to groups also meant that young people had varying experiences. While modern (structured) mentoring relationships are not characterised by the spontaneity of more traditional approaches, there still needs to be some sense of affiliation between mentor and mentee. Thought therefore needs to be given to the matching of mentors to mentees (DuBois *et al.* 2002) and, importantly, to if and how spontaneous mentoring relationships can be supported. Researchers have noted the importance of having 'appropriate' individuals involved with the delivery of youth physical activity programmes and have highlighted the need for enthusiastic, effective and inspirational leadership (e.g. Petitpas *et al.* 2008). This discussion would seem to suggest that for mentors, too, particularly those who are working with vulnerable or challenging youth, the need to be informed and aware of the role they are expected to play is equally important.

The most effective mentors in the HSBC/OB project were those, like Nick, who were fully involved in all aspects of the mentoring process, committed to actively engaging with the young people within and beyond project activities, willing to facilitate the on-going development of teaching-learning relationships, and interested in furthering their own understanding regarding the mentor role ('. . . it is completely dynamic; the role, it changes all the time'). Such findings point to the need for adults involved in 'engagement mentoring' projects with vulnerable youth to be carefully selected, in order to ensure that they have a clear sense of their role and a willingness to engage in an active, developmental process. Moreover, there is perhaps a need for adults working with vulnerable youth to undergo specific training, in order to increase their sensitivity to the issues these young people face and ensure that they are equipped with the skills necessary to foster learning and development over time (Fresko and Wertheim 2006). DuBois *et al.* (2002) also argue that effective mentor training can help to equip mentors and enhance their 'adaptive persistence' (p. 29) when faced with obstacles in establishing and maintaining relationships with young people. This would appear to be corroborated by Nick, when he states that '[i]t was why the on-going training was important . . . and why those who have kept up with that, who really bought into it, have stayed involved more'. The training provided to mentors involved in the HSBC/OB project was viewed positively by many and, interestingly, the inclusion of informal education as a learning strategy within this training appeared to enhance the mentors' capacity to reflect and gain a critical perspective on their role in supporting young people's learning (see Sandford *et al.* 2010).

As with other studies (e.g. Philip and Spratt 2007), some young people involved in the HSBC/OB project valued the opportunity to sustain an informal relationship with mentors beyond the end of the initiative ('I got on really well with one mentor . . . I was glad when my teacher said she'd help us keep in touch outside of school'). For this project, however, this was the exception rather than the norm. Rappaport (2002) acknowledges that maintaining mentoring relationships over time can be challenging, stating that the often 'contrived' nature of the relationship can render it 'susceptible to premature termination' (p. 109). The location of mentoring initiatives within the school context can also render them particularly challenging. Indeed, Rhodes et al. (2002) point out that mentoring programs located in and through schools are often limited in their impact, due to various ethical, structural and contextual restrictions. This would explain why some mentors and mentees in the HSBC/OB project found it easier to maintain relationships, with the support of school staff, outside of the formal project structure ('It was really difficult to [keep in touch] through the school, to be honest').

Philip et al. (2004) have argued that organised mentoring initiatives, particularly those with an 'engagement mentoring' focus, often neglect the process of ending the relationship. They note that this can have a significant impact on the young people involved, leading to a perceived sense of rejection that can potentially undermine any positive gains. Within the HSBC/OB project, a number of mentors bemoaned the lack of opportunities to have sustained contact with young people ('[H]ow do we keep in touch with these kids and build on what we've started?'). There is perhaps a need, therefore, for clear routes to be established and/or enabled at the end of any planned programme of mentoring activities, in order for mentors and mentees to maintain contact and further develop their relationship if desired. Such 'paths to progress' (Sandford et al. 2008) would facilitate the long-term impact of youth mentoring initiatives.

Lessons learned . . . What could we add to the Mentor Pedagogy Toolbox?

This analysis highlights a number of key points relating to the process of mentoring vulnerable youth and identifies several factors that can enhance the potential for positive impact through mentoring initiatives:

- **Mentoring as a panacea.** Mentoring cannot 'remedy all the ills facing vulnerable young people' (Philip et al. 2004, p. 324) but it can be a valuable resource to be employed, where appropriate, within a range of interventions.
- **Careful planning and preparation.** Programmes focused on promoting positive development among young people (particularly vulnerable youth) must be clearly planned, organised and delivered. They should have strong leadership and be built with firm theoretical foundations, underpinned by clear models of how, when and why change will come about.
- **Clarity of role.** Mentors should be informed about the role they are to play and be committed to the process of supporting and enhancing young people's learning. The careful selection, preparation and on-going development of mentors is vital, and mentor 'buy-in' should be a primary requirement of programme participation.
- **Developing networks.** There should be a clear understanding of how mentors can and will work together with other practitioners (e.g. teachers) in order to establish open communication mechanisms and enable a holistic approach to supporting young people's development. This can usefully feed into an effective mentor training programme.

- **Mentors as 'informal educators'.** Using informal education (IE) as a learning strategy within mentor training can be a useful means of supporting mentors' pedagogical development and enhancing their capacity to function effectively as educational practitioners.
- **Sharing mentoring experience.** Facilitating the on-going development of mentor training programmes, using feedback from those involved in existent mentoring relationships, is a valuable approach and can help to enhance the development of a supportive mentor community.
- **Long-term strategy.** Thought should be given to how youth mentoring relationships are set up, supported and sustained, in order to ensure the process is effective and meaningful for all involved. Included within this should be some element of planning for the end of structured mentoring relationships, with the identification of clear pathways to additional and alternative follow-on support.

Newburn and Shiner (2006) have noted that 'simply providing opportunities for change may be a necessary condition for achieving change, but is rarely a sufficient condition' (p. 39). Likewise, we can perhaps say that providing mentors, and encouraging mentoring relationships, may give an opportunity for positive impact, but without clear planning, guidance, support and commitment (on both sides), there is no guarantee that these effects will be seen. It is therefore important that we take on board the lessons learnt through previous initiatives and seek to identify and apply principles of best practice, such as those outlined here, in order to develop more effective programmes and enhance all participants' experiences of youth mentoring.

Key terms: engagement mentoring, informal education, positive youth development.

Notes

1 HSBC stands for Hong Kong and Shanghai Banking Corporation. The sponsors of the HSBC/OB project are 'HSBC in the Community', a sub-group of HSBC's corporate social responsibility arm that has responsibility for promoting positive relationships with the local community.
2 Informal Education (IE) is a term that has gained significant currency in recent times and has perceptible links to concepts such as situated learning, experiential learning, mentoring and reflection. Drawing on the theories of educationalists such as Dewey, Freire and Bruner, IE views learning as being a fluid, adaptable and collaborative process (Jeffs 2001). However, it is also argued that IE is, fundamentally, deliberate and purposeful (Sandford *et al.* 2010).
3 Residential activity sessions lasted between three and fourteen days and took place at outdoor centres around the UK. During these periods, the young people were split into mixed school groups (each led by a trained instructor) and undertook a timetable of activities designed to provide individual/group challenges and develop skills relating to team building, communication, and responsibility (e.g. rock-climbing, gorge walking and raft-building).

References

Armour, K. M. and Sandford, R. A. 2013. Positive youth development through an outdoor physical activity programme: Evidence from a four-year evaluation. *Educational Review*, 65(1), 85–108.

Bennetts, C. 2003. Mentoring youth: Trend and tradition. *British Journal of Guidance and Counselling*, 31(1), 63–76.

Colley, H. 2003. *Mentoring for Social Inclusion: A Critical Approach to Nurturing Mentor Relationships*. London: Routledge Falmer.

DuBois, D. L. and Karcher, M. J. 2005. Youth mentoring: Theory, research, and practice. In D. L. DuBois and M. J. Karcher (Eds.) *Handbook of Youth Mentoring*. Thousand Oaks, CA: Sage pp. 2–11.

DuBois, D. L., Neville, H. A., Parra, G. R., and Pugh-Lilly, A. O. 2002. Testing a new model of mentoring. In J. Rhodes (Ed.) *A Critical View of Youth Mentoring: New Directions for Youth Development*. San Francisco, CA: Jossey-Bass.

Fresko, B. and Wertheim, C. 2006. Learning by mentoring: Prospective teachers as mentors to children at-risk. *Mentoring and Tutoring*, 14(2), 149–161.

Lerner, R. M., Lerner, J. V., Almerigi, J. B. Theokas, C., Phelps, E., Naudeau, S., *et al.* 2005. Positive youth development, participation in community youth development programs, and community contributions of fifth grade adolescents: Findings from the first wave of the 4-H study of positive youth development. *Journal of Early Adolescence*, 25, 17–71.

Newburn, T. and Shiner, M. 2006. Young people, mentoring and social inclusion. *Youth Justice*, 6(1), 23–41.

Petitpas, A., Cornelius, A. and Van Raalte, J. 2008. Youth development through sport. In N. Holt (Ed.) *Positive Youth Development and Sport*. London: Routledge.

Philip, K., Shucksmith, J. and King, C. 2004. *Sharing A Laugh? A Qualitative Study of Mentoring Interventions with Young People*. York: Joseph Rowntree Foundation.

Philip, K. and Spratt, J. 2007. *A Synthesis of Published Research on Mentoring and Befriending for The Mentoring and Befriending Foundation*. The Rowan Group, University of Aberdeen.

Rappaport, N. 2002. Can advising lead to meaningful relationships? In J. Rhodes (Ed.) *A Critical View of Youth Mentoring: New Directions for Youth Development*. San Francisco, CA: Jossey-Bass.

Rhodes, J. E., Grossman, J. B. and Roffman, J. 2002. The rhetoric and reality of youth mentoring. In J. Rhodes (Ed.) *A Critical View of Youth Mentoring: New Directions for Youth Development*. San Francisco, CA: Jossey-Bass.

Sandford, R. A., Armour, K. M. and Stanton, D. J. 2010. Volunteer mentors as informal educators in a youth physical activity programme. *Mentoring and Tutoring*, 18(2), 135–153.

Sandford, R. A., Duncombe, R., and Armour, K. M. 2008. The role of physical activity/sport in tackling youth disaffection and anti-social behaviour. *Educational Review*, 60(4), 419–435.

Resources

www.infed.org – for those interested in learning about Informal Education and for those working in this area.

www.mandbf.org – the website of the Mentoring and Befriending Foundation, UK.

The Joseph Rowntree Foundation (http://www.jrf.org.uk) has a number of publications/reports available that look at the concept of youth mentoring.

Colley's (2003) book on engagement mentoring (see *References*).

5

MENTORING, 'RACE' AND ETHNICITY

Liam O'Callaghan

Overview

This chapter looks at mentoring of physical education (PE) teachers and the challenges posed by issues of 'race' and ethnicity. It is important at the outset to distinguish between the two concepts. 'Race' refers to the categorization of human beings along the lines of biological and physical characteristics. It is a term that has received much scholarly criticism due to the inequality that it is said to have engendered worldwide and the faulty scientific assumptions upon which it is based. Ethnicity is a more wide-ranging concept that categorises human beings according to all manner of social and cultural characteristics such as religion, language, place of birth and nationality (Hoberman 1997; Carrington and McDonald 2001). Any assessment of the relationship between mentoring, physical education and ideas of 'race' and ethnicity, needs to first outline briefly the broader context in which societies have become multi-ethnic in the last fifty years. In the case of the British Isles, this process can be traced back to the post-Second World War period when Britain, for instance, first became a host to significant numbers of migrants from the Caribbean and Asia. This led to a transition from a predominantly white, Christian society to one which comprised people from many different religious, cultural and ethnic backgrounds. This gave rise to a number of problems that newly arrived migrants and successive generations of British-Asians and British Afro-Caribbean people would encounter such as racial abuse and discrimination, and difficulty accessing educational and professional opportunities. In the post-war period, also, the concept of ethnicity replaced 'race' as a means of categorizing different groups. While the concept of 'race' was associated with biological characteristics of different peoples, ethnicity encompassed culture and the fluid nature of different identities. Problematically, however, cultural characteristics are often seen as fixed or innate among certain groups, and discrimination, therefore, persists (McDonald and Hayes 2003, p. 156). Indeed, this is a pattern that has been observed across countries that have a tradition of sustained inward migration of peoples from different ethnicities (Hoberman 1997; de Knop *et al.* 1996). The focus of this study is provided by Flintoff *et al.* (2008a). Though set in a UK context, many of the issues raised therein have application and resonance globally.

Vignette

Background

Flintoff *et al.* (2008a) carried out their study on black and minority ethnic experiences of initial teacher training in physical education in the UK. The underlying research problem was under-representation of black and minority ethnic (BME) teachers in physical education. At the time of the study, just 3 per cent of trainees in the physical education teaching profession were of BME background compared to 11 per cent of new entrants to teaching overall (p. 4). The aim of the study was to find out why there was such an under-representation of BME trainees in physical education and to investigate whether or not aspects of the subject itself were at fault for this. Moreover, a lack of previous research on the topic also provided a strong rationale for the undertaking.

The study recruited BME students from five universities across the UK, all with a strong tradition of PE teacher training, and all running undergraduate and graduate programmes leading to qualified teacher status (QTS). The principal method of data collection involved semi-structured interviews, of which twenty-five were completed, while questionnaires (completed by a further twenty-four people) were also used to offer participants an opportunity to provide information anonymously. The researchers, while careful to avoid over-simplifying the definition of BME, managed to gather the views of trainees from a diverse range of ethnic and religious backgrounds: from Eastern-European, to Black African to Islamic Asian. The authors showed self-awareness as they acknowledged that carrying out research exclusively on people from a BME background could, in itself, contribute to the notion their participants were somehow separate from the dominant culture and that the term BME itself was limited and did not capture the diversity of contemporary society.

Methods

The use of interviews as the principal source of data collection was designed to enhance existing quantitative research which points to membership of an ethnic minority having a strong negative correlation with achievement in higher education. Thus the overarching methodological rationale was to capture qualitative experiences in order to illuminate already established statistical trends.

Findings

The findings of the study were divided into different categories investigating the participants' perceptions of official ethnic categories, motivations for entering the teaching profession, positive and negative influences on career choice, and experiences while on teacher training. The researchers found that most participants were uncomfortable or ambiguous about official categories of ethnicity used by government and other official bodies and felt that the complexity of their backgrounds was not captured within these categories, especially those participants of mixed heritage. In terms of motivation, participants chose teaching for a variety of reasons ranging from a desire to work with children and wanting to be a role model for BME children through to more pragmatic considerations such as pay and leave entitlements. Most participants cited teachers as being a key positive influence in their decision to pursue a teaching career, while on the negative side, some were advised not to enter PE teaching due to the apparent 'low status' of the subject. This was a trend specifically observed among Asian participants where parents encouraged children towards higher-status professions such as medicine, law and so on.

Participants reported a wide range of experiences, both positive and negative, while on their teacher training course. Most trainees experienced 'culture shock' at realising that they were the sole BME student, or one of a small number, on the course (Flintoff et al. 2008a, p. 8). The most rewarding and challenging experiences for trainees came about during their school placement. Though widely acknowledged as the most important aspect of training, placement was also where difficulties, some related to trainees' ethnic and cultural background, arose. Some participants reported encountering difficulties in their relationships with white fellow students, school staff and importantly, in terms of this chapter, mentors. While many of these difficulties were of a kind that could arise in any inter-personal relationship, some participants reluctantly reported what could be termed subtle racism from school staff and fellow trainees. These attitudes ranged from bitterness on the part of white peers who felt that BME trainees were only accepted on the course to fulfil some imagined racial 'quota' through to comments relating to supposed innate physical characteristics associated with members of certain ethnic groups, a problem heightened in the context of physical education. The findings also showed that the mentor could play an important role in such circumstances as trainees being subject to racial abuse from pupils, BME trainees being placed in a school that was predominantly white, or where the school ethos was in some way at odds with the cultural norms of the trainee's ethnic group.

The study concluded that though BME trainees had much in common with their white counterparts, their ethnic background often had an impact on their experiences of teacher training. This was especially evident when trainees were immersed in the school environment via placement.

Analysis

This study gives rise to key questions about the role of the mentor in the professional development of BME physical education teacher trainees. It is clear that mentors need specific training to become aware of the various complexities which mentoring across cultural boundaries can bring to the fore. There are a number of key headings under which this can be considered: (a) There are *environmental factors* such as the school in which the trainee has been placed and how the mentor can help the mentee adapt to what could be unfamiliar and potentially hostile surroundings; (b) there is the *nature of the mentor/mentee relationship* itself and how the hierarchical structure of this arrangement can be exacerbated by ethnic differences and (c) there are also *cultural factors*: what potentially racist views does the mentor possess or how does the mentor help a BME mentee who is subject to racial prejudice? This racism can be both direct and subtle. Subtle racism may be particularly relevant to PE where the body is a key component in theory and practice (Evans *et al.* 2008).

Ethnic make-up of placement schools

On a fundamental level, this study and other research literature highlight how the mentor/mentee relationship can help or hinder a BME trainee overcome such difficulties as working in a predominantly white school. One participant, for instance, felt he received unfavourable treatment from his mentor compared to white peers. He claimed that he 'was basically told to do what I liked'. 'This had made him feel uncomfortable and unsupported, yet he was reluctant to label this as racially discriminatory treatment' (p. 66). Another trainee placed in a predominantly white school experienced what she labelled 'bullying' and constant 'snide remarks' from school staff and felt that the school had unreasonably high expectations of her. In this instance, the apparent inexperience of her mentor was a compounding factor (p. 66). When she eventually moved to another, more ethnically mixed school, she felt far more comfortable and was helped by the guidance of a new mentor. It has been observed in other studies that the perception of racism among mentors held by BME mentees also leads to the assumption of more favourable treatment for members of the dominant culture. With regard to placement, again in the UK context, there is a feeling among BME students that the most favourable positions are reserved for 'tall, white middle-class people' (Interviewee, cited in Basit *et al.* 2006).

Given that it would arguably be contrary to the spirit of multiculturalism and integration to intentionally place BME trainees in schools comprising mainly ethnic minority pupils, the role of school staff, and critically the trainee's mentor, becomes crucial. Indeed, some participants cited the positive influence of mentors in scenarios created by the trainee's ethnic background. One participant who was subject to a racist remark received strong support from their mentor, who dealt with the issue professionally. In scenarios where BME trainees are being placed in schools largely comprising the dominant culture, the selection of mentor needs to be carefully considered, however. Mentors need be selected on the grounds of suitability and need to possess the empathy and awareness to guide the mentee through an environment that, as research suggests, BME mentees can find difficult.

Racism: subtle and direct

While none of the participants in Flintoff's study reported outright racist abuse from mentors, it has been observed elsewhere that school-based mentors are sometimes seen as racist by BME mentees. Stuart and Cole, in their study of African and British Asian student teachers in southeast England, reported that a number of their participants felt that they received unfavourable treatment compared with white counterparts and that this treatment, in turn, 'had racist undertones' (p. 360).

In a study by Basit et al. (2006), twelve trainees claimed that 'course tutors/ mentors and/or fellow trainees' were perpetrators of 'deliberate racial harassment' (Basit et al. 2006, p. 401). One trainee who left the course claimed: 'I would have stayed if they changed my mentor who was clearly racist' (Basit et al. 2006, p. 406). In a study conducted by Cole and Stuart (2005), there was a report of a 'mentor invoking genetics to explain what she perceived to be a personality trait of one of her dual heritage students. She suggested that his "relaxed" presence in the classroom was related to his African descent' (p. 360).

Of greater importance in the physical education context, perhaps, is the continued prevalence of a more subtle form of racism in society related to the supposed innate physical characteristics of people from different ethnic backgrounds. This is particularly relevant to black athletic achievement and the assumption that black aptitude for sprinting, for instance, is somehow related to genetic factors (McDonald and Hayes 2003). The opposite has been the case with Asians, who are assumed to lack athletic prowess and are more adept at academic pursuits (Burdsey 2004). In Flintoff's study, black participants experienced stereotypical comments about their physicality that participants from other ethnic groups were not subjected to. Three black trainees experienced such comments in PE classes. Theories linking athletic achievement with supposed racial biological characteristics have long been dismissed by social scientists as scientific racism, with 'race' now seen as purely a social construct (Hoberman 1997). Physical education can also present challenges in other cultural contexts. Muslim women, for instance, with their cultural imperative to maintain their modesty, only wear restrictive clothing and find events like swimming a particular challenge (Benn et al. 2011).

The mentor/mentee relationship and power

It has been observed in educational research that the mentor/mentee relationship is an important factor in the successful completion of teacher training by BME trainees. Though mentoring fails for a variety of reasons relating to the aptitude, professionalism and approach of the mentor, a critical factor in the context of UK teacher training is the level of power possessed by the mentor within the relationship. As Flintoff et al. (2008a) conclude, 'the inevitable uneven power relations that exist between mentor and trainee may be heightened by "race" and ethnicity' (p. 10). In the view of BME trainees, the power of the mentor to fail a student is often used unfairly and is influenced by racist assumptions on the part of the mentor. Research has revealed that BME students feel as if their performance is subject to a greater degree of scrutiny because of preconceived notions, based on cultural background, on the part of the mentor (Basit *et al.* 2006, p. 401–403).

This issue, again, is one that can be solved by structured training for mentors, which develops strong listening and communication skills and, in the case of mentoring across different ethnicities, cultural awareness. Moreover, mentors need to be aware of any assumptions based on race or ethnicity, however harmless these may seem to be, that they themselves possess. This, in turn, can facilitate a process of exchange between mentor and mentee where the mentor can develop 'more knowledge, empathy and skills related to interacting with individuals from different social groups' (Johnson-Bailey and Cervero 2004, p. 17). Mentorship should encapsulate what Hodge has termed 'proper sensitivity to cultural styles'. This, in turn, could lead to the 'enrichment of interaction between the dyad and the improvement of mentor-protégé communications' (Hodge 1997, p. 181). If the purpose of the mentor-mentee relationship is 'engagement in professional sharing', then the mentor stands to gain significant experience in the cross-cultural context.

Basit (2006) has asserted that '[it] is pointless to waste valuable resources on specialist advisors, coordinators and race officers, when the money can be more productively spent on training . . . school mentors to increase their knowledge and sensitivity to issues of race' (p. 406). This, in essence is what this chapter argues. As the next section shall detail, the study by Flintoff and colleagues raises a number of critical issues that mentors involved in cross-cultural mentoring need to be equipped to deal with.

Ultimately, the mentor and the PE teacher are in a position to take a progressive stance on ethnic and cultural differences and social justice in general and promote an atmosphere of tolerance and celebration of differences in their professional duties. Mentor training should include the development of pedagogies that strive for this goal.

Lessons learned . . . What could we add to the Mentor Pedagogy Toolbox?

- **Schools are now obliged to take the issue of 'race' and ethnicity seriously.** Yet every effort needs to be made to ensure that teachers from ethnic minorities can operate in a productive, non-hostile environment. As Cole and Stewart have relayed: 'We need to say to all mentors and Professional Tutors that they should have a strategy for ensuring a Black African teacher can work in your school, even if you don't have one' (Cole and Stewart 2005, p. 361). Moreover, failure to develop an appropriate strategy for such cases amounts to unintentional institutional racism (McDonald and Hayes 2003).
- **A pedagogy that challenges racialised thinking needs to be developed (Dowling and Flintoff 2011).** In the first instance, mentors need to be aware of the broader context of racism in society, its historical background, its prevalence and its many forms. This should facilitate a socially progressive role for both the mentor and mentee. As Flintoff *et al.* (2008a) point out in arguing that cultural diversity needs to be built into the learning process during

placement, 'these [cultural awareness] sessions should help trainees to understand the educational importance of ethnicity and "race" to students' achievements in and experiences of schooling, and their role as teachers in promoting good "race" relations' (p. 11).

- **Mentor training in PE needs to have a strong reflexive component which challenges the mentor to develop a mature awareness of their own racial assumptions.** This is especially relevant to assumptions made about the athletic body on the grounds of 'race'.

   There needs to be a clear focus in training that emphasises how PE can both encompass and challenge 'racialised thinking, stereotyping and inequalities' (Flintoff et al. 2008a, p. 11). In this way, physiological myths about athletic achievement and its connection with 'race' can be eradicated.

- **Cross-cultural mentoring in the physical education context requires considerable interpersonal skills, emotional maturity and empathy on the part of the mentor.** While the importance of the role of the mentor in the subject-related professional development of the mentee is vital, the mentor should also be in a position to provide personal support to the mentee. This can be complicated by the composition of a dyad. Building such key elements of a successful dyad as trust can be made more difficult if the individuals are from different ethnic or cultural backgrounds, an issue further compounded by gender (Flintoff et al. 2008b).

- **Purposeful matching of mentor and mentee would be appropriate.** By implementing this approach, empathy and understanding within the dyad can potentially be established.

Key terms: 'race', biological racism, culture, ethnicity, scientific racism, cross-cultural mentoring.

References

Basit, T. N., Roberts, L., McNamara, O., Carrington, B., Maguire, M. and Woodrow, D. 2006. Did they jump or were they pushed? Reasons why minority ethnic trainees withdraw from initial teacher training. *British Educational Research Journal*, 32(3), 387–410.

Benn, T., Dagkas, S. and Jawad, H. 2011. Embodied faith: Islam, religious freedom and educational practices in physical education. *Sport, Education and Society*, 16(1), 17–34.

Burdsey, D. 2004. 'One of the lads'? Dual ethnicity and assimilated ethnicities in the careers of British Asian professional footballers. *Ethnic and Racial Studies*, 27(5), 757–779.

Carrington, B., and McDonald, I. 2001. Introduction: Race, sport and British society. In B. Carrington, and I. McDonald (Eds.), *'Race', Sport and British Society*. London: Routledge, pp. 1–26.

Cole, M., and Stuart, J. S. 2005. 'Do you ride on elephants' and 'never tell them you're German': The experiences of British Asian and black, and overseas student teachers in South-east England. *British Educational Research Journal*, 31(3), 349–366.

De Knop, P., Theeboom, M., Wittock, H., and de Martelaer, K. 1996. Implications of Islam on Muslim girls' sport participation in Western Europe. Literature review and policy recommendations for sport promotion. *Sport, Education and Society*, 1(2), 147–164.

Dowling, F. and Flintoff, A. 2011. Getting beyond normative interview talk of sameness and celebrating difference. *Qualitative Research in Sport, Exercise and Health*, 3(1), 63–79.

Evans, J., Rich, E., Allwood, R. and Davies, B. 2008. Body pedagogies, P/policy, health and gender. *British Educational Research Journal*, 34(3), 387–402.

Flintoff, A., Chappell, A. and Gower, C. 2008a. Black and minority ethnic trainees' experiences of physical education initial teacher training. Report to the Training and Development Agency. Carnegie Research Institute, Leeds Metropolitan University.

Flintoff, A., Fitzgerald, H. and Scraton, S. 2008b. The challenges of intersectionality: Researching difference in physical education. *International Studies in Sociology of Education*, 18(2), 73–85.

Hobermen, J. A. 1997. *Darwin's Athletes: How Sport Has Damaged Black America and Preserved the Myth of Race*. New York: Houghton Mifflin.

Hodge, S. R. 1997. Mentoring: Perspectives of physical education graduate students from diverse cultural backgrounds. *Physical Educator*, 54(4), 181.

Johnson-Bailey, J. and Cervero, R. M. 2004. Mentoring in black and white: The intricacies of cross-cultural mentoring. *Mentoring and Tutoring*, 12(1), 7–21.

McDonald, I. and Hayes, S. 2003. 'Race', racism and education: Racial stereotypes in Physical Education and school sport. In S. Hayes and G. Stidder (Eds.), *Equity and Inclusion in Physical Education*. London: Routledge, pp. 153–168.

Resources

Sporting Equals report on BME coaches: http://www.sportscoachuk.org/sites/default/files/Insight-BME-Coaching-December-2011.pdf

Long, J., Hylton, K., Spracklen, K., Ratna, A. and Bailey, S. 2009. A Systematic Review of the Literature on Black and Minority Ethnic Communities in Sport and Physical Recreation [carried out for Sporting Equals]. Carnegie Research Institute. Accessed from http://www.sportengland.org/media/39689/systematic-review-of-the-literature-on-bme-communities-in-sport.pdf

6

MENTORING

Special educational needs and disability

Hayley Fitzgerald

Overview

The challenges and opportunities of mentoring Physical Education Teacher Education (PETE) students towards inclusive schooling should not be underestimated. In this chapter specific consideration is given to how mentoring can enable PETE students to work towards inclusion for students with Special Educational Needs (SEN) and disabilities. These students may experience a range of learning, sensory or physical impairments that schools and teachers need to consider in order to support more inclusive and equitable learning experiences. Indeed, the premise underpinning contemporary understandings of inclusion, SEN and disability is founded upon the belief that disablement within society (including in education and physical education) is a consequence of a society that is organized to accommodate a non-disabled rather than SEN/disabled norm (Shakespeare 2013). The challenge for PETE students, then, is to better understand how they can develop as practitioners to support inclusion instead of reinforcing disablement. This chapter considers how mentoring can aid PETE students through their journey towards inclusive practice.

Vignette

To help them grow. To help them with their career and when they see other people, when they come across other people with differences, to see them as not just different . . . but in a positive way because when they teach they can forget, they think 'I've got to do this report. I've got to do this and that', but we need to show them that they have to go 'Hang on I've got a student with a disability, I need to slow down and get good advice and good resources'.

Mentor

It is a win/win situation. I think there is a certain amount of ignorance in relation to disability and I think it opens your eyes to what people with disabilities
are capable of . . . . Another thing for me is that it restores faith in the school
system because [of] my experiences at school, what happened to me and how
my disability was treated. So it sort of restores faith for me in what we are doing.

Mentor

Background

The 'mentors' featured in recent research from Raphael and Allard (2012) have a clear
vision of the outcomes they would like for the professional learning and practice of
teacher education (TE) students. Their aspirations are couched in a climate where
internationally, education and youth sport continues to be expected to respond to
legislation, policy and programmes that advocate the wider inclusion of young, disabled people and those with special educational needs (SEN) in mainstream schooling
and youth sport (Peters 2007; Rioux and Pinto 2010). Of course, the reality is that
the transition towards inclusive schooling and youth sport will be a long journey, one
that continues to expose vulnerabilities to the current practices in schools, youth sport
and teacher and coach education (Barton 2009; Haycock and Smith 2011; Slee 2010).
Indeed, student teachers often have many concerns on their journey to becoming a
teacher: Will I be able to control the class? How can I gain respect? How can I make
my lessons stimulating and interesting? How can I engage all my students? Alongside
this myriad of concerns, there can also be anxiety about whom they teach. More often
than not, there are significant concerns about supporting disabled students. Many years
ago, Hellison and Templin (1991) highlighted an array of questions:

How prepared are you to teach the child with Down Syndrome, or the student with muscular dystrophy, or the kid with a congenital heart defect, or the
hyperactive student? What are the needs and rights of these students or any
other students with disabilities? Do you want to teach these children? Are you
legally obligated to teach them? Should they be mainstreamed into your class?

Hellison and Templin 1991, p. 33

I suggest these questions have stood the test of time and remain equally relevant to
TE students, teacher educators and teachers in our schools today. For example, the
recent small-scale qualitative study by Raphael and Allard (2012) highlights some
of the concerns that TE students continue to have:

Having not had much exposure or experience with students with disabilities,
part of me as a teacher has a fear that I won't adequately be able to cater for
them in the classroom.

Student Teacher

For this, much work needs to be done to fulfill the aspirations of the mentors featured at the beginning of the chapter. Indeed, mentoring-related activities have a

pivotal role to play in developing confidence and instilling commitment to inclusive pedagogies that better equip TE students to work in schools. Initial teacher education is a key context in which student teachers can be supported to develop their inclusive practice with disabled students. Within this setting, teacher educators continue to grapple with how mentoring-related activities can be used to promote such inclusive practice.

Methods

In seeking to explore just what kind of mentoring activities best support TE students to work with disabled students, Raphael and Allard (2012) reflect on how a hands-on drama workshop organized and led by people with learning disabilities increased understandings and enhanced a sense of competency with regard to working with disabled students. The workshop was planned and led by five people with learning disabilities who were part of a theater company and aimed to:

> [p]rovide pre-service teachers with the opportunity to make contact with and engage in conversations with people with disabilities; position the pre-service teachers as learners in relation to people with learning disabilities who are the experts, able to talk about their own personal experiences of disability and education and encourage pre-service teachers to think critically about issues of diversity and SENs based on this form of experiential learning.
>
> *Raphael and Allard 2012, p. 209*

The workshop formed part of a wider learning experience situated within a fourth-year module/unit, 'Teaching for Diversity'. The workshop took place following the students' teaching placement (TP) where most had experience working with disabled/SEN students. Following the workshop, the module/unit tutorials further explored issues of inclusion and equity in teaching and learning. In capturing the views of the fifty-seven TE students during and after the workshop, data were generated through questionnaires and written reflections.

Findings

The written reflections reveal a range of feelings and thoughts about the workshop and aspirations about future practice. The following student responses reflect some of the themes emerging from the findings.

> [I]t gave me a truly authentic learning experience by allowing me the opportunity to hear about diversity from people experiencing difficulty within, not only schooling but also society as a whole. This is so much better than doing a reading on disability because being able to relate to each other as human beings, rather than 'labels' gives a much truer perspective on how similar we all are with regards to our basic desire and need to be shown dignity and respect as individuals.
>
> *Student Teacher*

A lot of the time it is seen as 'us' and 'them' and I feel that the workshop broke down barriers and gave insight into students' diverse needs.

Student Teacher

It illustrated to me that learning about difference helps to break down false ideas about people with disabilities with the hope of creating a friendlier social environment.

Student Teacher

I saw people with disabilities having fun, being in charge and enjoying life. I thought that everyone here is having a good time and that half way through I did not think of them as disabled but as fellow participants doing drama.

Student Teacher

The reflections of the TE students illustrate that they valued the privileging of the voices and stories of people with disabilities and recognized the importance of positioning the learning disabled workshop leaders as 'experts'. Moreover, TE students appreciated experiencing practical examples of inclusive teaching and learning activities during the workshop. The TE students also reflected that they felt more motivated at the prospect of teaching students with disabilities. After presenting the findings of this research, Raphael and Allard (2012) discuss a number of key issues emerging from the research that may be relevant to other settings. First, they argue that involvement of learning disabled people within the TE curriculum challenges negative views often constructed about disabled people. Second, by offering space to have frank discussions with disabled people, TE students may be more receptive in their practice to pro-actively engage with disabled students in order to promote more inclusive learning experiences. Third, the opportunities for the TE students to be reflective by assessing confidence and acknowledging anxieties relating to their learning needs was seen as important in relation to efficacy in teaching disabled students. On a number of levels this research piece invites the reader to think differently, and in the next section specific aspects of the paper are reflected upon in relation to thinking differently about mentoring within physical education.

Analysis

The drama workshop and associated research outlined by Raphael and Allard (2012) represents one approach for supporting TE students to better understand and work with disabled students in schools. Whilst the paper does not specifically feature physical education teacher education (PETE) students, nor is it explicitly about mentoring, I believe it raises some interesting points for discussion that are relevant to those seeking to initiate mentoring activities in order to promote inclusive practice in physical education and youth sport. Next, I discuss four key points for consideration, including (1) positioning disabled people as experts/mentors, (2) asking who can be a mentor, (3) mentoring beyond a physical education setting, and (4) understanding the challenges of initiating a mentoring programme. Taken together, these points represent a theoretical and practical analysis of the mentee and mentor experiences revealed within Raphael and Allard's research piece.

Positioning disabled people as experts/mentors

As Raphael and Allard (2012) describe, a unique feature of the workshop was that people with learning disabilities were positioned as the experts leading this activity. Indeed, at the beginning of this chapter I describe these individuals as 'mentors' (see initial extracts). Situating the learning-disabled mentors in this way is an interesting inversion of how disabled people are often understood within social life. That is, society typically perceives disabled people to be in need of care and requiring help from others (including education, social welfare and health). This positioning is driven by a medical model view of disability that renders disabled people inferior to a superior non-disabled 'norm' (Shakespeare 2013). As the workshop demonstrates, by re-positioning disabled people as the leaders or mentors within a learning context, an opportunity occurred to simultaneously empower these individuals and also broaden TE students' understanding of what it means to be disabled. As Danforth and Smith (2005) suggest, the TE students were encouraged to begin to rethink the notion of disability from a more critical perspective. Beyond this workshop, there are a number of possible approaches that a PETE mentoring process could instigate in order to develop mentoring representation from the disability community. For instance, by collaborating and building relations with a local advocacy organization for disabled people, their expertise could be drawn upon to facilitate a similar workshop to that undertaken by Raphael and Allard (2012), for example, an 'equity in youth sport', 'inclusive youth sport' or 'living in a non-disabled world' workshop. Moreover, consideration could be given to how such activities and the learning disabled mentors are embedded within wider curriculum activities of a PETE programme and subsequent continuous professional development (CPD) opportunities.

Who can be a mentor?

Situating the learning-disabled leaders as mentors also contributes to wider debates about who and what constitutes a mentor and what characteristics and experiences a good mentor should hold. It is also acknowledged that good teachers do not necessarily make good mentors (Harrison et al. 2006; Hobson et al. 2009; Desimone et al. 2014). This observation invites us to consider who else could take on the role of mentor for PETE students? More specifically, how could disabled mentors with expertise and experiences extending beyond education effectively mentor PETE students in their journey towards developing better understandings of inclusive learning? According to Raphael and Allard (2012), the TE students in their study benefited from the engagement with the learning disabled mentors by developing confidence, becoming more sensitive towards issues of disability and enhancing their ability to self-reflect, particularly in relation to inclusive teaching.

These are some of the key features that a mentor strives to work towards with a mentee. However, it is also clear that mentor-mentee partnerships often develop over time, and perhaps a limitation of the drama workshop reviewed in this chapter concerns the short time-frame in which the TE students engaged with the learning disabled mentors. Indeed, there was no opportunity to build an on-going collaborative mentor-mentee relationship outside of the workshop. As indicated previously, consideration could be given to embedding mentor-related activities within the wider PETE curriculum. With this in mind, future developments could address how a more sustained relationship between the (learning) disabled mentors and PETE students may be nurtured. For example, workshop activities could be extended by utilizing a 'circle of support' (Shridevi and Petroff 2011) in which PETE students work over a concentrated period of time in a reciprocal way with disabled mentors. Of course, in suggesting the possibility of a (learning) disabled person becoming a mentor to PETE students, there would need to be consideration to how other forms of formal mentoring (e.g. teacher mentor–university tutor) could continue to support PETE students to more broadly develop their professional practice. Indeed, careful thought would need to be given to how these different mentoring roles could dovetail each other and best support PETE students. Avoiding superficial representations that reinforce stereotypical views of the (learning) disabled mentors would also need to be carefully thought out when developing this kind of mentoring process.

Mentoring beyond a physical education setting

For PETE students, learning and associated mentoring often takes place within a physical education setting. In this arena, PETE students and teachers frequently make normative assumptions about how the bodies of their students will move – to catch a ball, swing a tennis racket, or hurdle. These activities require a willing and adaptable body, one that, through practice, improves techniques and skills in order to become a competent performer. It is precisely these attributes of physical education that can make visible disability as something associated with inability and incompetence. As already indicated, the drama workshop outlined by Raphael and Allard (2012) offers an alternative perspective of disability reflecting empowered and competent individuals. More specifically, their findings suggest this helped the TE students to become sensitized to the person first rather than just seeing their disability. Taking this kind of broader perspective in the professional preparation of PETE students, and associated mentoring, could prove to be fruitful for enabling PETE students to see beyond the physical abilities of students and instead begin to recognize a student in a much more holistic way. In this respect, the drama workshop activity signals how learning (and related mentoring) for PETE students should perhaps move beyond the domain specific to the physical education and offer a pedagogical encounter which enables '[o]ur children throughout the world . . . to find personally meaningful, engaging, and reflective approaches to be "in" movement. These programs will be boundless, integrated, and cross-disciplinary with pedagogy and assessment woven as one seamless educative enrichment' (Ennis 2013, p. 115). This would be a challenge within a PETE programme, but is one that could potentially enable PETE students, with mentoring, to understand disabled students beyond their physical self and in a more holistic way.

The challenges of initiating a mentoring programme

By looking beyond the traditional triadic relationship between mentor–university tutor–PETE student and supporting disabled mentors to work with PETE students, it is important to reflect upon the potential challenges this may bring. For example, careful attention and planning would need to be given to how potential disabled mentors are selected and what on-going development support could be offered (to these mentors and those they will work with, including other mentors and university tutors). Of course, these are issues that continue to be grappled with in PETE mentoring in general, but they would be magnified when developing an initiative to support disabled mentors. Moreover, the parameters for this kind of mentoring role would need to be clearly defined and considered in relation to wider mentoring opportunities (e.g. offered by the university tutor). The task of supporting such a mentoring initiative should not be underestimated – it would require sustained commitment and a willingness to extend notions of who is understood to be a mentor and what role they would take. By investing in an initiative that develops disabled people as mentors, it could be argued that this is singling out issues of disability over other markers of inequality. And to some extent this would be the case; however, repeatedly research has found that PETE students and PE teachers continue to struggle to support disabled students in physical education (Vickerman and Coates 2009; Fitzgerald 2012). With this evidence in mind and the broader legislative and policy commitments to promote inclusive physical education and youth sport for disabled young people, it is perhaps time to adopt a more radical approach to supporting our PETE students.

Lessons learned . . . What could we add to the Mentor Pedagogy Toolbox?

The drama workshop outlined in the paper featured in this chapter (Raphael and Allard 2012) provides a number of examples of mentor pedagogy that promote aspects of the Capability Maturity Model for Mentor Teachers (CM³T). Specific competences that emerge from the research findings include 'subject knowledge' (cognitive), 'empathy' (affective) and 'self-confidence' (hybrid). Whilst recognizing cognitive and affective competencies is core to the work of mentors, the challenge remains, with the disabled mentors, to more fully explore how support could be offered to enable progression along the mentor pathway to capability and beyond. The extent to which the disabled mentors could engage with and navigate the CM³T in order to support PETE students would need to be carefully considered. In part, university mentors and school-based mentors would have a key role to play in assisting the disabled mentors to understand the relevance and usefulness of CM³T.

Key terms: inclusion, mentoring, empathy, self-confidence, subject knowledge, disability, social model of disability, inclusive schooling.

References

Barton, L. 2009. Disability, physical education and sport: Some critical observations and questions. In H. Fitzgerald (Ed.) *Disability and Youth Sport*. London: Routledge, pp. 39–50.

Danforth, S. and Smith, T. J. 2005. *Engaging Troubling Students: A Constructivist Approach*. Newbury Park, CA: Corwin Press.

Desimone, L. M., Hochberg, E. D., Porter, A. C., Polikoff, M. S., Schwartz, R. and Johnson, L. J. 2014. Formal and informal mentoring: Complementary, compensatory, or consistent? *Journal of Teacher Education*, 65, 88–110.

Ennis, C. D. 2013. Implementing meaningful, educative curricula, and assessments in complex school environments. *Sport, Education and Society*, 18, 115–120.

Fitzgerald, H. 2012. 'Drawing' on disabled students' experiences of physical education and stakeholder responses. *Sport, Education and Society*, 17, 443–462.

Harrison, J., Dymoke, S. and Pell, T. 2006. Mentoring beginning teachers in secondary schools: An analysis of practice. *Teaching and Teacher Education*, 22, 1055–1067.

Haycock, D. and Smith, A. 2011. Still 'more of the same for the more able?' Including young disabled people and pupils with special educational needs in extra-curricular physical education. *Sport, Education and Society*, 16, 507–526.

Hellison, D. R. and Templin, T. J. 1991. *A Reflective Approach to Teaching Physical Education*. Champaign, Illinois: Human Kinetics Publishers.

Hobson, A. J., Ashby, P., Malderez, A. and Tomlinson, P. D. 2009. Mentoring beginning teachers: What we know and what we don't. *Teaching and Teacher Education*, 25, 207–216.

Peters, S. J. 2007. 'Education for All'? A historical analysis of international inclusive education policy and individuals with disabilities. *Journal of Disability Policy Studies*, 18, 98–108.

Raphael, J. and Allard, A. C. 2012. Positioning people with intellectual disabilities as the experts: Enhancing pre-service teachers' competencies in teaching for diversity. *International Journal of Inclusive Education*, 17(2), 205–221.

Rioux, M. H. and Pinto, P. C. 2010. A time for the universal right to education: Back to basics. *British Journal of Sociology of Education*, 31, 621–642.

Shakespeare, T. 2013. *Disability Rights and Wrongs Revisited*. London: Routledge.

Shridevi, R. and Petroff, J. 2011. He is more like us, looking for a person to date and eventually share his life with: Perspectives of undergraduate students on being a member of a 'circle of support'. *Disability and Society*, 26, 463–475.

Slee, R. 2010. *The Irregular School: Exclusion, Schooling and Inclusive Education*. London: Routledge.

Vickerman, P. and Coates, J. K. 2009. Trainee and recently qualified physical education teachers' perspectives on including children with special educational need. *Physical Education and Sport Pedagogy*, 14, 137–153.

Resources

Grant, G., Ramcharan, P., Flynn, M. and Richardson, M. 2010. *Learning Disability: A Life Cycle Approach*. Maidenhead: McGraw-Hill Education.

Mentoring and Befriending Foundation 2010. *Disabled People: Research Summary 4, A List of Key Findings from Research Studies and Evaluations that Show the Positive Impact of Mentoring and Befriending*. Manchester: Mentoring and Befriending Foundation.

O'Mahony, C. 2010. *Pushing for Change: The Role of Disabled People's Organisations in Developing Young Disabled Leaders of the Future*. London: The Alliance for Inclusive Education.

7

MENTORING AND GENDER

Liam O'Callaghan

Overview

Inequalities along the lines of gender are common in sport and physical education (PE). In the mainstream sports arena we can see this in divergent numbers of men and women participating in sports, the domination by men of the powerful administrative positions within sporting organisations, the subordination of women's sports in the media and the labelling of certain sports as being more appropriate for one gender over the other (Pfister and Hartmann-Tews 2005). In this, we can see both strong structural inequalities affecting sport and also the social construction of gender, where certain qualities or aptitudes are seen as being desirably masculine or feminine (Jarvie 2012, pp. 293–294, 386–387). In other words, discrimination against women is visible both in the numbers involved in participation and administration within sport and also the manner in which women are perceived or stereotyped within sport and physical activity more generally. The stereotyping largely refers to what society deems to be acceptably feminine behaviour. In that regard a lot of sports, particularly team sports, are seen to embrace 'masculine' qualities such as aggression and competitiveness, while more aesthetic activities such as dance and gymnastics are more appropriate for girls.

Some of these trends are reproduced in PE. Though the numbers of male and female PE teachers in the UK are roughly equal, according to a Department for Education report for 2009–10, boys consistently take part in more PE than girls across all ages, with the gap between the genders increasing as pupils get older. Overall, 52 per cent of girls participated in at least three hours of PE or extracurricular sport, compared to 58 per cent of boys. By year 11 of school, 46 per cent of boys maintained this level of participation while the equivalent figure for girls was just 33 per cent (Department for Education 2010, p. 16). Furthermore, these are trends that have been observed and documented by scholars in countries across the world (Gibbons and Humbert 2008; Camacho-Minano *et al.* 2011).

One of a number of explanations consistently advanced for the disadvantaged status of girls in PE is the gendered nature of PE and school sport and the dominance and promotion of masculine behaviours within these disciplines (Kirk 2005; Evans 2006). With an emphasis on competition, strength, physicality and independence, the nature of PE runs 'precisely counter to the socially sanctioned identity – this acceptable way of being [a] "teenage girl" . . . and the images of teenage girls and young women being physically active are non-congruous with the traditional ideologies of acceptable femininity' (Cockburn and Clarke 2002, p. 654). In other words, the way society feels women should look and behave when physically active is at odds with the required qualities to succeed in PE and sport more generally. Moreover, these behaviours can become conflated with sexual orientation, with boys participating in PE in an insufficiently masculine manner being positioned as effeminate and girls showing excessive 'masculinity' being seen as lesbian (Pfister and Hartmann-Tews 2005). This general theoretical framework, referred to as 'The Gender Order', sees masculinity, femininity and heterosexuality being positioned in relation to the dominant or 'hegemonic' form of masculinity (Connell 1987 cited in Brown and Rich 2002, pp. 82–83). Problematically, differential treatment of boys and girls within the subject of physical education is seen as somewhat natural and is often defended as being legitimate and even desirable (Brown and Evans 2004).

In the studies that form the basis of this chapter, we will see that the teacher training process is crucial in perpetuating the Gender Order in PE. Not only are gendered pedagogies transmitted from generation to generation of teachers, but they are also appropriated by female PE teachers. The studies conclude that little has occurred in recent years to challenge the gendered positioning of PE pedagogies and that trainee teachers with progressive attitudes towards gender equality feel the need to conform while training. Where mentoring becomes important in this context lies in the position of the mentor in the transmission of ideas and attitudes from one generation of teacher to the next, and the potential change in attitudes that can be fostered in the mentor/mentee dyad.

Two vignettes

Study One: Background

Vignettes illustrating these social constructions in practice are offered by two studies conducted by Brown with different colleagues (Brown and Evans 2004; Brown and Rich 2002). These studies, importantly, discuss the role of the mentor/mentee dyad within teacher training in the production and reproduction of gendered pedagogies in physical education.

Brown and Evans (2004), hereunder 'Study One', conducted a qualitative study investigating the prevalence of gendered pedagogies among male physical education teachers in Britain. The principal concern of the study was the persistence of masculine qualities and values within PE lessons and the continued valorisation of these by PE teachers. In the words of the authors, these values and qualities included 'demonstrable practical sporting ability; a competitive sports orientation; informality; fun jokes and pranks; spontaneity; strength and independence; strong discipline when necessary; and an implicit demand for respect based on these qualities' (p. 57). More specifically, the researchers were keen to establish the manner in which these gendered pedagogies are transmitted from generation to generation of PE teacher through the trainee teachers' own experiences of once having been taught PE in school and through their interactions with experienced teachers – in the case of this study, mentors – while on training.

Methods

The researchers gathered data by conducting in-depth, semi-structured interviews with eight male trainee PE teachers before, during and after their Post-Graduate Certificate in Education (PGCE) course. The interviews focused on gathering the 'life stories' of each individual teacher, allowing the researchers to probe the development of the participants' physical self and identity and to observe how broader social forces influence the individual's development over time.

Findings

The findings centre on three 'gendered links' that significantly shape the trainee teacher: the link between the trainee and their former PE teacher, the link between the trainee and their school-based mentor, and the link between the newly qualified teacher and the pupils that they will teach as their career progresses.

The principal finding of this research is that the structure and processes of teacher training, and the transmission of practices and pedagogies from one generation of teachers to the next, result in the reproduction of 'hegemonic masculinity' that is competitive, heterosexual, hierarchical and positional in nature. The term 'hegemonic masculinity', used frequently in the study, refers to the dominance and normalisation of certain male behaviours. The researchers conclude that the mentor is a vital part of this process of transmission and that there is little evidence of the mentor challenging the prevailing masculine pedagogy: 'the apprenticeships [mentor/mentee dyads] witnessed here reinforced and legitimated conventional patriarchal, gendered pedagogy and did very little to challenge underlying biological or social assumptions about boys and girls' (Study One, p. 61). In other words, the teacher-training process does little to challenge dominant masculine behaviours within the PE setting. Girls are expected to be weak and submissive and boys to be aggressive and competitive. Boys and girls behaving at odds with these social expectations are seen as unusual. Ultimately, the male teachers involved acted as 'cultural conduits' acquiring 'gendered dispositions' and passing them to the next generation of pupils.

Study Two: Background

Complementing this study was another by Brown and Rich (2002), hereunder 'Study Two', where the experiences of female trainee PE teachers were also included to give a fuller picture of how gendered pedagogies are transmitted through the teacher training process and the role of the mentor/mentee relationship within this phenomenon.

Methods

This study used data from intensive semi-structured interviews with female student PE teachers. Analysis of these data focussed on issues of gender and self-identity. The focus on life histories allowed the researchers to extrapolate the progression of the participants' gendered experiences of teacher-training.

Findings

The study concluded that the participants were eager to fit into the prevailing masculine gender order rather than challenging it. Particularly interesting in this regard, is the manner in which female teachers are observed to have appropriated gendered behaviours despite instinctively rejecting gender stereotypes. The remainder of this chapter will focus on specific themes arising from the studies and discuss both the observed and potential roles of the mentor in reaffirming or challenging gendered pedagogies in PE.

Analysis

At the core of Study One's observations of the role of the mentor is the idea that teaching practice, and in this case PGCE placements, are 'powerfully reproductive' experiences where mentees are given little incentive or opportunity to challenge the status quo and where 'mentors, who are charged with the task of supervising and teaching the teachers, may be instrumental in this process' (p. 58). In these two studies, this is evident from a gendered perspective in both generic teaching and communication methods and skills and contexts specific to physical education lessons.

Styles of teaching

In PE lessons both studies noted the prevalence of masculine styles of interacting with pupils and dealing with scenarios arising during a lesson. In Study One, a mentee recalled that his first mentor 'was excellent, he was quite [a] hard taskmaster, he was like old authoritarian schools, he was quite old fashioned . . . and he was good . . . He always like said, "oh you're too nice, you got to be this that and the other," do know what I mean? And I think part of that was it was just my first experience of teaching' (Study One, p. 60). This, to some degree, was the result of the prevailing atmosphere of the PE department where it 'was almost like the cadets you know, it was very structured, very rigid and very like, testosterone like, you know. You couldn't . . . it was charged, it was a charged atmosphere' (Study One, p. 60).

That trainee teachers are encouraged to develop 'masculine teaching identities' is also evident in Study Two where one female mentee was given the following advice from a female mentor:

> You've got to treat them like dogs. I talk to them like I do my own dog and that's the way that it has got to be because you've got to get them in a position whereby you've disciplined them, you've got control and they're ready to get on and learn. That's what they are there for. You have to remind them of the fact that we've all got to do things that we don't want to do but that's the way it is sometimes. You need to go right. You over there bang (points). You need to take a teacher-centred approach.
>
> *Study Two, p. 88*

One further extract clearly demonstrates different approaches to classroom management and the influence of gendered assumptions therein. In this instance a male trainee describes his experiences teaching girls:

> It was different . . . I don't know, they tended not to go off tasks so easily, as much as mess around . . . and to motivate them, but yes, you had to deal with them a bit more sensitively I think – do it a bit quieter during your teaching . . . when you are talking to them, and plenty of praise for the ones that weren't so motivated, and teach in a slightly lower tone perhaps, I don't know . . . I saw that with my mentor especially, the more caring side, with the girls you would tend to have to be a bit more, um, not so macho perhaps . . . Especially in the mixed PE situation, they [the girls] challenge the boys and they adopt some of the characteristics that perhaps they [the boys] have got.
>
> *Ibid., p. 89*

These extracts give rise to some key observations on the mentor/mentee dyad. We can observe an authoritarian style of teaching and interaction, with students being encouraged by mentors, and this, in turn, being absorbed by the mentee. Moreover, and as the authors in this case have observed, the perceived need to tone down the 'macho' disposition in front of girls implies that such an approach is available to the mentee and is, where appropriate, expected of him (Brown and Rich 2002, p. 89). In addition, implicit in the adoption of the boys' characteristics by girls is the assumption that this is somehow desirable and legitimate. Again, this displays the subtle prevalence of the Gender Order where masculine discourses are normalised and everything else is defined in relation to this hegemonic masculinity.

Choice of activity

Further evidence of positioning within a broader Gender Order was apparent in attitudes to certain types of physical activity. It has long been observed in sport research that the social construction of gender has resulted in the labelling of certain sports as being 'a man's sport' or a 'woman's sport'. While competitive, physical and exertive sports such as football and rugby have been seen as the preserve of men, more sedate, aesthetically graceful activities such as dance and gymnastics have been associated with femininity (Hargreaves 1994). This tendency, furthermore, has been observed in PE. Indeed, the most recent Department for Education report on PE in 2010 noted that provision of activities in secondary schools was still divided along gender lines, with girls more likely to take part in dance, rounders, cheerleading etc., and boys in football, rugby and cricket (Department for Education 2010). This is especially the case in single-sex classes where choice of activity again reinforces gendered perceptions of different sports and physical activities (Stidder and Hayes 2006).

These trends are, to some extent at least, perhaps attributable to gendered attitudes among teachers. In Brown and Rich's study, one trainee experienced this in his first teaching placement when he asked his mentor, "[H]ow much dance do you want me to do?' and received the answer, 'Oh none, I don't believe boys should do that" (Study Two, p. 86).

Another female mentee recalled the attitude of her mentor to the gender-appropriateness of different sports (p. 87):

> [H]e was a good laugh but some of the comments that he made to the kids were very derogatory, you know one of the lads had a buckle on his shoe and he was calling him a, I can't remember what he called him now . . . a dancer. He was saying, oh you look like a . . . I don't know if he actually called him a poof, but it was some term along that line. And I'd think, I don't really think you should have quite put it like that, and they make some comments to me about, you know, football, of what do you know about football. And just I'd give as good as I got for a bit, and then I'd just be like, oh carry on.

Here we have, on the part of the mentor, an implicit link being made between dance and homosexuality. Moreover, the comments on the trainee's assumed lack of knowledge about football shows that the experienced peer, who is guiding the future practitioner through the training process, clearly endorses the prevailing Gender Order.

The power of this shared intergenerational order is further evidenced by the marginalisation of some trainees' instinctively progressive attitudes to gender relations and associated perceptions of physical activities. One female participant in Brown and Rich's study showed a sophisticated understanding by claiming that:

> I think they are really important [the meanings of femininity/masculinity] because I am teaching PE, it's important to not have a stereotypical view of the body; so I am trying to get to grips with perhaps the correct terms to use. I haven't finalised anything definite . . . I want to give other people the chance to realise their potential and to realise that they are individuals that can achieve things . . . Enjoyment for everyone to feel safe, secure and happy.
>
> *Study Two, p. 85*

It was observed that she and other female participants possessed what the authors term a 'critical child-centred feminist' educational philosophy. The idea of a 'critical child-centred feminist' approach encompasses a commitment to achieving equality in gender relations and, in this context, removing the pressure that gendered expectations place upon children in PE lessons. In practice, however, they often felt forced to comply with more masculine pedagogies in order to succeed. One female participant, for instance, only gained acceptance from a group of boys when she displayed competence in football and basketball with the authors concluding that 'the demonstration of physical ability in these particular sports and contexts is in sharp contrast to the cultural conception of what it means to be stereotypically female' (Study Two, p. 92). In addition, this subversion of the Gender Order can have the effect of having a woman's sexual orientation called into question. In another study, Rich (2004) observed that female trainee teachers, while displaying a commitment to boosting female participation in PE, strove to do so within the parameters of the prevailing gendered pedagogies: 'Although the teachers in these cases held inclusive and intellectual positions of equal opportunities, the construction of "gender equality" seldom moved beyond a liberal notion of encouraging more girls into the current system of PE, rather than attempting to challenge the inequalities that are embedded within the structure, content and delivery of PE' (p. 232).

Many of the issues raised in the studies cited here have also been observed in coaching contexts. Indeed, in numerical terms women are glaringly underrepresented in coaching roles and in common with PE teaching, masculine behaviours and expectations have been seen to predominate (Fielding-Lloyd and Mean 2008).

Lessons learned . . . What could we add to the Mentor Pedagogy Toolbox?

- **A more gender-inclusive pedagogy in physical education needs to be inculcated.** For this broad aim to be achieved, the schools-based mentor, as a conduit between old and new generations of PE teachers, is in a position to interrupt the downward transmission of pedagogies centred on hegemonic masculinity.

- **An awareness of the socially constructed nature of gender in society needs to be embedded in mentor training.** As with other social constructs such as 'race' and sexuality, mentors needs to be self-aware and to recognise any assumptions, however subtle, that they make on the grounds of the supposed biological or emotional traits of one gender or another. Moreover, how this applies to certain sports also needs to be made clear. As Rich (2004) has observed in her study of female trainee PE teachers, participants who became frustrated at the lack of enthusiasm for PE among girls often reverted to a biological explanation of the issue.

- **Pedagogies that de-emphasise physical confrontation and muscularity need to be encouraged and promoted by the mentor.** As Gorely and her colleagues (2003) have argued, if PE has physical empowerment as its goal, it should not promote activities that favour physical prowess, strength and the causing of physical harm to young people.

- **PE curricula need to encompass a broad range of activities that mentors and trainees, irrespective of gender, are competent in delivering.** Problematically, it has been shown that in single-sex schools, the choice of PE activity is likely to be determined by gender and can, therefore, reinforce gender stereotypes (Stidder and Hayes 2006, p. 330).
- **Inclusion of 'alternative movement forms' that prioritise aesthetic above competitive components could reduce the potential alienating effects of the existing system** (Rich 2004, p. 236). Activities that minimise competitive elements such as dance and gymnastics, if accorded equal priority to competitive sports, can challenge dominant male behaviours.
- **Developing a pedagogy that tackles gender inequality requires a personal commitment to social justice on the part of the mentor and a desire to challenge the prevailing Gender Order.** Mentors, when confronted with issues of 'race', social class, disability, gender or any other structural or cultural inequality need, therefore, to take a 'micro-political' stance (Brown and Rich 2002, p. 94). By doing so, the mentor is perfectly positioned to interrupt intergenerational reproduction of gendered pedagogies.

Key terms: gender inequality, gendered pedagogies, hegemonic masculinity, femininity, gender order.

References

Brown, D., and Evans, J. 2004. Reproducing gender? Intergenerational links and the male PE teacher as a cultural conduit in teaching physical education. *Journal of Teaching in Physical Education*, 23, 48–70.

Brown, D., and Rich, E. 2002. Gender positioning as pedagogical practice in teaching physical education. In D. Penney (Ed.) *Gender and Physical Education: Contemporary Issues and Future Directions*. London: Routledge, pp. 80–100.

Camacho-Minano, M. J., LaVoi, N. M. and Barr-Anderson, D. J. 2011. Interventions to promote physical activity among young and adolescent girls: A systematic review. *Health Education Research*, 26(6), 1025–1049.

Cockburn, C. and Clarke, G. 2002. 'Everybody's looking at you!': Girls negotiating the 'femininity deficit' they incur in physical education. *Women's Studies International Forum*, 25(6), 651–665.

Department for Education, PE and Sport Survey 2009 to 2010.

Evans, B. 2006. 'I'd feel ashamed': Girls' bodies and sports participation. *Gender, Place & Culture: A Journal of Feminist Geography*, 13(5), 547–561.

Fielding-Lloyd, B. and Mean, L. J. 2008. Standards and separatism: The discursive construction of gender in English soccer coach education. *Sex Roles*, 58(1–2), 24–39.

Gorely, T., Holroyd, R. and Kirk, D. 2003. Muscularity, the habitus and the social construction of gender: Towards a gender-relevant physical education. *British Journal of Sociology of Education*, 24(4), 429–448.

Gibbons, S. L. and Humbert, L. 2008. What are middle-school girls looking for in physical education? *Canadian Journal of Education*, 3(1), 167–186.

Hargreaves, J. 1994. *Sporting Females: Critical Issues in the History and Sociology of Women's Sports*. London: Routledge.

Jarvie, G. 2013. *Sport, Culture and Society: An Introduction*. London: Routledge.

Kirk, D. 2005. Physical education, youth sport and lifelong participation: The importance of early learning experiences. *European Physical Education Review*, 11(3), 239–255.

Pfister, G. and Hartmann-Tews, I. 2005. Women and sport in comparative and international perspectives: Issues, aims and theoretical approaches. In I. Hartmann-Tews, and G. Pfister (Eds.), *Sport and Women: Social Issues in International Perspective*. London: Routledge, pp. 1–14.

Rich, E. 2004. Exploring teachers' biographies and perceptions of girls' participation in physical education. *European Physical Education Review*, 10(2), 215–240.

Stidder, G. and Hayes, S. 2006. A longitudinal study of physical education trainee teachers' experiences on school placements in the south-east of England (1994–2004). *European Physical Education Review*, 12(3), 317–338.

Resources

UNESCO report on the importance of Physical Education in empowering girls. Accessed at http://unesdoc.unesco.org/images/0021/002157/215707e.pdf

Women's Sport and Fitness Foundation's website (http://www.wsff.org.uk/), which contains useful resources, studies and papers dealing with girls' experiences of sport at school and the role of teachers in that context.

8

MENTORING AND VOLUNTEERISM

Julia Walsh

Overview

You need to invest if you want the best!

> It's easy to get somebody to come along and give a hand out, but when they
> are standing there and feeling out of their depth and two weeks on the trot and
> nobody is helping them, good luck and good bye, you know. It is a case that you
> have to give people some help as well when you get them in and make it kind
> of almost attractive for them as well, make them feel they are part of something.
>
> *Volunteer*

This quote highlights the learning needs of the volunteer sector. This research
explored volunteering insights and issues in a youth sport context specifically
investigating volunteer motivations, needs and capacities and how best to develop
and support them in their roles. The reoccurring theme was the need for a range of
support processes, in particular mentoring, as they moved through the 'volunteer
life cycle' (Scottish Government 2007).

Vignette

Background

The aim of the study was to explore volunteer recruitment and investigate motivations and barriers to volunteering. Volunteering is the lifeblood of sports programmes
across the world (Rowlands 2014; English Federation of Disability Sports 2014).
Volunteers, like the athletes, are participants and require investment and ongoing
support. Understanding the needs, barriers, and motivations of volunteers is pivotal
for the survival of sports organizations as volunteers make sport and physical activity
viable, affordable, and a healthy option for the community (Walsh *et al.* 2011).

Methods

A mixed methodology was used, comprising both qualitative and quantitative paradigms. Data collection tools used were two online questionnaires, one targeting the general volunteer population and the second, volunteer sport administrators. Six focus group interviews with volunteers investigated issues arising from the questionnaire. Quantitative data analysis was carried out to provide descriptive statistics. During qualitative data analysis, focus-group data were recorded, transcribed and analyzed using the constant comparative method for theme identification (Charmaz 2006). A total of 1,186 volunteers and 210 volunteer administrators participated in the study. The volunteers worked in 31 sports, and the volunteer administrators were involved in 27 sports across Ireland. Participants were recruited through regional sports partnerships, National Sport Governing Bodies, and the Irish Sports Council.

The Research Ethics Committee at Dublin City University approved the study protocol. All participants provided written consent to participate in the study.

Findings

The key findings comprised the following key themes: (a) the volunteer profile; (b) the recruitment, training and retention of volunteers; (c) volunteer education; and (d) club administration and development. These themes create a narrative on who volunteers, why they volunteer, what happens once they are engaged in volunteering, and how to retain volunteers.

Volunteer profile: Unpaid volunteers made up 97 per cent of the total workforce involved in junior sport. Typically they were parents aged between 35–54 years, working in a medium-sized club of at most 100 athletes. Over 80 per cent of the volunteers committed one day per week of their time and remained in the role between 3–10 years. This differs from volunteer research in other countries that typically cites 6 years or less in a volunteer role (Cuskelly 2008).

Recruitment, training and retention of volunteers: Pathways into volunteering were localized to personal connection, previous participation in sport or prior volunteer experience. The most common recruitment strategy was word of mouth, meaning club members talking to people they knew and trying to attract them to the club. Motivation to become a volunteer was related to either one or a combination of previous experience as a sport participant, enjoyment from working with young people, or a family connection:

> The children would have been definitely why I'm involved, before that it would have been because I played the sport myself and I loved it, and I realize what good it had done for me when I was a teenager.
>
> *Volunteer*

Ongoing commitment was motivated by personal, health, social, and skill outcomes:

> The stuff that I've achieved out of volunteering, the huge amount of life skills and learning and meeting other people, the stuff that I've taken, its trials and tribulations with like any coach, you reach the top, but you have huge, huge failings. And it's trying to learn from that and passing it on.
>
> *Volunteer*

Participants entered and remained in the volunteer role if they felt connected and benefited from that connection.

Volunteer education: The volunteers expressed the need to demonstrate competence and confidence in their role. This required investment in training, which they were prepared to do if their time was used efficiently and effectively.

Learning opportunities impact the participant experience and influence retention. Local support and mentoring for performing their role and pathway advancement were critical. Those pursuing a specialist pathway (i.e. coaches, officials, managers) indicated they required a combination of programs, for example, coach accreditation programs, engagement with other volunteers in similar roles, knowledge sharing through mentoring, and opportunities to gain experience. Volunteers also privileged procedural over declarative knowledge (Lyle 2002). In other words, they valued knowing how to do something *in situ* rather than the theory of what to do. They wanted knowledge to be forthcoming and shared from within the sporting organization as well as having access to external training programs.

Club administration and development: At the local club level, knowledge, skill sets and experience are a reflection of the current volunteer workforce. When skilled volunteers leave, so do the knowledge, skills and experience. There were limited examples of succession planning, mentoring, or shadowing at the local club level. This is further compounded and leads to negative experiences when volunteers are expected to take on roles for which they have no skills as indicated by the following quote:

> You are going to have secretaries, a treasurer, you know this sort of thing, and initially this is not what they signed up for. This puts volunteers off, I don't really want to do this and I don't know how to do this.
>
> *Administrator*

Management of volunteers is a significant barrier to retention and the sustainability of the sport club or organization. Volunteers often have multiple roles, some of which stretch their skill set and act as a barrier to volunteer retention. The following quote demonstrates the volunteer's exasperation in having the manpower but lacking the knowledge and skills to perform the role:

I think one of the problems is that there are lots of people to help, but the problem with it is there's nobody there willing to help the people, you know, to actually give them information, you know.

Volunteer

Recommendations

The findings illuminate the need to invest in volunteers during all stages of their tenure from recruitment to retirement. They want to be effective in their roles and expect efficient use made of their limited time (Hughes 2006). This requires sports clubs and organisations to think about how best to distribute knowledge and support volunteers through all stages of involvement in the sport organisation. Volunteers have suggested shadowing and mentoring programs as processes for transferring knowledge and sharing cultural practice within the organisation. This will challenge sport organisations given limited financial resources, time, and expertise to develop and manage these processes. Yet, it might be the only answer if volunteers are to be retained and program outcomes are to be achieved. Sport organisations are unique because of their dependence on a volunteer workforce. Therefore, creating a learning environment that both serves and retains volunteers will require a unique context-driven solution that engages and encourages volunteers to collaborate, share knowledge, build a learning community and embed the knowledge within people and the organisation.

Analysis

Mentoring has a long history and has been used extensively as a learning tool in work and training environments (Clutterbuck 2009). It makes good sense to position mentoring as a learning hub in the volunteer sport sector. The volunteer sector brings its own set of challenges that differ from the work environment and these need to be analyzed and considered in the design and implementation of a mentoring program.

To most people in the community, a 'volunteer' is someone who contributes time to help others with no expectation of pay or other material benefits (Wilson and Musick 2000). However, this does not mean that volunteer work is of no consequence for the volunteer; they do expect fulfillment for themselves. For the volunteer, active contribution to building social capital, the collective social benefits derived through co-operation between individuals and groups (Putnam 2000), working in an environment of trust and reciprocity, and being socially connected are important outcomes. In performing their volunteer role, they aspire to display competence and confidence. Those who do will have more reason to continue volunteering than those with no confidence and under stress (Hughes 2006). The volunteers in this study clearly demonstrated this need and articulated what was required during the volunteer life cycle to retain their services and goodwill. Mentoring and other support mechanisms dominated this discourse.

Shadowing and mentoring were highlighted as ways of creating a rich learning environment and establishing social and cultural connections for volunteers. Shadowing referred to opportunities for volunteers to watch and learn from someone performing a similar role. For example, a volunteer appointed to a club secretary role shadows the current secretary for six months to understand the skills, processes, and temporal components of the job. Volunteers discussed mentoring as short- and long-term solutions for their learning. The short-term solutions focused on mentoring that was interactive, targeted skill and knowledge deficits, and provided an opportunity to apply learning in practice and receive feedback in action from other more experienced members in the sports club. This short-term mentoring is more reflective of coaching, it is targeted and instructional and it relates to some aspect of performance (Jones *et al.* 2009). For some volunteers, their learning needs had much more holistic intentions, were based on developing identity in their role and were associated with career outcomes. It reflected a long-term formalized arrangement where a more knowledgeable person supports and oversees a less experienced but knowledgeable person so as to facilitate that person's goals and aspirations (Roberts 2000). Hence, volunteers used the term *mentoring* broadly to mean anything from induction into the club to career pathway planning.

In general there is confusion about the nature of mentoring (Corrigan and Loughran 2007). From this study, it lacks a shared definition, agreed processes, and is yet to be grounded in an accepted theoretical framework. In some ways, this is understandable as mentoring is built upon relationships, all of which will be different. Equally, these relationships are context-bound which makes it impossible to develop a one-size-fits-all theory or program. This is a challenge for the local sport organization that decides to embark on a mentoring program to support volunteers. The club will need to consider how to create and implement a mentoring program that is sustainable. The study participants provided rich information about their support needs. This critique informed the design of the mentoring program.

In this study, the investment was predominately at recruitment, with limited opportunities for ongoing development. However, the volunteers were vividly aware of what they needed, who should deliver it, how it should be delivered, and when. Understanding the volunteer life cycle illuminates the broader volunteering context beyond recruitment. In a well-organized sport, a volunteer is recruited, and then enters a cycle that has several phases: (a) orientation and induction, (b) training and development and (c) progression, i.e. sustaining the development of volunteers (Scottish Government 2007). During orientation, a person's view of the club or organisation is strongly influenced by early impressions (Hughes 2006). The orientation provides basic information about the club, how it works, and points of contact, and ensures that volunteers know their value and the difference they make through their contribution. The induction assists volunteers to transition into the organisation and is seen as a continuous process until the volunteer understands their role and how the club operates (Scottish Government 2007). Potentially, volunteers remain longer, volunteers become more effective in their role, and it sets the framework for further professional development (Walsh *et al.* 2011). The training and development foci include volunteers' understanding of legislation (i.e. legal guidelines for working with youth), investment in training based on their role, previous experience and personal development goals so that they can perform to the best of their capabilities. Management and leadership training are offered to expand volunteers' horizons by providing opportunities to support and organize other volunteers. The final phase is progression where opportunities to advance are provided to keep volunteers motivated, engaged and up to date. These cycles are not necessarily hierarchical; for example, a volunteer could be engaged in induction, training and development concurrently (Scottish Government 2007).

Volunteers are particular about how support needs to be structured based on their limited availability. For the majority of volunteers, context-specific mentoring in practice at the local level was what was required. The pedagogical encounter was about learning in context and having opportunities to build upon that learning (Armour 2011). Mentoring is influenced by culture, context, and purpose (Clutterbuck 2009, p. 1). The uniqueness of the volunteer work environment means that context as well as skills must be part of the support package. Hence mentoring programs for volunteers should be context balanced in combination with competence development, and provide an opportunity for volunteers to feel that they are part of something (Hughes 2006).

For volunteers, human interaction and relationship building was paramount. It was not just about access to bodies of knowledge (resources); they wanted bodies with knowledge to share their expertise. Procedural knowledge, knowing how to perform aspects of their role (Lyle 2002), was more valued than formal knowledge delivered outside the context of their volunteer role. Procedural knowledge also provided a temporal understanding of the task or role that is rarely delivered in formal education settings. Solutions that connect learning to and through practice and enable volunteers to meet their goals and motives in their role are more likely to be effective (Snyder *et al.* 2000).

Mertz (2004) has proposed a conceptual mentoring framework that aligns closely with volunteers' support needs. It takes into consideration level of commitment (time and effort required), needs analysis and the type of support relationship best suited to the need.

The model identifies three categories of intent and aligns them to different support relationships:

Intent	*Relationship*
Psychosocial Development	Modeling
Professional Development	Advising
Pathway Advancement	Brokering

In the volunteer context, psychosocial development would enhance an individual's sense of competence, identity and effectiveness (Kram 1985). This reflects volunteers' needs to be effective and efficient in their roles. Professional development activities are

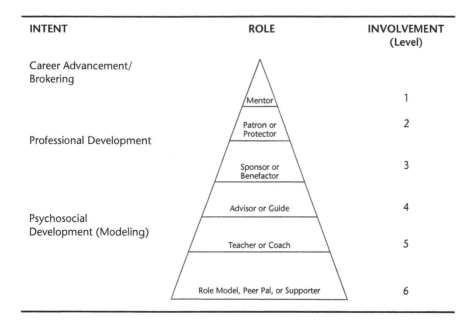

INTENT	ROLE	INVOLVEMENT (Level)
Career Advancement/ Brokering	Mentor	1
Professional Development	Patron or Protector	2
	Sponsor or Benefactor	3
Psychosocial Development (Modeling)	Advisor or Guide	4
	Teacher or Coach	5
	Role Model, Peer Pal, or Supporter	6

FIGURE 8.1 Supportive work relationships arranged hierarchically in terms of primary intent and level of involvement

Mertz 2004, p. 551

designed to help individuals grow and develop professionally in their current context. At the brokering stage, the primary intent is on volunteers' needs into the future. For example, the volunteer is provided with opportunities to engage with the mentor's networks and the mentor looks for opportunities to share power with the mentee.

Involvement within the conceptual framework focuses on the critical elements of time and of intensity of the involvement for the mentor and mentee. Volunteers are time-poor, i.e. they want support but it must be effective and efficient in its delivery if they are to personally invest. Mertz's (Mertz 2004) conceptual framework could form the basis of questions for identifying the mentee's needs, the most appropriate type of supportive relationship, and the amount of time the mentor and mentee have to invest.

Designing and implementing a mentoring program for volunteers is complicated for sports clubs and organizations; it requires people to share and build expertise within the organisation as compared to a model that temporarily imports people with expertise and when those people leave the expertise is gone. Commitment to a mentoring program is long term as it takes time to train and empower people as mentors and mentees. The conundrum is that volunteers perform the majority of roles in the club and there is a high natural turnover of volunteers (Cuskelly 2008).

> Mentoring programs enjoy sustainability over time when mentoring is embedded in an organisational cultural that values continuous learning.
>
> *Zachary 2000, p. 167*

Until organizational change has occurred, mentoring programs may only last as long as someone in the club champions the program. The program requires time to attach itself to the club's cultural roots. Not unlike a club that has over time established a particular game style for which it is known, mentoring programs need to be seen internally and externally as the learning hub for the organisation.

Mentoring programs require resources, time, expertise and cultural acceptance, particularly in the early stages of development. Responsibility for large-scale volunteer mentoring programs may best be located with national bodies who have access to financial resources and can distribute knowledge to their feeder organizations economically. Diversity of volunteer expertise requires a flexible mentoring programme, not a one-size-fits-all programme. The volunteer sector is unique and will require a unique mentoring solution where context, time, and the mentoring pedagogy are considered.

Conclusion

There are numerous challenges in setting up a mentoring program in the volunteer sport sector: time is limited, volunteering is optional, and sharing knowledge is yet to become a cultural practice in many sports clubs. Having noted this, the volunteer voice has indicated very clearly what they value and what they need. Making mentoring the hub for learning addresses some of these issues, but it must be relevant and meaningful for the mentor, mentee and the organisation in a work environment that has its own set of limitations and opportunities.

Lessons learned . . . What could we add to the Mentor Pedagogy Toolbox?

- **Mentoring programs are an investment in volunteer and club development.** This is an attractive incentive for local sports clubs to encourage people to volunteer and to retain them.
- **Time-poor volunteers.** The challenge for any mentoring program in a time-poor environment is to provide the mentor and mentee ample time to build and secure this relationship. Allocating time in the planning phase and being considerate of the context-specific issues will be essential.
- **The majority of people who volunteer commit 3–6 years to the organization** (Cuskelly 2008). Learning needs for those new to volunteering or to a specialist role (i.e. coaches, managers, club secretary) require a combination of knowledge, skills, and social connection. Volunteers want personal contact when learning, and their preference is that it be locally available.
- **The challenge for any local sport club is to build an environment where learning is central and knowledge is distributed** across all members. It is a long-term investment requiring cultural change and buy-in from all participants. It should be seen as a long-term project.

Key terms: mentoring, volunteers, youth, sports mentoring.

References

Armour, K. 2011. *Sport Pedagogy: An Introduction for Teaching and Coaching.* London: Routledge.

Charmaz, K. 2006. *Constructing Grounded Theory: A Practical Guide through Qualitative Analysis.* London: Sage Publications.

Clutterbuck, D. 2009. Coaching and mentoring in support of management development 1. In S. J. Armstrong and C. V. Fukami (Eds.) *The SAGE Handbook of Management Learning, Education and Development.* Thousand Oaks, CA: SAGE, 477–497.

Corrigan, D. and Loughran, J. 2007. *Snapshots of Mentoring: Vignettes of Practice.* Melbourne: Faculty of Education, Monash University.

Cuskelly, G. 2008. Volunteering in community sport organisations: Implications for social capital. In M. Nicholson and R. Hoye (Eds.) *Sport and Social Capital.* London: Butterworth-Heinermann.

English Federation of Disability Sports. 2014. Volunteer engagement (Online). Available at http://www.do-it.org.uk/articles/types-of-volunteering/sport-and-outdoor-activities/sports-volunteers/ (accessed 23 February 2014).

Hughes, L. 2006. *A Guide for Training Volunteers. Part A.* Melbourne: Volunteering Australia.

Jones, R. L., Harris, R. A. and Miles, A. 2009. Mentoring in sports coaching: A review of the literature. *Physical Education and Sport Pedagogy*, 14, 267–284.

Kram, K. 1985. *Mentoring at Work: Developing Relationships in Organizational Life.* Glenview, IL: Scott, Foresman and Company.

Lyle, J. 2002. *Sports Coaching Concepts: A Framework for Coaches' Behaviour.* London: Routledge.

Mertz, N. 2004. What's a mentor, anyway? *Education Administration Quarterly*, 40, 541–560.

Putnam, R. 2000. *Bowling Alone: The Collapse and Revival of American Community.* New York: Simon and Schuster.

Roberts, A. 2000. Mentoring revisited: A phenomenological reading of the literature. *Mentoring and Tutoring: Partnership in Learning*, 8, 145–168.

Rowlands, O. 2014. Do-it: Volunteering made easy (Online). Available at http://www.efds.co.uk/our_work_in_sport/volunteer_engagement (accessed 23 February 2014).

Scottish Government. 2007. Volunteering in the youth work sector (Online). Available at www.scotland.gov.uk/publications/2007/11/26110321/3 (accessed 19 January 2014).

Snyder, M., Clary, E. G. and Stukas, A. A. 2000. The functional approach to volunteerism. In G. R. Maio and J. M. Olson (Eds.) *Why We Evaluate: Functions of Attitudes.* Mahwah, New Jersey: Lawrence Erlbaum Associates, Inc.

Walsh, J., Tannehill, D. and Woods, C. B. 2011. The Children's Sport Participation and Physical Activity Study (CSPPA): Volunteer Study. Dublin: Dublin City University.

Wilson. J. and Musick, M. 2000. The effects of volunteering on the volunteer. *Law and Contemporary Problems*, 62, 141–168.

Zachary, L. J. 2000. *The Mentor's Guide: Facilitating Effective Learning Relationships.* San Francisco: Jossey-Bass.

Resources

AFL. 2014. Finding a coach mentor (Online). Available at http://www.aflcommunityclub.com.au/index.php?id=326 (accessed 23 December 2013).

Zuztertu, Ltd. 2012. Mentor's toolbox (1.0) (Mobile application software). Retrieved from https://itunes.apple.com/au/app/mentors-toolbox/id490954383?mt=8

SECTION 3

Mentoring and physical education

9

EFFECTIVE MODELS OF MENTORING FOR SCHOOLS

Policy and practice

Sinéad Luttrell

Overview

Research on Initial Teacher Education highlights the integral role of the school placement component of such programmes, and positions mentors as exhibiting 'the most significant influence on pre-service teachers' (Kirk *et al.* 2006, p. 447). This case study seeks to address a gap in the research literature which centres on how the process of learning to teach, scaffolded by mentoring support, is enacted in practice. As Cullingford notes, '[t]here are many books on how to introduce and practice mentoring programs, but far fewer which provide a scrutiny of what actually takes place' (Cullingford 2006, p. xii). This study is set against the backdrop of radical systemic changes in Teacher Education in Ireland, viewed as 'the most creative of eras' where changes in policy may potentially serve as a catalyst 'to transform teacher education in Ireland and the engagement of the teaching profession with its development' (Coolahan 2013, p. 9). The policy and practice of mentoring student teachers as stipulated in the Teaching Council's 2013 *Guidelines on School Placement* aims to ensure 'greater consistency in the school placement experience' and to facilitate 'enhanced collaboration' (ibid., p. 3) between the university and schools. Mentoring student teachers is recognised as a complex and multi-faceted role: 'Mentoring encompasses all those means by which the student teacher on placement is supported, advised and encouraged and his/her practice and thinking is affirmed and challenged, as appropriate' (ibid., p. 6).

Vignette

> As a mentor, you see them grow and I want to try to open their eyes, rather than tell them what to see. It is like watching a bird learn to fly. You want to protect and nurture the student teacher as they learn to teach, but at the same time support and encourage them to take flight.
>
> *Mentor Focus Group*

The research questions underpinning this study are as follows:

1.   What is the nature of student teacher learning during teaching practice?
2.   How do the relationship and nature of support evolve in the mentoring dyad?
3.   What are the prerequisites for an effective learner-centred model of mentoring?

Wang and Odell (2007, p. 473) identify three facets that are prevalent in teacher education mentoring programmes: (a) humanistic assumptions (helping novice teachers to overcome personal problems and feel comfortable in the profession); (b) situated apprentice (helping novice teachers to move into the existing school culture and supporting the development of survival skills in particular contexts); and (c) critical constructivist (transforming teaching by posing questions and challenging existing teaching practices). Zachary (2011) proposes a mentee-centred or learner-centred mentoring paradigm in which the mentee plays a more active role in the learning process, in contrast to mentor-driven paradigms whereby the mentee adopts a more subservient role: 'There has been a shift away from the more traditional authoritarian teacher-dependent student-supplicant paradigm, where the passive mentee sits at the feet of the master and receives knowledge' (Zachery 2011, p. 3). Broadening the scope of mentoring to encompass the professional growth of student teachers requires 'emotional support and professional socialisation in addition to pedagogical guidance' (He 2009, p. 263) and legitimising the dual roles of student and learner.

Methods

The methodologies deployed in this study were closely interwoven with the research questions, and operated within a constructivist paradigm. The rationale for the selection of constructivism as the most apt research paradigm resides in the fact that realities are arguably socially constructed and both the school context and experiences of mentees and mentors present a specific version of social reality whereby knowledge is viewed as indeterminate. The situated social constructivist approach suggests that 'knowledge is constructed by a person in transaction with the environment' (Richardson 2000, p. 925). The qualitative data collection methods employed consisted of sixteen interviews, one hundred observation sheets, a card sort and two focus groups. Research participants were self-selected and pseudonyms have been used throughout to protect the identity of the participants and their respective schools. The qualitative data was analysed using a grounded theory approach (Strauss and Corbin 1998) which is an inductive method of theory generation. Grounded theory (Strauss and Corbin 1998; Charmaz 2006) was selected since mentoring is idiosyncratic and context-dependent.

Findings

The main findings of this study are summarised below and presented thematically in the next section to capture the voices of mentors and student teachers.

- Mentoring requires a dynamic, flexible framework to support student teachers' individual progress through stages of teacher development.
- Mentors have the capacity to accelerate student teacher learning.
- Learning to teach can be both an exciting and painful journey.
- Mentors are viewed as agents of socialisation in school context, role models and facilitators of student teacher learning.
- The school context is a rich site for professional learning and growth.
- The role of a mentor is multi-faceted and challenging; it evolves since it is driven by mentee needs and their stage of teacher development.
- Mentors navigate the mentee journey through guidance and support, facilitating the potential personal and professional development of both parties.

Analysis

Theme 1: Mentoring as a personal and professional odyssey

This case study exemplified the personal satisfaction mentors derived from their mentoring experiences and an altruistic motivation for involvement transpired in both the focus group and interviews.

> As a PE teacher I welcome the chance to help, support and guide pre-service teachers into the profession because I know what it's like for them, how hard it can be and I kind of feel like that it's only right to give something back to the profession and it's rewarding to see the next generation of PE teachers grow and develop, especially over the course of a year teaching practice.
>
> *Mentor 5 Interview*

This closely resonates with the research literature regarding the role of the mentor to 'support all trainees in discovering the teacher within or in transforming themselves from non-teacher into teacher' (Malderez *et al.* 2007, p. 239) and empowers mentors 'to revitalise their career and to bring personal satisfaction' (Ehrich 2008, p. 31). Mentors co-navigate the journey with student teachers through guidance and support, merging personal and professional development.

> Yeah it was good because he was very approachable, encouraged me and was just really nice. I also got to see how the students reacted to him and I can adapt some of his routines in PE . . . and try things out . . . You get confidence when strategies work. He would encourage me and shared in my success, praising me for a good lesson.
>
> *Mentee 7 Interview*

Theme 2: The role of mentor evolves

Fletcher (2000, p. 18) highlights the benefits of dynamic mentoring, aligned to the specific stages of student teacher development: 'we need to start our mentoring at the point where trainees are, rather than where we think they should be'. The prospect of such alignment proved somewhat challenging for mentor teachers in this study, who expressed uncertainty in both determining the actual stage of teacher development and the type of support or challenge required to meet the needs of mentees.

> I suppose trying to gauge where they are at, like what kind of help or support do they actually need at a particular time of the year. They develop professionally at their own pace.
>
> *PE Mentor 5 Interview*

The implication is that the role of mentor teacher evolves and cannot be reduced to a shopping list of duties and responsibilities; it changes in accordance with the specific needs and stages of student teacher development.

> The role of mentor can be dictated by a list of jobs, it is personal and must suit the needs of the student teacher. . . . I think it actually changes according to the time of year, like at the start it is all about familiarisation with the school ethos, rules, classroom management. Then when they are settled in and comfortable, content, teaching strategies, giving feedback to students becomes more important. It isn't until after Christmas that student teachers feel confident about trying out new ideas, taking risks.
>
> *Mentor Focus Group*

There was a consensus regarding the initial stage encompassing socialisation into the school context and classroom management issues; it was the distinct rates of progression between stages of student teacher development which proved problematic. Fuller (1969) posits a three-stage 'concerns theory', following a hierarchical pattern. Reeves and Kazelskis (1985, p. 267) define concerns as 'something he or she thinks frequently about and would like to do something about personally'. The first stage of teaching is concern for *Self*, revealed in such concerns as survival in the classroom or gym, acceptance by peers, feelings of inadequacy, lack of confidence and obtaining a good grade on teaching practice. The second stage is concern about the teaching *Task*, as evidenced by concerns about the teaching situation (e.g. duties and responsibilities, resources, number of pupils, classroom management and pedagogical content knowledge). The third stage of concern is *Impact* of teaching on pupils, indicated by concerns for meeting diverse student needs and adapting to meet these needs. The mentor focus group identified with Fuller's model (1969), presented as a stimulus for discussion, but the recognition of the specific stage and the tendency to oscillate between stages posed the most difficulty for mentors.

The student teachers whom I've mentored over the years didn't quite follow that pattern, the concern of teacher as *self* seems to be a dominant one, although the *impact* one was definitely the last, the focus on meaningful student learning certainly isn't there from the outset.

Mentor Focus Group

This mirrors the findings of Conway and Clark (2003, p. 472), who reported an overdominance of self-as-teacher concerns permeating the teaching practice journey, rather than 'remaining frozen in self-survival concerns as Fuller predicted'. Their extension of Fuller's (1969) concerns-based model of teacher development, terms the shift from self to tasks to students as 'a journey outward' and incorporates concerns about 'their personal capacity to grow as a teacher and person, as their understanding of teaching and all that it involves changed – an inward journey' (ibid., p. 465). The implications are firstly to assist mentors in the recognition of their mentees' actual stage of teacher development and secondly to facilitate progression to the next level. There is a danger in viewing stages of teacher development as linear in nature. Student teacher learning is progressive and individual needs and rates of progress differ.

Daloz's (1999) model of mentoring locates the student teacher within a context of support and challenge. This model is based upon the view that where support is low, there is little opportunity for any challenge to occur and the student teacher may withdraw from the mentoring relationship. Conversely, if support is high, new knowledge and images of teaching become possible for the student teacher. Sensitivity and diplomacy are key attributes for effective feedback and a key challenge for effective mentor pedagogy is the simultaneous provision of both high support and high challenge as advocated by Daloz (1999).

If mentor teachers are unwilling to criticize, perhaps out of fear of negatively affecting the relationship shared with the student teacher, progress will be slow. Unless student teachers know where their areas for improvement lie, they are likely to flounder with no direction.

Glenn 2006, p. 91

This study suggested that diplomatic articulation of teaching difficulties is only the first step; the mentor is faced with two possible and concurrent actions, to try to get the mentee to engage in practical reasoning or to prescribe the solution deemed appropriate by the mentor or opt for a 'directive' or 'enquiry-oriented' approach, as labelled by Zeichner *et al.* (1988 p. 61). Little (1990, p. 298) echoes this view that the mentor teacher should help student teachers 'confront difficult problems of practice and use their teaching as a site for learning'.

I think that observing the student teacher teaching and providing them with feedback, addressing their concerns and giving them both reassurance or praise on their strengths, as well as identifying areas for improvement, without being too critical because they are quite sensitive and vulnerable, [is important].

PE Mentor 1 Interview

Theme 3: Learning to learn: The metamorphosis of student teachers on teaching practice

Schools are more than sites for teaching practice placements; they are the platforms for meaningful student teacher learning and growth. Fletcher (2000, p. xi) defines mentoring through a process-orientated lens 'to participate in life growing'. Mentor selection based on suitability and a compatible mentor-mentee match (Chambers *et al.* 2012), were deemed desirable features by the student teachers in this study.

> It is really important to match up student teachers with mentors who actually want to be mentors. Like, volunteers are interested. You definitely need to get on well with the mentor, you both have to make an effort, and personalities come into it when you are working closely for like the whole year, you develop a good personal relationship as well as the professional TP one.
>
> *Mentee Focus Groups*

While Dolloff (2007, p. 17) contends that student teachers are ultimately the 'architects of their own development', the findings of this study indicate that mentors have the capacity to accelerate both the process and progress of student teacher learning.

> My professional learning and development as a teacher would've occurred anyway but it wouldn't have occurred at the same pace, it would've taken a lot, lot longer because the mentors point you in the right direction . . . and it's just like they are kind of role models, so they reduce the time that it takes you to learn things.
>
> *Mentee 1 Interview*

Maynard (2000, p. 27) posits that a lot of energy on teaching practice is afforded to 'keeping the relationship right' and '[e]xperience of school-based teacher education . . . can simply mean learning to fit in, while not disrupting the precarious equilibrium of existing classroom practices' (Ellis 2010, p. 110). Similarly, one student teacher felt that in the interest of preserving a positive mentoring relationship, he was reluctant to take risks in planning and to use teaching strategies which differed from the mentor teacher:

> I didn't want to suggest alternative PE programme content areas or even chance using different instructional models, it's just you don't want to upset the status quo. The PE programme was quite structured and we were getting on so well.
>
> *Mentee 8 Interview*

Learning to teach can be both a stressful and exciting process: 'By understanding the ways students cope with the stresses of learning to teach, teacher educators may be better informed about how to help students become more resilient teachers' (Murray-Harvey 2001, p. 118). Student teacher professional learning that is scaffolded by mentor support may alleviate the 'reality shock' of initial teaching experiences. Can effective models of mentoring in schools bridge the gap between what Duffield (2006, p. 167) termed 'safety net and free fall' for student teachers on teaching practice?

Lessons learned . . . What could we add to the Mentor Pedagogy Toolbox?

The researcher proposes that the 'Mentor Pedagogy Toolbox' contains a rich tapestry of dynamic and adaptive core principles which seek to scaffold a learner-centred model of mentoring.

Different strokes for different folks. The learner-centred model outlined in this chapter recognises that mentor pedagogy is 'essentially idiosyncratic' because 'each instance of mentoring is based on a unique relationship involving an extremely complex interplay of cognitive, affective and interpersonal factors' (Hawkey 1997, p. 326). The role of mentor evolves and is inextricably linked to the specific needs of each student teacher and their relative stage of teacher development. 'Mentoring support is most effective when it is adjusted to the needs of student or beginning teachers' (Krull 2005, p. 147).

Mentors as co-learners. Enabling teachers to continue to grow, learn, and be excited about their work depends on both ongoing, high-quality learning opportunities and career opportunities that enable them to share their expertise in a variety of ways (Darling-Hammond and Lieberman 2012, p. 164).

Mentoring may be viewed as a reciprocal relationship, mutually beneficial for both mentor and mentee. Mentors engage in a process of self-reflection as they articulate and model best practice for student teachers whom they mentor: 'Serving as a mentor pushes one not only to model but also to be accountable for that modelling' (Weasmer and Woods 2003, p. 69).

Professional learning is a marathon, not a sprint. The Teaching Council's Continuum of Teacher Education (2011) identifies Initial Teacher Education as the start-line of teacher education, spanning the entire teaching career. Teachers are viewed as career-long professional learners, from Initial Teacher Education, through Induction and Continuing Professional Development (CPD). To extend the analogy, it is viewed as a marathon rather than a sprint (Luttrell and Chambers 2013, p. 429). Each stage of the continuum is underpinned by 'innovation, integration and improvement' (Teaching Council 2011, p. 8). The provision of opportunities to share best practice and engaging in meaningful mentor pedagogy, challenges traditional and cultural norms congruent with the 'legendary autonomy' of Irish teachers (OECD 1991), in favour of a more collaborative and synergetic approach. Mentor training is advocated as a form of continued professional development;

'mentors should view the development of this knowledge and skills as opportunities to strengthen professional practice as lifelong learners' (Kajs 2002, p. 62).

Key terms: student teacher learning, mentors, teaching practice, learner-centred mentoring, policy and practice of mentoring.

References

Chambers, F. C., Armour, K., Luttrell, S., Bleakley, E. W., Brennan, D. A. and Herold, F. A. 2012. Mentoring as a profession-building process in physical education teacher education. *Irish Educational Studies*, 31(3), 345–362.

Charmaz, K. 2006. *Constructing Grounded Theory: A Practical Guide through Qualitative Analysis*. London: Sage Publications.

Conway, P. F. and Clark, C. M. 2003. The journey inward and outward: a re-examination of Fuller's concerns-based model of teacher development. *Teaching and Teacher Education*, 19(5), 465–482.

Coolahan, J. 2013. Towards a new era for teacher education and the engagement of the teaching profession. *Irish Teachers' Journal*, 1(1), 9–26.

Cullingford, C. 2006. *Mentoring in Education: An International Perspective*. Aldershot, UK: Ashgate Publishing Ltd.

Daloz, L. A. 1999. *Mentor Guiding the Journey of Adult Learners*. San Francisco: Jossey-Bass.

Darling-Hammond, L. and Lieberman, A. 2012. *Teacher Education Around the World: Changing Policies and Practices*. London and New York: Routledge.

Dolloff, L. A. 2007. "All the things we are": balancing our multiple identities in music teaching. *Action, Criticism and Theory for Music Education*, 6(2), 1–20.

Duffield, S. 2006. Safety net or free fall: the impact of cooperating teachers. *Teacher Development*, 10(2), 167–178.

Ehrich, L. C. 2008. Three P's for the mentoring of women educators: purpose, power, propriety. *Journal of the Association of Women Educators*, 17(2), 31–36.

Ellis, V. 2010. Impoverishing experience: the problem of teacher education in England. *Journal of Education for Teaching*, 36(1), 105–120.

Fletcher, S. 2000. *Mentoring in Schools: A Handbook of Good Practice*. London: Routledge.

Fuller, F. 1969. Concerns of teachers: a developmental conceptualisation. *American Educational Research Journal*, 6, 207–226.

Glenn, W. J. 2006. Model versus mentor: defining the necessary qualities of the effective cooperating teacher. *Teacher Education Quarterly*, Winter, 33(1), 85–95.

Hawkey, K. 1997. Roles, responsibilities and relationships in mentoring: a literature review and agenda for research. *Journal of Teacher Education*, 48(5), 325–335.

He, Y. 2009. Strength-based mentoring in pre-service teacher education: a literature review. *Mentoring and Tutoring: Partnership in Learning*, 17(3), 263–275.

Kajs, L. T. 2002. Framework for designing a mentoring program for novice teachers. *Mentoring and Tutoring: Partnership in Learning*, 10(1), 57–69.

Kirk, D., Macdonald, D. and O'Sullivan, M. 2006. *The Handbook of Physical Education*. London: Sage Publications.

Krull, E. 2005. Mentoring as a means for supporting student and beginning teachers' practice-based learning. *TRAMES: A Journal of the Humanities and Social Sciences*, 2, 143–158.

Little, J. W. 1990. The mentor phenomenon and the social organization of teaching. *Review of Research in Education*, 16, 297–351.

Luttrell, S. and Chambers, F. C. 2013. *Senior Cycle Physical Education Curriculum and Instructional Models: Pathways for Teacher Implementation*. Dublin: ePrint Limited.

Malderez, A., Hobson, A. J., Tracey, L. and Kerr, K. 2007. Becoming a student teacher: core features of the experience. *European Journal of Teacher Education*, 30(3), 225–248.

Maynard, T. 2000. Learning to teach or learning to manage mentors? Experiences of school-based teacher training. *Mentoring and Tutoring*, 8, 17–30.

Murray-Harvey, R. 2001. How teacher education students cope with practicum concerns. *The Teacher Educator*, 37(2), 117–132.

Reeves, C. K. and Kazelskis, R. 1985. Concerns of preservice and inservice teachers. *The Journal of Educational Research*, 78, 267–271.

Richardson, L. 2000. Writing: a method of inquiry. In N. K. Denzin and Y. S. Lincoln (Eds.) *Handbook of Qualitative Research* (2nd edition). Thousand Oaks, CA: Sage Publications, pp. 923–948.

Strauss, A. and Corbin, J. 1998. *Basics of Qualitative Research: Techniques and Procedures for Developing Grounded Theory* (2nd edition). Thousand Oaks, CA: Sage.

Teaching Council 2011. *Policy on the Continuum of Teacher Education*. Maynooth: Teaching Council.

Teaching Council 2013. *Guidelines on School Placement* (1st edition). Maynooth: Teaching Council.

Wang, J. and Odell, S. J. 2007. An alternative conception of mentor-novice relationships: learning to teach in reform-minded ways as a context. *Teaching and Teacher Education*, 23, 473–489.

Weasmer, J. and Woods, A. M. 2003. Mentoring: professional development through reflection. *The Teacher Educator*, 39(1), 64–77.

Young, J. R., Bullough, R. V., Draper, R. J., Smith, L. K. and Erikson, L. B. 2005. Novice teacher growth and personal models of mentoring: choosing compassion over inquiry. *Mentoring and Tutoring: Partnership in Learning*, 13(2), 169–188.

Zachary, L. J. 2011. *The Mentor's Guide: Facilitating Effective Learning Relationships*. San Francisco: Jossey-Bass.

Zeichner, K. M., Liston, D. P., Mahlios, M. and Gomez, M. 1988. The structure and goals of a student teaching program and the character and quality of supervisory discourse. *Teaching and Teacher Education*, 4.

Resources

Chambers, F. C., Armour, K., Luttrell, S., Bleakley, E. W., Brennan, D. A. and Herold, F. A. 2012. Mentoring as a profession-building process in physical education teacher education. *Irish Educational Studies*, 31(3), 345–362.

Teaching Council 2011. *Policy on the Continuum of Teacher Education*. Maynooth: Teaching Council.

10

TRAINING MENTOR TEACHERS ACROSS THE CAREER-SPAN

Fiona C. Chambers, Frank A. Herold, Paul McFlynn, Deirdre A. Brennan and Kathleen Armour

Overview

Sir Ken Robinson (2010) describes the change in culture needed radically to shift the current teacher education system, using the words of Abraham Lincoln (1862):

> The dogmas of the quiet past are inadequate to the stormy present. The occasion is piled high with difficulty, and we must rise with the occasion. As our case is new, so we must think anew, and act anew. We must disenthrall ourselves, and then we shall save our country.

Teacher Education in the twenty-first century must therefore be 'capable, agile and sustainable' (Department of Education and Training Queensland 2011), which will itself shape an agile teaching workforce.

Agility is defined as the quality of being agile; readiness for motion; nimbleness, activity, dexterity in motion (Oxford English Dictionary, 2013). *Workforce agility* is often defined as the ability of employees to respond strategically to uncertainty (Glinska *et al.* 2012, p. 2):

> Agility is a capability; it is an organization's capacity to respond rapidly and effectively to unanticipated opportunities and to proactively develop solutions for potential needs. It is the result of an organization and the people in it, working together in ways that benefit the individual, the organization, and their customers.
>
> *Nelson and Harvey 1995*

Arguably, this capability is central to creating an agile organization (Prahalad and Hamel 1990). There is a need to 'mobilize employees to meet the demands of the unpredictable education landscape with speed, flexibility and nimbleness' (p. 2).

Educating the teacher workforce to be agile is achieved through carefully designed professional development and training opportunities across the three-phase continuum of teacher education (Teaching Council of Ireland 2011). This is essentially about teachers learning, learning how to learn, and transforming knowledge into practice for the benefit of their professional and pedagogical growth (Darling-Hammond 2006b; Darling-Hammond 2006a; Darling-Hammond and Rothman 2011).

According to the Queensland Department of Education and Training (2011, p. 6), mentoring plays a pivotal role in the professional development of an agile workforce:

> Mentoring is a relationship designed to build confidence, encourage participants to take responsibility for their own learning, help them apply greater initiative to their own development, and assist less experienced staff to 'navigate' the organization.

Mentor training

Currently, mentor selection can be a haphazard process as mentors are chosen on the basis of (a) being excellent classroom teachers, even though some do not have the potential to be effective mentors (Fletcher 1998; Tannehill and Goc-Karp 1992) or (b) being available rather than suitable (Fletcher 1998). Riggs (2000) concurs, saying most mentor teachers generally are selected on the basis of their expertise as a teacher and position in the Career Cycle (Hennissen *et al.* 2011). Because expertise is domain-specific (Berliner 2001), good teachers are not automatically good mentors (Zanting 2001). Coupled with this, formal mentor training programmes may not exist even though studies identify a need for serious on-going mentor training (Rikard and Veale 1996; Hardy 1999). It is argued that such training programmes should contain the following approaches: role-modeling, observation, data collection and feedback-focused analysis (Randall 1992; Metzler 1990) underpinned by a strong reflective purpose (Korthagen 2001). In this way, the mentor will be equipped to address issues of power and the effect of phases of personal and professional life in the mentor-mentee relationship. Hennissen *et al.* (2011) state that 'apart from expertise as a teacher, it is important that mentor teachers develop attitudes, knowledge and skills in the specific domain of mentoring' (p. 207). It may be helpful at this point to tease out how mentor suitability can be gauged using the concepts of mentor capacity and capability.

Mentor capacity and capability

In dictionary definitions, *capacity* is defined as the power to hold, accommodate, or receive something. The word is also used to describe the abilities or powers of human beings to do or understand something; the power to learn or retain knowledge; mental ability; innate potential for growth, development or accomplishment; faculty. *Capability* is a feature, an ability, or competence that can be developed in a person or a potential aptitude. It could refer to an ability that exists in an individual but can be improved upon – e.g. a novice mentor may support the mentee in a very directive style but the mentor trainer might feel that with training he or she could move to a more collaborative style (Glickman *et al.* 2001). According to the dictionary, capability, therefore, is the sum of existing *ability* or capacity plus the potential for development of that ability (*potentiality*).

Capacity building

> For all practical purposes, building teacher capacity is, ultimately, engendering development, growth and excellence within an education system.
>
> *Egbo 2011, p. 2*

The contention here is that this will also apply to mentor teacher capacity – i.e. the investment in building mentor teacher capacity will have a direct impact on the quality of the overall education system. There is a range of approaches to mentor training in the three jurisdictions in the vignette reported in this chapter. In Ireland and Northern Ireland, there is no formal training, compared to England where mentors are selected, trained and paid for their mentoring work. Clearly, inconsistent or non-existent mentor training is inimical or hostile to pre-service teacher learning.

Egbo's (2011) model of capacity building in teachers is useful in this context. She states (p. 13) that:

> [i]n building teacher capacity, the focus should be several but, in particular, the following broad areas: policy, training, and pedagogy, infrastructure development and, teacher welfare and empowerment.

Perhaps, the same facets apply to building mentor capacity (see Figure 10.1).

According to Egbo (2011), the end result of successful capacity building initiatives should be effective and transformative teaching and learning. Through the mentor-capacity building process, a curiosity is awakened within the learner, allowing them to engage critically with the commonplace and the familiar and to grow more mature pedagogies (Freire 1970). Mentor capacity building encourages the learner to understand the teaching self and, indeed, the mentor-self. Egbo (2011, p. 12) argues that:

> [c]rucially, for capacity building to be effective, it must respond to the growth and development needs of the individual as well as those of the relevant institutions.

Capacity and capability are symbiotic terms and can be best understood within the notion of a Capability Maturity Model.

Capability Maturity Model

To begin, a definition of the core elements of a Capability Maturity Model will be helpful. Clarke *et al.* (2013) defines capability in relation to processes, as follows:

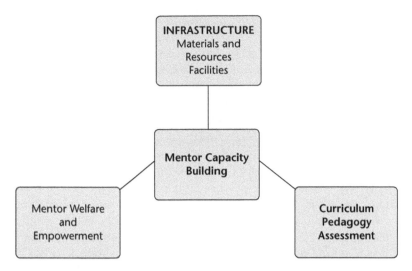

FIGURE 10.1 Adapted from 'A Contextualised Model of Teacher Capacity Building'
Egbo 2011, p. 8, in Chambers *et al.* 2013, p. 37

the capability of a process used by an organization (e.g. the Teacher Education System) is an indication of how well it does what it is designed to do. Rosemann and De Bruin (2005) describe how the combined influence of the capabilities on a given aspect of the organization, in this case mentor teacher education, is a sign of maturity. Iversen, Nielsen and Nørbjerg (1999) speak of aspects, which can have levels of maturity, i.e. be more or less mature. The maturity rating of these aspects can impact on the process of mentor teacher training within the education system. Mentor-teacher education capability improves based on the increased maturity of these aspects. A model is defined as:

> [a] theoretical representation that simulates the behaviour or activity of systems, processes or phenomena and by ordering all of the theoretically possible incremental improvements into a continuum, it is possible to generate a model that summarises the maturity of the capabilities for that organization.
>
> *Clarke et al. 2013, p. 2*

The integration of these three ideas produces the capability maturity model[1], which:

> [r]epresents a continuum of incremental improvements, evolving from a less to a more mature or effective level . . . clustered into a series of stages or levels where process capability – how capable a process is of achieving what it is designed to do – can be described within each level in terms of key processes and between levels as a logical maturational development from one level to the next. The dominant level provides the global indicator of maturity.
>
> *Ibid., p. 4*

The Capability Maturity Model (CMM) has its genesis in the information technology (IT) industry – e.g. the CMM (Paulk 1999) is a classic example of such a model which was level-oriented. Marshall and Mitchell (2002) evolved a model that replaced levels with a more holistic, dimension-driven structure. Marshall (2010) is careful to point out that the CMM is not a linear and hierarchical tool. Instead, it is the synergistic and holistic nature of the dimensions concept where maturity is interpreted as a complex, interactive product of all of the dimensions. Marshall and Mitchell (2006, p. 1) explain:

> The key idea underlying the dimension concept in contrast, is holistic capability. Rather than the model measuring progressive levels, it describes the capability of a process from synergistic perspectives. An organisation that has developed capability on all dimensions for all processes will be more capable than one that has not. Strong capability at particular dimensions that is not supported by capability at the other dimensions will not deliver the desired outcomes.

Even more complexity is inherent in development of capabilities, as not all mentors learn in the same way.

Vignette

Background

This study (Chambers *et al.* 2013) builds on the previous Standing Conference on the Teacher Education North and South (SCoTENS) funded study (reported in Chapter 3), which interrogated current mentoring practice in three Physical Education Teacher Education (PETE) programmes (Ireland, Northern Ireland and England). Using the same three research sites, this study aimed to prepare a detailed Charter of Mentor Competencies in PETE.

Methods

Research participants comprised six university tutors (UTs) and ten PE mentor teachers across the three research sites. This study employed a mixed method approach to data collection (focus groups and a survey). Data were analysed thematically either using a constructivist version of grounded theory as a framework for data analysis (Strauss and Corbin 1998, p. 141; Charmaz 2000) or using Descriptive Statistics.

Findings

This study moved beyond the initial aim to produce a Charter of Mentor Competencies in PETE and formulated a Capability Maturity Model for Mentor Teachers (CM³T) across a new Mentor Career Cycle framework.

The CM³T can be used as both (a) a diagnostic tool to ascertain mentor training needs within the Mentor Career Cycle and (b) a planning tool for designing bespoke training programmes for mentors at each phase of the Mentor Career Cycle. The mentor competencies are assigned to Bloom *et al.*'s (1956) (i) cognitive domain, (ii) affective domain or (iii) hybrid cognitive/affective domains. The CM³T also shows the level within each domain taxonomy using a colour–coding system. A Mentor Career Cycle was also generated based on Huberman's Career Cycle (1989). Mentor teachers in the study expressed dissatisfaction with the titles for some of the phases in Huberman's Career Cycle (1989) and changed these as follows: *Career entry* to *Novice, serenity/ relational distance* to *consolidation/maturity* and *moving toward disengagement* to *Expert*.

How to use the CM³T

From this study, data have shown that *all capabilities* in the CM³T Chart have to be developed by the mentor across each phase of the Mentor Career Cycle. In each phase of the Mentor Career Cycle, the domain level of each mentor capability is clearly outlined in the CM³T Chart. The definitions of the levels of each capability (cognitive and affective [hybrid]) are outlined in Table 10.3. The CM³T Chart helps the mentor trainer to diagnose the positioning of the mentor in the Mentor Career Cycle and the capability level the mentor must attain within this phase. This may serve as a useful diagnostic and training tool for mentor teachers. Two worked examples using the complete CM³T Chart are now presented in relation to development of a particular mentor capability.

Example 1

Capability: Planning
Domain: Cognitive
Mentor: Conor, Republic of Ireland
Mentor Career Cycle phase: Novice
CM³T Novice phase level required: Level 5: *Synthesis* – involves the putting together of elements and parts so as to form a whole.
Therefore, mentor training required: How to develop long-term and short-term Mentee Development Plan comprising the following:
  Aims/goals, learning outcomes, assessment tools, tasks, outputs and impact. This involves identifying challenges and barriers as well as new goals, strategising resolution, revising timelines, prioritizing and developing an action plan. Regular time-tabled meetings, Mentee teaching workload, etc. (Department of Education and Early Childhood Development 2010).

Example 2

Capability: Empathy
Domain: Affective
Mentor: Andrew, England

TABLE 10.1 Capability Maturity Model for Mentor Teachers (CM³T)

Competency	Domain	Novice	Stabilisation	Experimentation	Consolidation/Maturation	Expert
Empathy	Affective	3	4	5	5	5
Trust	Affective	3	4	5	5	5
Fostering positivity	Affective	3	4	4	5	5
Defining mentee expectations	Affective	3	4	5	5	5
Protective	Affective	2.5	3	4	5	5
Support	Affective	3	3.5	4	5	5
Flexibility	Cognitive	4	5	5.5	6	6
Leadership	Cognitive	4	4.5	5	6	6
Planning	Cognitive	5	5	6	6	6
Organisation	Cognitive	4	5	5	6	6
Subject knowledge	Cognitive	4	5	6	6	6
Observation	Cognitive	4	5	6	6	6
Cross-fertilisation of mentoring skills from one subject to another	Cognitive	3.5	4.5	5	6	6
Role model	Cognitive	5	5	6	6	6
Recognising excellent performance	Cognitive	5	5	6	6	6
Advisor	Cognitive	4	5	6	6	6
Facilitator	Cognitive	4	5	6	6	6
Multi-task	Cognitive	4	5	6	6	6
Empowering the mentee	Cognitive	3	4	5	6	6
Context knowledge	Cognitive	4	5	5	6	6
Facilitating appropriate progression	Cognitive	4	5	5	6	6
Resourceful	Cognitive	4	5	5	6	6

Fostering teamwork	Cognitive	4	5	6	6	6
Discerning	Cognitive	4	4	5	6	6
Delegate	Cognitive	4	5	6	6	6
Collaborative	Cognitive	4	5	5	6	6
Guided discovery	Cognitive	3	4	5	6	6
Advisor	Cognitive	4	5	6	6	6
Team teaching	Cognitive	3	5	6	6	6
Decision making	Cognitive	4	5	6	6	6
Issuing feedback and corrective action	Hybrid	App,Resp	S,V	E,O	E,I	E,I
Building rapport	Hybrid	Ana,V	S,O	E,I	E,I	E,I
Non-directive	Hybrid	Ana,V	Ana/S,O	S,O	E,I	E,I
Self-confidence	Hybrid	Ana,V	S,O	S/E,O	E,I	E,I
Objective	Hybrid	App,V	Ana,V	S,O	E,I	E,I
Developing the mentee	Hybrid	Ana,V	Ana,V	S,O	E,I	E,I
Interacting with triad partners	Hybrid	S/Ana,V/O	S,O	S/E,I	E,I	E,I
Mentee focused	Hybrid	App,V	Ana,V	S,O	E,I	E,I
Unthreatened	Hybrid	Ana,V	S,O	E,I	E,I	E,I
Negotiation	Hybrid	Ana,V	S,O	S,I	E,I	E,I
Recognising success	Hybrid	Ana,V	S,O	S,O/I	E,I	E,I
Delivering criticism	Hybrid	App,V	Ana,O	S,O	E,I	E,I
Approachable	Hybrid	S,V	S,O	E,I	E,I	E,I
Interactive	Hybrid	S,V	S,V/O	E,I/O	E,I	E,I
Application of mentoring styles	Hybrid	Ana,V	S,V/O	S/E,I/O	E,I/O	E,I
Coexistence of professional and personal relationships	Hybrid	Ana,V	S,O	E,I	E,I	E,I
Conflict management	Hybrid	Ana,V	Ana/S,O	S,O	E,I	E,I

Chambers *et al.* 2013, p. 84

TABLE 10.2   Key for CM³T

Level	Level Description
Cognitive Domain	
6	Evaluation (E)
5	Synthesis (S)
4	Analysis (Ana)
3	Application (App)
2	Comprehension (C)
1	Knowledge (K)
Affective Domain	
5	Internalizing (I)
4	Organisation (O)
3	Valuing (V)
2	Responding (Resp)
1	Receiving (Rec)

Chambers *et al.* 2013, p. 84

TABLE 10.3   Level descriptors of cognitive and affective domain [hybrid]

Cognitive and Affective (Hybrid) Capabilities	
Cognitive	Affective
1 **Knowledge** *involves the recall of specifics and universals, the recall of methods and processes, or the recall of a pattern, structure, or setting.*	**Receiving** *involves awareness, willingness to hear and selected attention.*
2 **Comprehension** *refers to a type of understanding or apprehension such that the individual knows what is being communicated and can make use of the material or idea being communicated without necessarily relating it to other material or seeing its fullest implications.*	**Responding** *refers to active participation on the part of the learners. The individual attends and reacts to a particular phenomenon. Learning outcomes may emphasize compliance in responding, willingness to respond, or satisfaction in responding (motivation).*
3 **Application** *refers to the use of abstractions in particular and concrete situations.*	**Valuing** *refers to the worth or value a person attaches to a particular object, phenomenon, or behavior. This ranges from simple acceptance to the more complex state of commitment.*
4 **Analysis** *represents the breakdown of a communication into its constituent elements or parts such that the relative hierarchy of ideas is made clear and/or the relations between ideas expressed are made explicit.*	**Organisation** *involves organizing values into priorities by contrasting different values, resolving conflicts between them, and creating a unique value system. The emphasis is on comparing, relating, and synthesizing values.*
5 **Synthesis** *involves the 'putting together of elements and parts so as to form a whole.'*	**Internalising** *involves having a value system that controls one's behavior. The behavior is pervasive, consistent, predictable, and most importantly, characteristic of the learner.*
6 **Evaluation** *engenders judgments about the value of material and methods for given purposes.*	
(Bloom et al. 1956, pp. 201–207)	*(Krathwohl et al. 1973)*

Cited in Chambers *et al.* 2013, pp. 93–94

Mentor Career Cycle phase: Expert
CM³T Expert phase level required: Level 5: *Internalising* – Has a value system that controls their behavior. The behavior is pervasive, consistent, predictable, and most importantly, characteristic of the learner.
Therefore, mentor training required: How to be consistently empathic with mentee while maintaining professionalism.

In sum, the findings in this study have allowed interrogation of the CM³T from a number of standpoints: (a) duality/hybridity of domains, (b) moving from competency to expertise and (c) phases of the Mentor Career Cycle.

Analysis

Duality/hybridity of domains

It is interesting to note that there were a number of competencies in this study which mentors lay in *both* the cognitive and affective domain. Empathy is one such capability. This aligns with the work of Birbeck and Andre (2009) who assert that 'the affective and cognitive domain teaching should not be seen as a dualism' (p. 3). Rather, many competences have a cognitive-affective aspect (e.g. empathy, although, in this study mentors allocated empathy as an affective competence). Krathwohl *et al.* (1964) describe the affective domain in relation to the cognitive domain as follows: 'in the cognitive domain we are concerned that the student shall be able to do the task when requested. In the affective domain we are more concerned that he does do it when it is appropriate after he has learned he can do it' (p. 60).

From competencies through capabilities to expertise

The terms capability, capacity and competency are use interchangeably in the literature. There are overlaps in these terms but it is clear that *competency* is a much narrower concept than the idea of *capability*. Parry (1996, p. 48) described a competency as:

> [a] cluster of related knowledge, skills and attitudes that affect a major part of one's job (role or responsibilities), that can be measured against some sort of occupational standards and can be improved by training and development. In other words, it is a measure of the current knowledge, skill or attitude of an individual.

Capability is a more holistic idea, which not only delineates the person's current knowledge, skill and attitudinal status but also their potential for improvement in each of these learning domains 'and is to do with future competence' (Chartered Society of Physiotherapists 2005). 'Competencies are a range of applied abilities and skills that relate to capability' (ibid.) or in the case of mentor training, cognitive and affective competencies that lead to mentor capability. According to Konkel (2008), the route to expertise begins by grounding key

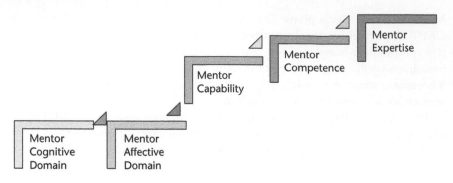

FIGURE 10.2   A stairway to expertise

Chambers *et al.* 2013, p. 99 (adapted from Konkel *et al.* 2008)

competencies. In this study, mentors identified cognitive and affective competencies as being core to their work. The step change from attaining these competencies to achieving the status of capability is achieved through training. Thereafter, the shift from capability to overall competence is acquired by experience, peer review and reflective practice (ibid.). The diagram in Figure 10.2 depicts this relationship and is adapted from Konkel (2008). The CM³T represents the pathway to realizing the mentor's potential to develop in each of the capabilities and leads to future overall competence and ultimately mentor expertise.

Lessons learned . . . What could we add to the Mentor Pedagogy Toolbox?

- The CM³T can be used as both (a) a diagnostic tool to ascertain mentor training needs within the Mentor Career Cycle and (b) a planning tool for designing bespoke training programmes for mentors at each phase of the Mentor Career Cycle.
- According to Konkel (2008), the route to expertise begins by grounding key competencies. In this study, mentors identified cognitive and affective competencies as being core to their work. The step change from attaining these competencies to achieving the status of capability is achieved through training. Thereafter, the shift from capability to overall competence is acquired by experience, peer review and reflective practice (ibid.).

Key terms: capacity, capability, agile workforce, Capability Maturity Model for mentor training.

Note

1 Both Capability Maturity Model and Maturity Model are used in the literature.

References

Berliner, D. C. 2001. Learning about learning from expert teachers. *International Journal of Educational Research*, 35, 463–482.

Birbeck, D. and Andre, K. 2009. The affective domain: beyond simply knowing. *ATN Conference*. RMIT University.

Charmaz, K. 2000. Grounded theory: objectivist and constructivist methods. In N. K. Denzin and Y. S. Lincoln (Eds.) *Handbook of Qualitative Research*. London: Sage Publications.

Chambers, F. C., Herold, F. A, McFlynn, P., Brennan, D. A. and Armour, K. 2013. Developing effective mentor pedagogies to support pre-service teacher learning on Teaching Practice (Mentor-Ped): A Capability Maturity Model for Mentor Teachers [CM³T]. Standing Conference on Teacher Education North and South. Armagh, Co. Antrim.

Chartered Society of Physiotherapy. 2005. *Core Standards of Physiotherapy Practice*. London: The Chartered Society of Physiotherapy, 2005.

Clarke, J. A., Nelson, K. J. and Stoodley, I. D. 2013. The place of higher education institutions in assessing student engagement, success and retention: a maturity model to guide practice. In *Higher Education Research and Development Society of Australasia*. University of Auckland.

Darling-Hammond, L. 2006a. Constructing 21st century teacher education. *Journal of Teacher Education*, 57, 300–314.

Darling-Hammond, L. 2006b. *Powerful Teacher Education: Lessons from Exemplary Programs*. San Francisco: Jossey-Bass.

Darling-Hammond, L. and Rothman, R. 2011. *Teacher and Leader Effectiveness in High Performing Education Systems*. Washington, DC: Alliance for Excellent Education, and Stanford, CA: Center for Opportunity Policy in Education.

Department of Education and Early Childhood Development 2010. *A Learning Guide for Teacher Mentors*. Department of Education and Early Childhood Development: East Melbourne,Victoria.

Department of Education and Training 2011. *The Department of Education and Training Annual Report 2010–11*. Brisbane: Queensland Government.

Egbo, B. 2011. Teacher capacity building and effective teaching and learning: a seamless connection. *Proceedings of the 2011 International Conference on Teaching, Learning and Change*. Omoku, Rovers State Nigeria: International Association for Teaching and Learning (IATEL).

Fletcher, S. 1998. Attaining self-actualization through mentoring. *European Journal of Teacher Education*, 21, 109–118.

Freire, P. 1970. *Pedagogy of the Oppressed*. New York: Herder and Herder.

Glickman, C. D., Gordon, S. P. and Ross-Gordon, J. M. 2001. *SuperVision and Instructional Leadership: A Developmental Approach*. Needham Heights, MA: Allyn & Bacon.

Glinska, M., Carr, S. D. and Halliday, A. 2012. *Workforce Agility: An Executive Briefing*. Transforming Society Through Entrepreneurship and Innovation. Batten Institute.

Hardy, C. A. 1999. Preservice teachers' perceptions of learning to teach in a predominantly school-based teacher education program. *Journal of Teaching in Physical Education*, 18, 175–198.

Hennissen, P., Crasborn, F., Brouwer, N., Korthagen, F. and Bergen, T. 2011. Clarifying pre-service teacher perceptions of mentor teachers' developing use of mentoring skills. *Teaching and Teacher Education*, 27, 1049–1058.

Huberman, M. 1989. The professional life cycle of teachers. *Teachers College Record*, 91, 31–57.

Iversen, J., Nielsen, P. A. and Nørbjerg, J. 1999. Situated assessment of problems in software development. *The DATABASE for Advances in Information Systems*, 30(2).

Konkel, S. 2008.A Competence-Based Curriculum for Environmental Health. *Environmental Health Planning and Policy*. Environmental Health Sciences Institute at ARROW@DIT: Dublin Insitute of Technology.

Konkel, R. S., Brennan, M. and Lewis, T. 2008. Developing an International Competence-based Curriculum for Environmental Health. *10th World Congress on Environmental*

Health, Brisbane, Australia, January 2008. Accessed on 28th June 2013 from http://works.bepress.com/steve_konkel/7

Korthagen, F. A. J. 2001. *Linking Practice and Theory: The Pedgaogy of Realistic Teacher Education*. Mahwah, NJ: Lawrence Erlbaum Associates.

Krathwohl, D. R., Bloom, B. S. and Masia, B. B. 1964. *Taxonomy of Educational Objectives: The Classification of Educational Goals. Handbook II: Affective domain*. New York: David McKay Company.

Marshall, S. 2010. A quality framework for continuous improvement of e-Learning: The e-Learning Maturity Model. *Journal of Distance Education*, 24, 143–166.

Marshall, S. J. and Mitchell, G. 2006. Assessing sector e-learning capability with an e-learning maturity model. In D. Whitelock and S. Wheeler (Eds.) *Proceedings of the 13th International Conference of the Association for Learning Technologies Conference*. Edinburgh, UK, pp. 203–214.

Marshall, S. M. and Mitchell, G. 2002. An E-Learning maturity model? In winds of change in the sea of learning. *ASCILITE*. Auckland.

Metzler, M. W. 1990. *Instructional Supervision for Physical Education*. Champaign, IL: Human Kinetics.

Nelson, A. and Harvey, F. A. 1995. Technologies for training and supporting your agile workforce. In *Creating the Agile Organization: Models, Metrics and Pilots*. Proceedings 4th Agility Forum Annual Conference. Agility Forum, Bethlehem, PA.

Oxford English Dictionary (2013). c.v. *Agility*. http://www.oed.com/view/Entry/3983?redirectedFrom = agility#eid. Accessed on 4th September 2013.

Parry, S. B. 1996. The quest for competencies. *Training*, 33(7), 48–54.

Paulk, M. C. 1999. Using the software CMM with good judgment. *ASQ Software Quality Professional*, 1, 19–29.

Prahalad, C. K. and Hamel, G. 1990. The core competence of the corporation. *Harvard Business Review*, 68, 79–91.

Randall, L. E. 1992. *Systematic Supervision for Physical Education*. Champaign, IL: Human Kinetics.

Riggs, I. M. 2000. The impact of training and induction activities upon mentors as indicated through measurement of mentor self-efficacy. San Bernardino: California State University.

Rikard, G. L. and Veale, M. L. 1996. Cooperating teachers: insight into their preparation, beliefs and practices. *Journal of Teaching in Physical Education*, 15, 279–296.

Robinson, K. 2010. Bring on the education revolution, in *TED*, Ted (ed.). UK: TED.

Rosemann, M. and De Bruin, T. 2005. A model to measure business process management maturity and improve performance. *13th European Conference on Information Systems*, Regensberg.

Strauss, A. and Corbin, J. 1998. *Basics of Qualitative Research: Techniques and Procedures for Developing Grounded Theory*. London, Sage Publications.

Tannehill, D. and Goc-Karp, G. 1992. The student teacher practicum: placement trends and issues. *The Physical Educator*, 49, 39–48.

Teaching Council of Ireland 2011. *Policy on the Continuum of Teacher Education*. Maynooth: Teaching Council of Ireland.

Zanting, A. 2001. *Mining the Mentor's Mind: The Elicitation of Mentor Teachers' Practical Knowledge by Prospective Teachers*. Doctoral thesis, Leiden University.

Resources

Mindrum, C. 2008. Agility training for the learning organization. *Chief Learning Officer*, 7(12), 36–87.

Gladwell, M. 2008. *Outliers: The Story of Success*. New York: Little Brown.

11

MENTORING PRE-SERVICE TEACHERS WITHIN A SCHOOL–UNIVERSITY PARTNERSHIP

Fiona C. Chambers

Overview

In effective teacher education programmes, the strength of the school-university relationship in supporting pre-service teacher learning is pivotal (Darling-Hammond 2006). A robust school-university partnership offers a collective, commonsense approach to pre-service teacher education (McIntyre *et al.* 1996; Hardy 1999) and according to Walsh *et al.* (2000), is centred on the critical intersection of theory and research (university) with implementation and practice (school). Walsh and Backe (2013, p. 595) describe the sharing of intellectual capital by schools and universities:

> As schools have sought to identify new strategies in instruction, leadership, and student support, universities have had the capacity to identify new approaches based on theory and research and to evaluate innovations in practice. The overarching goal is to link inquiry with action.

Intellectual capital is 'material that has been formalized, captured, and leveraged to produce a higher-valued asset' (Klein and Prusak 1994, p. 2). It comprises human, structural and relational components. In this case, the asset is effective and meaningful pre-service teacher training. The fusion of intellectual capital in the school and university occurs around:

> [t]he confluence points of the three major domains of schooling (i.e., curriculum and instruction, educational leadership, and student support) with the three functions of universities (i.e., teaching, research, and service). By finding ways to link the domains of schooling with the functions of the university, partners are able to create mutually beneficial relationships.
>
> *Walsh and Backe 2013, p. 596*

More recently, teacher training and professional development have been a key focus of school-university partnerships (Ladson-Billings and Gomez 2001; Teitel 1999; Goodlad *et al.* 2004). School-based teaching practice sites provide a mutual benefit for both sides of the partnership:

> The work of an individual partnership is typically defined by one partner's critical need and the other partner's capacity to respond. . . . Placement of student teachers in local schools addresses reciprocal needs of the partners by providing students with opportunities for experiential learning while also providing schools with expanded personnel and exposure to cutting-edge educational approaches.
>
> *Walsh and Backe 2013, p. 596*

Communities of practice, learning organisations and mentoring

In 1896, John Dewey introduced the idea of school-university collaboration in teaching through the University of Chicago laboratory schools. Over time, school university partnerships have had a variety of guises, e.g. professional practice schools (Levine 1992), communities of practice (Cobb *et al.* 2003) or professional learning communities (Hord and Sommers 2007). The central tenet of each 'version' is the idea that the school-university partnership is a learning organization which has a shared purpose to improve teacher education which in turn impacts on the quality of pupil learning (DuFour *et al.* 2005; Teitel 2001).

The study reported in this chapter is scaffolded by situative theories that focus on the social nature of learning (Barab and Duffy 2000, p. 26). Put simply, this means that learning is explained as a social phenomenon where individuals learn from each other and build upon previous experiences through this engagement. The decision to focus specifically on physical education (PE) pre-service teacher professional learning was taken in order to address the lack of research in this area in Ireland, and for its potential contribution to the wider pre-service teacher learning literature. In situative theories, learning is associated with an increase in the ability to participate effectively in the practices of a community. Learning is conceptualised as collaborative social practice, located in communities of practice and occurring through legitimate peripheral participation (LPP) in those communities (Lave and Wenger 1991). Lave and Wenger argue that '[t]o be able to participate in a legitimately peripheral way entails that newcomers have broad access to arenas of mature practice' (p. 110).

The school university partnership is itself a community of practice which fosters ongoing discussion, sharing and collaboration on commonly valued issues and concerns within pre-service teacher education (Mawer 1996; Anyon and Fernandez 2007). Walsh and Backe (2013, p. 599) describe how:

> [s]uccessful partnerships reach agreement early on about the goals of the partnership and develop a consensus around the social, political, and historical context of the work and the nature of change itself.

Zeichner's (2010) notion of the Third Space is helpful here to capture the shared learning space created by the school-university partnership, where academic and practitioner knowledge that exist in communities come together in new, less hierarchical ways in the service of teacher learning (p. 89). Further, Zeichner (2010) argues that within these hybrid spaces, establishment of conditions for learning in and from practice, as being both educative and enduring (p. 91), can occur. Quintessentially, through conversational and social processes, a new community of practice emerges (Bullough *et al.* 2004; Wenger 1998) in this Third Space. The hybrid area in which this new community of practice (COP) resides is characterised as 'a transformative space where the potential for an expanded form of learning and the development of new knowledge are heightened' (Gutiérrez 2008, p. 152; Martin *et al.* 2011). Moreover, it impacts learning of all members of the COP:

> Mediation of student teaching experiences through interactions within a partnership context has a transformative potential – for teacher candidates, as well as school-based and university-based teacher educators.
>
> *Martin et al. 2011, p. 299*

Within this hybrid COP, mentoring is a key formal mechanism of supporting effective pre-service teacher learning. However, the current reality for PE cooperating teachers (CTs) in Ireland is to work voluntarily in an informal, untrained and unpaid capacity during practicum. CTs, as a gesture of amity, offer learning support to pre-service teachers in the area of classroom management and pedagogical content knowledge (PCK) (Kiely 2005). In spite of this philanthropic work, a number of impediments have arisen in the quality of pre-service teacher support during practicum. Specifically, there is inconsistency in both the amount and quality of learning support offered to pre-service teachers by CTs (Chambers 2008). CTs seem to be confused about their exact role on practicum (ibid.). This can lead to difficulties in delineating the exact function of school and university personnel during practicum which, again, impacts on the quality of the practicum as a learning experience for pre-service teachers (ibid.). Therefore the school-university partnership does not provide a harmonious space with a common and shared view of how to support pre-service teacher learning.

The presence of experienced and trained mentors in formative field experiences is a vital component in ensuring meaningful work-based learning for pre-service teachers (McIntyre *et al.* 2005), leading to them becoming more effective practitioners (Evertson and Smithey 2000; Humphrey *et al.* 2000). In addition, trained mentors play a crucial role in the socialisation and enculturation of pre-service teachers (Wenger 1998) in the hybrid community of practice, which according to Armour *et al.* (2012) is a key professional learning space. In order to have a healthy COP, the school-university partnership must share a common vision of learning support for the pre-service teacher and invest in the transition from CT to trained mentor.

Vignette

Background

This study investigated the development of the Telemachus Project, i.e. cultivating school-university partnerships as learning organisations, which support the transition of CTs to a mentoring role in pre-service teacher education. The research was situated within a four-year Bachelor of Education Physical Education degree programme in the Republic of Ireland and was funded by the Teaching Council of Ireland.

Methods

Using a case study approach, this research harnessed a range of qualitative data-collection methods (open profile questionnaires, in-depth interviews, focus groups and a reflective journal), and data were analysed using a six-level approach to grounded theory (Harry *et al.* 2005).

Findings

Within a four-stage process (Reconnaissance, Open Consultation, Shared Language and Active Negotiated Meaning), 'double-loop learning' (Argyris 1976) is an effective guiding framework to develop a strong school-university partnership which co-designed a new and coherent mentor training programme for pre-service cooperating teachers.

One School Principal (SP) asserted that PE pre-service teachers 'needed to be given permission to be learners on teaching practice and they were often treated as fully-fledged teachers with little or no support' (SP, National Association of Principals and Deputy Principals Meeting 2009). It was clear that the values and assumptions inherent in existing school-university partnerships needed to change. To effect organizational change, Argyris's (1976) double-loop learning was employed in this study. Double-loop theory is based upon a "theory of action" perspective outlined by Argyris and Schon (1974) which examines reality from the standpoint of human beings as actors. Changes in values, behaviour, leadership, and helping others, are all part of, and informed by, the actor's (person's) theory of action. This has a pivotal role in learning at the organisational level (e.g., Argyris 1976; Schon and Argyris 1974). Four key steps in the action theory learning process were used: (1) discovery of espoused and theory-in-use, (2) invention of new meanings, (3) production of new actions and (4) generalisation of results. In double-loop learning, assumptions underlying current views from both schools and university personnel were questioned and theories about behaviour tested publically. An important aspect of the theory is the distinction between an individual's 'espoused theory' (what they believe/say) and their 'theory-in-use' (what they actually do); bringing these two into congruence is a primary focus of double-loop learning. Typically, dialogue with others is necessary to identify the conflict between what an actor says and what he does. Using double-loop learning theory (Argyris 1976), the Telemachus Project encouraged open dialogue between schools and university personnel toward a shared purpose of supporting pre-service teacher learning. The resultant mentor training programme, co-designed by both school and university personnel, was named in honour of the first mentee, Telemachus, who was guided/taught by Mentor when his father, Odysseus, left to fight the Trojan War (Encyclopaedia Britannica 2008). There were four key stages in this process: Reconnaissance, Open Consultation, Shared Language, and Active Negotiated Meaning. These are analysed in the following section.

Analysis

Stage One: Reconnaissance

The process began with reconnaissance, i.e. 'an inspection or exploration of the area or a preliminary survey to gain information' (Merriam-Webster Dictionary 2011) on the culture and discourse of TP in Ireland through familiarisation with (a) what is valued within teacher education in Ireland (historically and currently) and (b) the perceived distribution of power within teacher education and school-ing. It seemed clear at this point that school management were disgruntled with the lack of parity in the current school-university relationship, believing that the school was 'quite peripheral to the affair' (SP, Mr. Noonan, 16th February 2007). This stage was influenced by the first stage of Action Theory by establishing the 'theory-in-use' (Argyris and Schon 1974).

Stage Two: Open consultation

This phase moved to establish the 'espoused theory' (Argyris and Schon 1974) of all school-university stakeholders. Firstly, a relationship based on parity of esteem had to be built between the key stakeholders in Brookdale University (Head of School of Education and University Tutors) and within schools (SPs, DPs and CTs). The consultation process had to acknowledge the hierarchy of relationships within the school-university: (a) the University Tutor (UT) and SP/DP relationship and (b) the UT and CT relationship. Given that SPs and DPs are the 'gatekeepers' to school-based practice, consultation must begin with SPs and DPs, and thereafter progress to CTs. The journey towards such parity is precarious, often infused with suspicion and lack of mutual respect. According to Trubowitz (1986), when a school and university collaborate, there are eight key stages which must be tra-versed: (1) hostility and aggression, (2) lack of trust, (3) period of truce, (4) mixed approval, (5) acceptance, (6) regression, (7) renewal and (8) continuing progress. In November 2006, in order to navigate the preliminary stages – (1) hostility and aggression and (2) lack of trust – the author contacted both Mr. Bill McTeigue (SP), Executive member of the National Association for Principals and Deputy Principals (NAPD), and Mr. Fred Daly (SP) Executive member of NAPD, to be mentored by 'insiders' on how to engage with the organisation as they understood and shared the social capital of this group (Field 2005), with a view to understanding how the university might establish a strong partnership with schools in the region. The crucial element of this stage was persuading the school management that the university was willing to listen to their views and to act on them. This is an important first step in building partnerships (between school and university), defined as: a relationship between individuals or groups that is characterized by mutual cooperation and responsibility, as for the achievement of a specified goal (TheFreeDictionary.com 2009).

According to Graham (1988, p. 168), when collaboration occurs, the barriers between the university and the school often become less formidable with communication levels increasing:

> Aloofness or a feeling of superiority is a facade that is easy to maintain at a distance, but when people work together successfully, facades disappear. And that is a positive, potential benefit of collaboration.

As was noted earlier, eventually, in effective collaboration, parties come to value each other's contribution, which can lead to parity of esteem between the school and university.

Mr. Daly (SP) believed that opening a dialogue with the NAPD 'was a brave thing to do given the troubled history of the school-university partnership in teacher education' but added that he felt that the author was 'preaching to the converted' (Mr. Daly, SP, Interview, 22nd September 2009). Mr. Daly (SP) believed that 'changing the culture of the school-university partnership to a more collegial entity would take time particularly with older teachers who were very set in their ways' (Mr. Daly, SP, Interview, 22nd September 2009).

During this process, the 'theory-in-use' is compared to the 'espoused theory' (Argyris 1976). Interestingly, it was clear that the theory-in-use was congruent with the espoused theory (ibid.).

Stage Three: Shared language

In Action Theory, Argyris and Schon (1974) speak of the 'invention of new meanings' (the second step). This stage, however, begins by establishing a common language of teacher education between SPs, UTs and CTs, particularly in relation to mentoring practice – e.g. CTs must be selected to be PE teacher mentors (PTMs) on the basis of suitability, not availability (Fletcher 2000), in terms of *both* expertise and disposition (Chambers 2008). Once chosen, the CTs needed to question their espoused theory of teacher training and how this aligned with their actual theory-in-use (Argyris and Schon 1974). An important aspect of this process is the opportunity for stakeholders (SPs, UTs and CTs) to share best practice and to jointly delineate codes of practice in the area of (a) initial teacher education, (b) teacher competencies and (c) mentoring protocol (mentor role/mentee role/ university tutor role in teaching practice).

Stage Four: Active negotiated meaning

This stage focused on school-university partnership co-designing a shared mentor training programme for CTs which was underpinned by a shared philosophy, i.e. moving trainee mentors through Fuller and Brown's (1975) three-phase 'Concerns Model':

1. **Self-survival stage (concerns about self):** Will my mentee like me? Will he/she respect me?
2. **Task-instruction stage (concerns about tasks):** What should I focus on when observing mentee practice?
3. **Impact–pre-service teachers stage (concerns about impact):** How might I progress mentee/pre-service teacher learning?

Effective mentoring processes included additional training for mentors, which employed self-study (reflective practice) and consisted of two-hour training sessions (co-creating knowledge and critically analysing real-life mentoring case studies). It comprised (a) coaching/feedback skills, (b) adult learning techniques, (c) how to determine competency gaps, (d) goal-setting, (e) how to accelerate knowledge transfer and (f) how to address problems in mentoring relationships. In addition, stakeholders were encouraged to share their thoughts on the process and to shape the process through strategically timed focus groups.

Lessons learned . . . What could we add to the Mentor Pedagogy Toolbox?

- The success of the Telemachus Project was due to the development of a strong school-university partnership.
- This school-university partnership imbued mutual trust (Trubowitz 1986), reciprocal learning (Callahan and Martin 2007), reflective practice (Schon 1987) and ultimately, a shared, logical idea of teacher education (McIntyre *et al.* 2005; Hardy 1999). Therefore, this school-university partnership was ideally placed to provide a strong platform to support the transition of CTs to their new role as PE teacher mentors.
- Beyond knowledge and attitudes of mentoring, the nature and scope of professional development opportunities for CTs should be addressed.

Key terms: intellectual capital, social theories of learning, school-university partnership, third space, double-loop learning, reconnaissance, open consultation, shared language, active negotiated meaning.

References

Anyon, Y. and Fernandez, M. A. 2007. Realizing the potential of community-university partnerships. *Change*, 39, 40–45.

Argyris, C. 1976. *Increasing Leadership Effectiveness*. New York, John Wiley.

Argyris, C. and Schon, D. A. 1974. *Theory in Practice: Increasing Professional Effectiveness*. San Francisco: Jossey-Bass.

Armour, K., Makopoulou, K. and Chambers, F. C. 2012. Progression in physical education teachers' career-long professional learning: conceptual and practical concerns. *European Physical Education Review*, 18, 62–77.

Barab, S. A. and Duffy, T. M. 2000. From practice fields to communities of practice. In D. H. Jonassen and S. M. Land (Eds.) *Theoretical Foundations of Learning Environments*. London: Lawrence Erlbaum Associates, Publishers.

Bullough, R. V., Draper, R. J., Smith, L. and Birrell, J. R. 2004. Moving beyond collusion: clinical faculty and university/public school partnership. *Teaching and Teacher Education*, 20, 505–521.

Callahan, J. L. and Martin, D. 2007. The spectrum of school-university partnerships: a typology of organizational learning systems. *Teaching and Teacher Education*, 23, 136–145.

Chambers, F. C. 2008. *Irish Physical Education Teacher Education Students and their Professional Learning: The Teaching Practice Experience*. PhD thesis. Loughborough University.

Cobb, P., McClain, K., de Silva Lamberg, T. and Dean, C. 2003. Situating teachers' instructional practices in the institutional setting of the school and district. *Educational Researcher*, 32, 13–24.

Darling-Hammond, L. 2006. *Powerful Teacher Education: Lessons from Exemplary Programs*. San Francisco: Jossey-Bass.

DuFour, R., Eaker, R. E. and DuFour, R. 2005. *On Common Ground: The Power of Professional Learning Communities*. Bloomington, IN: Solution Tree.

Encyclopaedia Britannica, 2008. *s.v.* 'Fenelon'. *Encyclopaedia Britannica*. Chicago, Illinois: Encyclopaedia Britannica.

Evertson, C. M. and Smithey, M. W. 2000. Mentoring effects on proteges' classroom practice: an experimental field study. *The Journal of Educational Research*, 93, 294–304.

Field, J. 2005. *Social Capital and Lifelong Learning*. Bristol: Policy Press.

Fletcher, S. 2000. *Mentoring in School: A Handbook of Good Practice*. Routledge Falmer.

Fuller, F. and Brown, O. 1975. Becoming a teacher. In K. Ryan (Ed.), *Teacher Education: Seventy-fourth Yearbook of the National Society for the Study of Education*. Chicago: University of Chicago Press.

Goodlad, J. I., Mantle-Bromley, C. and Goodlad, S. J. 2004. *Education for Everyone: Agenda for Education in a Democracy*. San Francisco: Jossey-Bass.

Graham, G. 1988. Collaboration in physical education: a lot like marriage? *Journal of Teaching in Physical Education*, 7, 165–174.

Gutiérrez, K. 2008. Developing a sociocultural literacy in the third space. *Reading Research Quarterly*, 43, 148–164.

Hardy, C. A. 1999. Preservice teachers' perceptions of learning to teach in a predominantly school-based teacher education programme. *Journal of Teaching in Physical Education*, 18, 175–198.

Harry, B., Sturges, K. and Klinger, J. 2005. Mapping the process: an exemplar of process and challenge in grounded theory analysis. *Educational Researcher*, 34(2), 3–13.

Hord, S. M. and Sommers, W. A. 2007. *Leading Professional Learning Communities: Voices from Research and Practice*. Thousand Oaks, CA: Corwin Press.

Humphrey, D. C., Adelman, N., Esch, E. E., Riehl, L. M., Shields, P. M. and Tiffany, J. 2000. *Preparing and Supporting New Teachers: A Literature Review*. Menlo Park, CA: SRI International.

Kiely, E. 2005. *The Mentoring Phenomenon in Educating Pre-service Science Teachers through School-Based Collaborative Partnership*. Doctor of Philosophy, University of Limerick, Ireland.

Klein, D. A. and Prusak, L. 1994. *Characterising Intellectual Capital*. Cambridge, MA: Ernst and Young.

Ladson-Billings, G. and Gomez, M. L. J. 2001. Just showing up: supporting early literacy through teachers' professional communities. *Phi Delta Kappan,* 82, pp. 675–680.

Lave, J. and Wenger, E. 1991. *Situated Learning: Legitimate Peripheral Participation*. Cambridge: Cambridge Press.

Levine, M. (Ed.) 1992. *Professional Practice Schools: Linking Teacher Education and School Reform*. New York: Teachers College Press.

Martin, S. D., Snow, J. L. and Franklin Torrez, C. A. 2011. Navigating the terrain of third space: tensions with/in relationships in school-university partnerships. *Journal of Teacher Education,* 62, 299–311.

Mawer, M. 1996. *Mentoring in Physical Education: Issues and Insights*. London: Falmer Press.

McIntyre, D., Hagger, H. and Wilkin, M. 2005. *Mentoring: Perspectives on School-based Teacher Education*. London: Routledge Falmer.

McIntyre, D. J., Byrd, D. M. and Foxx, S. M. 1996. Field and laboratory experiences. In J. Sikula, T. J. Buttery and E. Guyton (Eds.) *Handbook of Research on Teacher Education: A Project of the Association of Teacher Educators*. New York: Macmillan.

Merriam-Webster Dictionary 2011. c.v. *Reconnaissance. Merriam-Webster Online Dictionary,* Accessed on 4th April 2011.

Schon, D. 1987. *Educating the Reflective Practitioner: Toward a New Design for Teaching and Learning in the Professions*. San Francisco: Jossey-Bass.

Teitel, L. 1999. Looking toward the future by understanding the past: the historical context of professional development schools. *Peabody Journal of Education,* 74, 6–20.

Teitel, L. 2001. *How Professional Development Schools Make a Difference: A Review of the Research*. Washington, DC, National Council for Accreditation of Teacher Education.

TheFreeDictionary.com 2009. c.v. *Partnership*. Retrieved from http://www.thefree dictionary.com/partnership and accessed on 3rd March 2009.

Trubowitz, S. 1986. *When a College Works With a Public School: A Case Study of School-College Collaboration*. Boston: Institute of Responsive Education.

Walsh, M. E., Brabeck, M. M., Howard, K. A., Sherman, F. T., Montes, C. and Garvin, T. J. 2000. The Boston College–Allston/Brighton partnership: description and challenges. *Peabody Journal of Education,* 75, 6–32.

Walsh, M. E. and Backe, S. 2013. School–university partnerships: reflections and opportunities. *Peabody Journal of Education,* 88(5), 594–607.

Wenger, E. 1998. *Communities of Practice: Learning, meaning and identity*. Cambridge, UK: Cambridge University Press.

Zeichner, K. 2010. Rethinking the connections between campus courses and field experiences in college- and university-based teacher education. *Journal of Teacher Education,* 61, 89–99.

Resources

Meister, J. C. and Willyerd, K. 2010. Mentoring millennials. *Harvard Business Review,* May 2010.

University of Cambridge, UK (School-University Partnership for Educational Research): http://www.educ.cam.ac.uk/research/projects/super/

12

THE VOICE OF THE PRE-SERVICE TEACHER IN THE GROUP MENTORING PROCESS

Pilvikki Heikinaro-Johannsson, Mirja Hirvensalo, Terhi Huovinen and Sanna Palomäki

Overview

Mentoring offers a conduit to reach the primary objective of the physical education teacher education (PETE) programme at the University of Jyväskylä (JyU), Finland, i.e. to graduate physical educators who have the ability to reflect critically on their experiences, their actions, and on the appropriate application of their knowledge and beliefs in different teaching situations and contexts (Mezirow 1990). The programme employs a model, termed the Integrative Pedagogy Model, in which learners' reflections are linked to their theoretical and practical knowledge (Korthagen 2008). This model sees educational theory, teaching practice, pedagogical content knowledge and subject didactics in reciprocal interaction.

Example One

> During the group mentoring meeting, we discussed fitness tests and I asked my second-year pre-service teachers (PSTs): 'How many of you, as physical education teachers, will include fitness tests in your physical education programme?' Of my fourteen mentees, only one male student said that he would not organize fitness tests in school physical education. He said: 'I don't believe fitness tests are the best way to motivate those children and adolescents who are least fit and most in need of physical activity promotion'. Following this comment the group had a rich research-informed conversation critiquing the positive and negative aspects of fitness tests in school-based physical education. When we finished this group meeting, another PST said: 'I think that physical education teaching is more complicated than I had assumed. There are so many aspects which I have to consider carefully.'
>
> *Extract from mentor's journal following a group meeting with second-year mentees*

Example Two

Dear Terhi,

Here is my e-learning plan for my bachelor's degree. I was not quite sure which minor subjects I should choose for this degree and which ones I should save for my master's. I would also like to discuss some elective courses when we meet next week. Is it possible to simply go and begin some courses in dance pedagogy? Also, I have a dream to study abroad, maybe next year. Could you give me some information about that?

See you!

Minna

Email from a second-year female mentee

These quotations showcase the types of interactions that take place between mentors and mentees in the JyU PETE mentoring programme. Becoming a reflective teacher involves a long process of growth, which requires guidance and support. Mentoring is a process which continues, for both mentor and mentee, throughout the five years of the PETE programme. Each mentor meets his or her group of mentees several times during the academic year (Huovinen *et al.* 2007). The mentoring process involves group discussions and one-to-one discussions between mentors and mentees, in addition to written assignments such as analytical tasks, portfolios and self-assessment tasks. The mentoring programme supports PSTs as they progress through their studies. A personal learning plan, devised by each PST, is the basis for this support system and mentors monitor the progress of PSTs through their plans (Heikinaro-Johansson *et al.* 2007).

Critical reflection is a tool for thinking and problem solving that assists PSTs to find solutions to the different issues that arise during their initial teacher education and during their subsequent professional lives (Griffiths 2000; Hirvensalo *et al.* 2009). The mentoring programme, established within the PETE programme in 2000, fosters reflective thinking of PSTs as a core principle.

Each year, four to five staff members act as mentors for the new intake of physical education PSTs ($n = 60$). At any given time, approximately 25 staff members (lecturers, researchers and professors) and 350 PSTs are participating in the JyU PETE mentoring programme. In order to ensure the effectiveness of the programme, it is important that PSTs, faculty and school personnel have a shared vision of both PETE and the mentoring system. Mentors meet regularly to share their mentoring experiences.

Vignette

Background

This chapter, written by four experienced mentors, examines the experiences of PSTs and physical education teacher educators as they experience the mentoring process. In our view, mentoring is a reciprocal relationship between persons relatively more experienced (mentors) and those less experienced (mentees) (Kram 1985; Schunk and Mullen 2013). Group mentoring refers to groups with one mentor and multiple mentees that are engaged in structured activities. The group setting is known to provide a safe environment in which to develop social skills and receive constructive feedback from peers (Karcher *et al.* 2006). Each mentoring group is given space to grow in its own direction, depending on the needs of mentees and on the mentor's personality and teaching philosophy. This feature has proved to be extremely important in keeping mentors and their mentees motivated and engaged in the process (Huovinen *et al.* 2007).

Methods

Each mentor in the PETE programme at JyU is an experienced physical education teacher educator. We followed the progress of 60 mentees, assigned to four mixed groups of 12–18 PSTs, each with one mentor. Mentee ages ranged from 20 to 25 years. For each group, the five-year mentoring process involved approximately fifteen group sessions and five to ten one-to-one meetings. Data were collected through individual and group interviews, mentoring journals, mentees' written reflective analyses and mentees' evaluation feedback at the end of their studies.

Findings

According to the results of an in-depth analysis of PST evaluations at JyU (Heikinaro-Johansson *et al.* 2007), the themes prioritised by physical education PSTs regarding their professional learning and development are (1) educational and professional orientation, (2) the learning process and (3) group dynamics and psychosocial support. These three areas were chosen as the focus for this chapter in discussing the perspectives of PSTs on the mentoring process.

Analysis
Educational and professional orientation

At the beginning of their studies, each PST formulated a personal learning plan. The mentor helped PSTs to understand the overall nature and content of the PETE programme and to choose elective courses and minor subjects, which suited their needs. At the beginning of each year, mentors scheduled an individual discussion with each PST in the group to discuss how the individual learning plan was progressing. The PST's goals for the academic year and more long-term career goals were also discussed. Areas of strength and weakness were identified and the learning plan was adjusted, as appropriate, to address the core needs of the PST. This support for the learning process intends to achieve both psychosocial and instrumental outcomes (Karcher *et al.* 2006). The development of the self-esteem of mentees and of their awareness of personal goals, strengths and weaknesses constitute the psychosocial outcomes, while the instrumental outcomes are focused on the improved study skills and results of PSTs leading to optimal progress through their studies to graduation.

In addition to individual mentor-mentee discussions, each mentor scheduled two to four group meetings per year (Heikinaro-Johansson *et al.* 2007). During group mentoring seminars, PSTs had the opportunity to discuss their studies with their peers. Through reflection on their experiences, collaborative planning of studies, and the process of giving feedback to lecturers, PSTs were encouraged to think about their own learning skills and to view their academic achievements within the peer group context.

> My student group has supported me in my studies. At the beginning of my studies I should have paid attention to those whose studies progressed fast. For me, it took a long time to learn how to study effectively. My studies are finally concluding now that I have gained effective learning skills.
>
> *Joni, male PST, 5th year interview*

> When trying to improve students' teaching skills, teacher educators should have the courage to place their trust in the power of discussions. It's not necessary to write essays about everything. Of course, this would require time and resources and more mentors with extensive knowledge of group dynamics. Only then could discussions be deep enough. I mean, you could express your real feelings and opinions. In my mentoring group, I felt we had very rewarding discussions about studying, and also about sport pedagogy.
>
> *Topi, male PST, 5th year interview*

Some PSTs are very independent and progress smoothly through their studies. In these cases, mentoring discussions remain collaborative and democratic (Orland-Barak and Klein 2005).

> *Mentor:* Your studies have progressed very well.
> *PST:* Yes, I'm happy with them. I had a very busy year last year but now I have more time to concentrate on my master's thesis. I will research communications skills in physical education.
> *Mentor:* Interesting. That is an important research area.
> *PST:* I think so too. I have noticed that communication skills may be more important than sport skills when you teach young children or teenagers in a school.

When PSTs need more support, this can result in mentors investing considerable time, and discussions can often be described as prescriptive and controlling (Orland-Barak and Klein 2005).

> *Mentor:* I can see that you still have not completed this course. Why is that?
> *PST:* I was ill when we had the exam for that course.
> *Mentor:* When do you have the next opportunity to take an exam?
> *PST:* No idea.
> *Mentor:* You should write [an] e-mail to the lecturer responsible for that course. Would you like to do it immediately?

The learning process

Mentors created learning opportunities for PSTs to better understand their teaching, learning, and learning about teaching. School practices and field experiences are combined with other studies throughout the five years of the PETE programme at JyU and mentoring forms a lens through which these pedagogical experiences can be understood. Group meetings provide a space for mentees to share their reflections and for mentors to bring knowledge and raise questions about relevant topics.

Personal experiences and life history play a critical role in the professional development of teachers (Placek *et al.* 1995; Matanin and Collier 2003). Mentors must understand the individual histories of their PSTs and systematically and repeatedly challenge them to discuss different beliefs and perspectives. Although some of the beliefs of PSTs persisted through professional training, PSTs also assimilated more sophisticated perspectives, developed their pedagogical content knowledge and became more student-centred in their decision making (Palomäki 2009).

> The best things about the PETE programme are that pedagogy is included throughout the five-year programme, progress is logical, we have a lot [of] courses in small groups, the team spirit is strong and the learning environment is secure.
>
> *Anna, female PST, comment at the end of 5th year*

Teaching is a human relations profession in which interaction is at the very core (Kansanen 2004, pp. 37–40). Effectiveness in the profession requires the ability to cope with a growing diversity of learners, the demands of the work environment, and ever-changing societal expectations. Teacher education must focus on the development of interpersonal, interaction and communication skills in order to build the capacity of PSTs to enter into dialogue with pupils, colleagues and parents, to overcome challenges as they arise, and to manage change effectively (Atjonen 2004). Mentoring is a mixture of collaboration and reflection, focusing on assessing options, weighing risks, considering ethical questions and analysing and rethinking meanings (Schunk and Mullen 2013).

> At the beginning of my studies, I believed that most of the work would centre on teaching sport skills and only being responsible for what happens during PE lessons. Through my studies, I have realized that as a teacher I will have several roles and responsibilities. One challenge as a PE teacher will be to get those pupils who are least interested in physical activity to be motivated to move.
>
> *Mikko, male PST, comment at the end of 5th year*

Group dynamics and psychosocial support

In the mentoring programme at JyU, the theoretical model of group development (Tuckman 1965; Öystilä 2002) is discussed and the groups are encouraged to be conscious of the stages they have reached (forming, storming, norming, performing, adjourning). We will take one group as a case in point. In this group everybody was quite satisfied with their group at first. 'We have a good group!' was the sentiment expressed by almost everybody to describe group relations. They noted: 'We must be in the group forming stage'. This was a comfortable stage for the PSTs. Theory suggests that conflict is unusual at this initial stage as individuals are driven by a desire to be accepted (Tuckman 1965).

During second year, some tension and arguments occurred. This stage of the group development process, storming, highlighted a sense of disapproval PSTs felt towards particular study tasks, and also against some lecturers. A core problem here was that PSTs were not comfortable to express their opinions honestly to each other. Two female PSTs took the opportunity to arrange a meeting with the mentor. They criticized one male PST for manipulating tasks and not giving them enough time to do their joint group work properly: 'He is deciding everything in our group'. Unresolved problems can prevent the group from proceeding and cause them to be frozen in this stage of the group development process. The mentor tried to solve the problem by encouraging the PSTs to express their feelings clearly to the male PST in question. The mentor also spoke with the male PST, listening to his point of view and asking him to pay attention to the opinions of his fellow PSTs.

It is worth noting that small groups can often form within a larger group. This is a natural occurrence as group members gravitate towards those with shared values and thoughts (Carron and Hausenblas 2005). A sense of cohesion can form within the smaller group but this can lead to the smaller group progressing through the group development stages at a different rate to the group as a whole. As one PST expressed: 'Our group is in storming and norming stage at the same time; we agree on many things but there are still many differing opinions'. After the first three stages of group development, the performing and adjourning stages follow. During the final group evaluation, all PSTs emphasized the importance of a good group: 'It was good that so many of us reached the final stage of teacher education together; it is so nice to be with people you know well, you know their good and bad sides'. The feeling of group unity was also evident in the free time choices of the PSTs. The group often engaged in fun social activities and planned an excursion together for the end of their studies. The mentor was especially satisfied with the development of this group, as she had strived to create a relaxed, open atmosphere and keep group dynamics at the centre of discussions.

Occasionally, PSTs shared study difficulties with the mentor. The responsibilities of PSTs, the opportunities available to them, and the rationale for various courses were often discussed in a collaborative group atmosphere. However, for the mentor difficulties sometimes arose. One of the male mentees in the group shared his study difficulties with the mentor many times, leading her to reflect in her journal after one meeting: 'What the hell will I do with him?' Although his sport studies went well, he neglected to write essays and could not concentrate on long-term courses. The mentor tried to help him to find solutions by, for example, working together to find effective study strategies for him. She was supportive and understanding at first, but after three years became frustrated. Other PSTs also reported their concerns to the mentor: 'We are worried about him; he will fail all the courses'. After seven years of study, the PST came to see the mentor and revealed that he may have been suffering from depression during those three first years of study. This example illustrates the complex issues that can sometimes lie on the periphery of the mentoring process and highlights the need for mentors to be alert to those needs of PSTs which are beyond the scope of the mentoring process and to be prepared to refer a PST to those appropriately educated to deal with such needs.

Conclusion

During their teacher education, PSTs undergo significant changes in their under-standing of the physical education profession, in their understanding of teaching and learning, in their professional orientation and in their social development. The mentoring process strives to ensure that PSTs are aware of these changes and are capable of articulating and reflecting upon them. When carried out effectively, mentoring allows PSTs to see first-hand what it is be a learner in a caring, collabo-rative and supportive educational setting, encouraging them to echo this style of teaching in their own classrooms.

Lessons learned . . . What could we add to the Mentor Pedagogy Toolbox?

- **Given a shared vision for the mentoring process, both mentors and mentees can have a valuable educational experience.** It is highly rewarding for mentors to feel that their learning and experience is esteemed by mentees and it can be empowering for mentees to have the opportunity to express and explore opinions in a supportive atmosphere.
- **The role of the mentor is ever evolving.** As the mentees progress through their studies and gain a level of academic independence, the role of the mentor changes from that of the expert in the room to that of sensitive listener, attend-ing to the needs of the group and facilitating educational growth.
- **Effective mentoring requires an understanding of group dynamics.** Being aware and making mentees aware of the stages of development that a group goes through allows for tensions to be dealt with calmly, and PSTs to learn how to facilitate group learning themselves.
- **Boundaries are important.** It is crucial to strike a balance between being supportive and being prescriptive. Mentors also need to be clear about what does and does not fall within their remit in order to ensure mentors do not take responsibility for issues with which they are not qualified to deal effectively.

Key terms: supportive and prescriptive mentoring, group dynamics and psycho-social support, learning process of mentee, mentoring, learning, teacher reflection, student feedback.

References

Atjonen, P. 2004. *Kasvatusta ja opetusta koskeva ydinaines opettajankoulutuksessa* [*The core of education and teaching in teacher education*]. In P. Atjonen and P. Väisänen, (Eds.) *Osaava opettaja* [The skillful teacher]. Joensuu, Finland: University of Joensuu, pp. 15–30.

Carron, A., Hausenblas, H. and Eys, M. 2005. *Group dynamics in sport*, 3rd edition. London, Ontario: Fitness Information Technology.

Griffiths, V. 2000. The reflective dimension in teacher education. *International Journal of Educational Research*, 33(5), 539–555.

Heikinaro-Johansson, P., Hirvensalo, M., Huovinen, T. and Johansson, N. 2007. *Ohjausta opintielle. Ryhmäohjauksen laatukäsikirja* [*Handbook for group mentoring*]. Jyväskylän yliopisto, Liikuntatieteiden laitos [University of Jyväskylä, Department of Sport Sciences].

Hirvensalo, M., Huovinen, T., Johansson, N. and Heikinaro-Johansson, P. 2009. Enhancing professional development of student teachers by including staff-tutoring in the physical education teacher education program. In P. Rossi, T. Hay, L. McCuaig, R. Tinning and D. Macdonald (Eds.) *Sport pedagogy research, policy and practice: International perspectives in physical education and sports coaching*. North meets South, East meets West. Proceedings of the 2008 AIESEP World Congress. University of Queensland.

Huovinen, T., Heikinaro-Johansson, P., Hirvensalo, M. and Johansson, N. 2007. Supporting the professional growth of pre-service teachers through staff-tutoring. In P. Heikinaro-Johansson, R. Telama and E.McEvoy (Eds.) *The role of physical education and sport in promoting physical activity and health*. Proceedings of the AIESEP World Congress. University of Jyväskylä, Department of Sport Sciences. Jyväskylä: Kopijyvä, pp. 186–189.

Kansanen, P. 2004. *Opetuksen käsitemaailma* [*Educational concepts*]. Jyväskylä: PS-kustannus.

Karcher, M. J., Kuperminc, G. P., Portwood, S. G., Sipe, C. L. and Taylor, A. S. 2006. Mentoring programs: A framework to inform program development, research, and evaluation. *Journal of Community Psychology*, 34(6), 709–725.

Korthagen, F. A. J. 2008. Building a realistic teacher education program. In F. A. J. Korthagen, J. Kessels, B. Koster, B. Lagerwerf and T. Webbels (Eds.) *Linking practice and theory. The pedagogy of realistic teacher education*. New York, NY: Routledge. pp. 69–87.

Kram, K. E. 1985. Improving the mentoring process. *Training and Development Journal*, 39(4), 40–43.

Matanin, M. and Collier, C. 2003. Longitudinal analysis of preservice teachers' beliefs about teaching physical education. *Journal of Teaching in Physical Education*, 22(2), 153–168.

Mezirow, J. 1990. How critical reflection triggers transformative learning. In J. Mezirow (Ed.) *Fostering critical reflection in adulthood: A guide to transformative and emancipatory learning*. San Francisco: Jossey-Bass, pp. 1–20.

Orland-Barak, L. and Klein, S. 2005. The expressed and the realized: Mentors' representations of a mentoring conversation and its realization in practice. *Teaching and Teacher Education*, 21(4), 379–402.

Öystilä, S. 2002. *Ongelmakohdat ryhmän ohjaamisessa* [*Instructing a group*]. In E. Poikela (Ed.) *Ongelmaperusteinen pedagogiikka – teoriaa ja käytäntöä* [*Problem-based pedagogy – theory and practice*]. Tampere: Tampere University Press, pp. 88–144.

Palomäki, S. 2009. *Opettajaksi opiskelevien pedagoginen ajattelu ja ammatillinen kehittyminen liikunnanopettajakoulutuksessa* [*Pre-service teachers' pedagogical thinking and professional development in physical education teacher education*]. Studies in Sport, Physical Education and Health. Jyväskylä: University of Jyväskylä.

Placek, J. H., Dodds, P., Doolittle, S. A., Portman, P. A., Ratliffe, T. A. and Pinkham, K. M. 1995. Teaching recruits' physical education backgrounds and beliefs about purposes for their subject matter. *Journal of Teaching in Physical Education* 14(3), 246–261.

Schunk, D. H. and Mullen, C. A. 2013. Toward a conceptual model of mentoring research: Integration with self-regulated learning. *Educational Psychology Review*, 25(3), 361–389.
Tuckman, B. 1965. Developmental sequence in small groups. *Psychological Bulletin*, 63(6), 384–399.

Resources

Korthagen, F. A. J. 2008. Building a realistic teacher education program. In F. A. J. Korthagen, J. Kessels, B. Koster, B. Lagerwerf and T. Webbels (Eds.) *Linking practice and theory. The pedagogy of realistic teacher education*. New York, NY: Routledge, p. 69–87.
Kram, K. E. 1985. Improving the mentoring process. *Training and Development Journal*, 39(4), 40–43.
Tuckman, B. 1965. Developmental sequence in small groups. *Psychological Bulletin*, 63(6), 384–99.

13

PEER-MENTORING AND THE POWER DYNAMICS OF THE HPETE TRIADIC RELATIONSHIP

Louise McCuaig, Simone Hare and Sue Monsen

Overview

> Siren song (n.): An enticing plea or appeal, especially one that is deceptively alluring; the enticing appeal of something alluring but potentially dangerous.
>
> *TheFreeDictionary.com, 2013*

In this chapter, we draw upon the notion of a siren song to inspire a review of a peer-mentoring strategy we employed in the Health and Physical Education Teacher Education (HPETE) practicum program at the University of Queensland's School of Human Movement Studies (UQHMS) in Australia. As Bullough Jr. and Draper (2004) explain, mentoring within the teacher education practicum experience is often 'complicated by the presence of not two but three players: a cooperating teacher or assigned mentor, a student or beginning teacher, and a university representative, most often designated as a supervisor rather than a mentor' (p. 407). Into this triad, we at UQHMS added an experienced, high-performing fourth-year HPETE peer-mentor. Findings from our HPETE peer-mentoring initiative were analysed according to a non-system/system actor analytic framework devised by scholars undertaking education policy implementation research (Cohen and Hill 2000; Coburn 2005). Our analysis provides insight into the benefits of peer mentoring and power differential dangers operating within the HPETE triadic relationship.

Vignette

Background

Faced with the challenges of providing cost effective and appropriate support for our HPETE students during their school practicum experience, peer mentoring floated into our imaginaries like a beguiling siren song. Our entrée into the world of mentoring was humble and ill informed, arriving amidst one of our team meetings:

> Louise: No matter what we have tried in order to provide more support for our students on their initial secondary school practicum, the truth is we have had little success.
>
> Sue: Yes, and next semester we are really up against it because we have very few experienced tutors who can visit the schools and provide students with the feedback they want.
>
> Louise: Clearly we can't ask any more of the teachers and we've got no funds to pay them . . . what if we tried to create a peer-mentoring program involving our experienced fourth-year HPETE students who could work with the thirds?
>
> Sue: Hmm . . . maybe that would work . . . what we could do is . . .

Methods

Having identified peer mentoring as a strategy, HPETE staff at UQHMS, energetically went ahead devising and implementing a school practicum peer-mentoring program. The practicum experience of concern involved groups of third-year HPETE students placed at partnership schools one day/week over a ten-week period. During this time, students were required to explore advanced student-centred teaching styles in the middle years of schooling (students 12–15 years of age). A university tutor facilitated group tutorials, attended school practicum, provided feedback on students' teaching practices and determined a final grade for practicum performance. This experience thus entailed the typical practicum triadic relationship of a student, university tutor and cooperating teacher.

Into this triad, we added an experienced, high-performing fourth-year HPETE student (Olivia) who would undertake the role of practicum experience peer-mentor. Extending an invitation to be a peer-mentor resulted from Olivia's in-depth understanding and successful implementation of contemporary HPETE pedagogical practices, as evidenced by her HPETE grades and supervising teachers' reports. A fundamental assumption of our program was that Olivia would enhance the learning of her mentees due to her recent HPETE practicum experiences and, as a consequence, would promote the advocated student-centred teaching philosophies of the UQHMS program. Providing Olivia with an opportunity to assist less experienced practicum students was intended to enhance her reflection practices and feedback skills within Health and Physical Education (HPE) learning contexts. It was further believed that, as the school context had been the site of her culminating practicum, Olivia would provide mentees with additional, context-specific teaching advice that would assist with school induction processes. To summarise, we anticipated a win (mentee): win (mentor): win (school teachers): win (UQHMS) for all involved.

Having agreed to participate, Olivia was subsequently asked to observe her mentees' teaching, provide feedback and facilitate mentees' reflective practice during the practicum. Importantly, Olivia's role involved no formal reporting or grading responsibilities. This peer-mentoring process provided the focus for a quasi-action research methodology (Kemmis and McTaggart 1988) involving the collection of mentee reflections, both verbal and written, in addition to gathering mentee, mentor and tutor feedback concerning the peer-mentoring initiative. Data gathered were analysed through the qualitative methods of constant comparison and thematic analysis (Emmison and Smith 2000).

Findings

Initial signs were promising, even exciting. Reflections and interview data indicated that our third-year HPETE students considered Olivia to be of significant benefit, providing 'relevant feedback' and an appreciation of 'what we are going through'. All mentees indicated that Olivia provided a different perspective on issues compared to those of the older, experienced cooperating teachers. Mentees were also keen to inform Olivia that lecturers, tutors and cooperating teachers did not see the issues faced by beginning teachers and had forgotten the learning involved in their early career teaching. Importantly, Olivia's feedback in relation to the application of a variety of pedagogies in schools was identified as fresh, accurate and more relevant to contemporary schooling:

> [The mentor] hasn't slipped into any bad habits . . . or had any bad experiences . . . the mentor's opinion [of pedagogies] is untarnished . . . they've got more fresh knowledge of all the pedagogies . . . and it makes it more relevant to us.
>
> *Sanchez*

Mentees also valued the considerable support Olivia provided through the building of self-confidence, career affirmation and assistance with induction. As anticipated, Olivia's 'inside knowledge' of the processes and expectations within the school setting eased the students' induction into the teaching practicum site, with Emma stating that Olivia 'knew all the teachers and policies and it helped us settle in a little smoother'.

However, the dangers and flaws of our 'eyes wide shut' engagement with the alluring strategy of peer-mentoring were soon to emerge. Although mentees were seeking more time and input from Olivia, she was quietly trying to negotiate the increasing demands of her mentor responsibilities. Olivia experienced an initial lack of understanding with respect to her role, was apprehensive about how mentees would accept her and found it challenging to provide valuable feedback in some situations. Additionally, as she was also completing full-time study, Olivia felt the burden of the large time commitment.

Aside from this, Olivia was faced with additional challenges that were specific to the school in which she had previously completed her culminating practicum. In this context, Olivia's mentees shared the same supervising teacher that she had worked with in her own practicum experience. This situation resulted in the teacher allocating organisational tasks to Olivia and treating her as a pre-service teacher instead of recognising her role as peer-mentor:

> I felt obliged to do as I was asked, as I didn't want to leave a bad impression even though it limited my ability to observe students and provide them with feedback. While this didn't seem to affect the students' perception of my role as a mentor, I found it difficult to define my role as a mentor with the other staff.
>
> *Olivia*

In addition to this, Olivia increasingly found herself undertaking the role of advocate for the organisation, content, philosophies and privileged pedagogical approaches of her university's HPETE program:

> At morning tea I felt like I had to advocate for the program on many occasions. Staff were commenting on how stupid they thought the structure of the one-day-a-week practicum was for everyone.
>
> *Olivia*

It was Olivia's positioning as advocate of the UQHMS pedagogical philosophies that truly led to the shipwreck of our peer-mentoring program. To understand this state of affairs, we need more insight into why peer mentoring in HPETE practicum experiences is so seductive and yet, potentially dangerous for peer-mentors.

Analysis

Peer mentoring within tertiary settings typically encompasses more advanced students helping less experienced students improve their academic performance (Colvin and Ashman 2010). Research conducted by Hansford, Ehrich and Tennent (2004) found that for mentees, the benefits of peer-mentoring programs include friendship, increased confidence, enhanced risk-taking behavior and interpersonal development. For mentors, an important benefit is the opportunity to observe mentees' teaching practices, which exposes mentors to new ideas and encourages reflection on their current beliefs and practices (Hansford *et al.* 2004).

Findings from our study provide confirmation of this literature. Nonetheless, they also draw attention to the influence of power dynamics operating within teacher education triadic relationships (Anderson 2007; Bullough Jr. and Draper 2004). Work by researchers exploring the implementation of instructional policy within schooling provides a useful analytic framework that reveals both the benefits of peer mentoring and the impact of power differentials (Cohen and Hill 2000; Coburn 2005). In her research, Coburn (2005) argued that teachers 'learn about new approaches to teaching and learning through a diverse and at times loosely connected set of policies, organizations, and actors' (p. 24). A range of actors who have formal roles within the education system (school and policy leaders) exert considerable influence on teachers' connections and uptake of policy messages. Additionally, there are numerous individuals and organisations, independent of the formal schooling system, who typically promote policy messages, enhance the relevance of these messages and assist policy uptake through the delivery of strategies that convey classroom implications to teachers. According to Coburn (2005), non-system actors are significant players, demonstrating 'a greater capacity than policy actors to reach teachers in ways that are substantive, sustained, and situated in their day-to-day work in the classroom' (p. 44).

Drawing on this non-system/system actor theoretical framework, we suggest that Olivia was afforded the role of non-system actor through her provision of support to pre-service teachers from a position that lay 'outside' the formal roles of the school system. As with instructional policy, HPETE programs focus on the uptake and implementation of 'sanctioned' curriculum and pedagogy messages. Such messages are however conveyed to (pre-service) teachers through 'a web of interactive and, at times, reciprocal linkages' (Coburn 2005, p. 25) that typically comprises university and school-based personnel competing for the hearts, minds and actions of (pre-service) teachers. According to Coburn (2005), Olivia's effectiveness as a non-system actor and key mediating link in the translation of HPETE 'policy' into practice can be determined by the extent to which her work demonstrates greater intensity, greater proximity to the classroom, greater depth and voluntariness.

From this perspective, Olivia's success can be attributed to her achievement in the twin dimensions of *classroom proximity* and *voluntariness*. For Coburn (2005), the degree to which non-system actors provide teachers with practical advice related to the pedagogical demands and core business of teachers' day-to-day work characterises their proximity to the classroom. Analysis of comments from mentees indicates that this factor was the most significant contributor to the success of the peer-mentoring program. While the mentor, tutor and supervising teachers all provided mentees with advice, mentees considered the mentor's proximity to the practicum experience to be greater than that of their tutor or supervising teachers. Olivia's recent and successful engagement with the mentees' practicum site and slightly more advanced stage of development ensured that feedback was relevant to the current and near-future concerns of mentees. From the mentees' perspective, university tutors and supervising teachers 'don't know what they know'. Olivia thus had a greater capacity to encourage her mentees' acceptance and application of new pedagogical philosophies.

Voluntariness considers the extent of pressure associated with the professional development provided by non-system actors (Coburn 2005). She further identifies the regulative, normative and cognitive pressures exerted through policy messages that are intended to shape an individual's actions and beliefs. In contrast to regulative pressures which enforce a 'this is what you must do' message, normative pressures employ a tone of 'this is what you could or should do', while cognitive pressures promote a practice as natural or 'common sense'. As university tutors and supervising teachers are typically involved in the business of judging and assessing pre-service teachers' performances, their feedback and guidance inevitably exerts a 'you must' tone throughout the practicum experience. Olivia's freedom from the formalities of assessment reduces the regulative tone of the messages circulating within the triadic relationship. As the peer-mentor's advice focuses on what pre-service teachers could or should do to improve their performance, the normative and cognitive nature of the support enhanced the 'voluntariness' dimension of the mentor's contribution.

Through the analytic lens of *greater intensity and greater depth*, it is possible to identify some of the factors that compromised Olivia's effectiveness. *Greater intensity* refers to an ongoing partnership that emerges within the context of 'sustained and ongoing interactions with high-quality professional development or one-on-one interactions over time' (Coburn 2005, p. 35). In this study, a relative degree of intensity was achieved through Olivia's observation, reflection and feedback on mentees' teaching practices. According to mentees, Olivia's one-on-one provision of feedback was rich, relevant and more useful than feedback from the tutor or supervising teachers. Yet it is worth noting that, given the short duration of the peer-mentoring partnership, the intensity of the program could not truly be classified as sustained, which ultimately compromised the degree of depth that our non-system actor could achieve with her mentee teachers. Greater depth concerns a non-system actor's capacity to move teachers beyond the superficial elements of classroom organisation, to examine and reflect upon personal teaching and learning philosophies (Coburn 2005). To a certain extent, Olivia's personal experiences in applying advanced HPETE pedagogical approaches facilitated some discussion pertaining to the values and beliefs shaping pre-service teachers' personal philosophies. Nonetheless, the immediacy of pre-service teachers' needs regarding behaviour management, organisation and student engagement resulted in relatively superficial commentary with few opportunities to explore deeper understandings.

Notwithstanding this insight, the overall success of the peer-mentoring program was ultimately compromised by Olivia's ambiguous non-system actor role. As earlier commentary indicates, Olivia found it difficult to define her role to teaching staff, particularly those who had contributed to her own practicum triadic relationship. For these teachers, Olivia was still an actor 'inside' their system and thus subject to the influence and expectations of the more immediate and powerful school system. Although we had hoped mentees would benefit from Olivia's insider knowledge, we failed to consider research indicating that student teachers' 'recognition of their cooperating teachers as their bosses' (Anderson 2007, p. 318) results in an entrenchment of the 'power differential inherent in the practicum' (ibid., p. 318). As Anderson (2007) further explains, pre-service teachers are acutely aware of the reward power, in terms of positive reports and future employment, that supervising teachers hold within the practicum triad relationship. Indeed, Olivia had been informed by her previous supervising teachers that they were actively petitioning school leaders to have her appointed to their school the following year. Consequently, Olivia's capacity to inspire her mentees' employment of innovative pedagogical practices was compromised by her own vested interests and positioning within the hierarchical relationships of the school system.

Olivia's uneasiness was further exacerbated when she found herself having to advocate on behalf of her university's HPETE program in response to critical commentary from supervising teachers. Teacher education research has revealed the extent to which pre-service teachers are required to negotiate the competing expectations of their teacher education programs and cooperating teachers (Marks 2007; Bullough Jr. and Draper 2004). Many argue that field experiences are often characterized by tug-of-war conflicts where university and school-based demands conflict (Marks 2007). The ambiguity surrounding Olivia's 'inside-outside' positioning within the triadic relationship resulted in her becoming the focal point around which this tug-of-war took place. Although the mentees found Olivia's familiarity with the school context of considerable use, these benefits were outweighed by Olivia's increasingly compromised role as peer-mentor.

At the conclusion of the practicum, we were forced to acknowledge our naivety and the ease with which we had been seduced by the siren song of peer mentoring. In our collaborative efforts to review the initiative, Olivia's experience and feedback revealed the extent to which 'questions of expertise, experience and power can complicate what appears to be a straightforward expert-novice interaction' (Smith 2007, p. 88). In our rush to embrace the ideal solution of peer mentoring, we failed to engage with the literature, which may have alerted us to the dangers associated with the misunderstanding or misuse of power that is often a feature of collaborative learning strategies (Bruffee 1994). As Colvin (2007) warns, successful peer mentoring is determined by the quality of relationships among pre-service students, supervising teachers and university instructors, which do not occur within a vacuum. Even when training is ongoing and established, assumptions cannot be made about the understanding of roles, risks and benefits and how these translate into issues of power and resistance (Colvin and Ashman 2010). The potential benefits to be garnered when peer-mentors function as non-system within the triadic relationships are mitigated when HPE teacher educators fail to stimulate critical reflection processes concerning the power dynamics of the professional experience. As Bullough Jr. and Draper (2004) have suggested, 'differences need to be recognized and a common space created . . . the meeting of a triad should become such a space: a place within which good talk across differences about good teaching occurs earnestly, honestly, and respectfully' (p. 419).

Lessons learned . . . What could we add to the Mentor Pedagogy Toolbox?

Our work confirms the appeal and usefulness of peer mentoring, but provides further insight into the potential dangers when such initiatives are hastily employed within the HPETE practicums. Mindful of the mutual benefits for mentors and mentees, peer-mentoring may well be offered to advanced HPETE students to enhance their professional development when:

- Peer-mentors work as non-system actors whose practices seek to achieve voluntariness, greater intensity, greater depth, and in particular, greater proximity to the classroom.
- The placement of peer-mentors within the context of the practicum triad relationship is accompanied by rigorous attention to the power differentials through practices of critical reflection (Mallett 2004). Creating opportunities for critical reflection should not be considered a mere luxury, but an essential pre-requisite to enhance, where possible, the congruency of messages within the triadic relationship and to ensure peer-mentors have the best possible opportunity to enact their role according to mutuality, collaboration and equality (Awaya *et al*. 2003; Stanulis and Russell 2000).
- These findings and our analysis of the data focus attention on the importance of reflective practices and their capacity to reveal the interactive nature of several aspects of the CM³T model of mentor competencies, including (a) *Affective* (trust, empathy, support), (b) *Cognitive* (context knowledge) and (c) *Hybrid* (building rapport, approachability, co-existence of professional and personal relationships).

Key terms: HPETE triad, peer-mentoring, power, non-system actor, system actor.

References

Anderson, D. 2007. The role of cooperating teachers' power in student teaching. *Education*, 128(2), 307–323.

Awaya, A., McEwan, H., Heyler, D., Linsky, S., Lum, D. and Wakukawa, P. 2003. Mentoring as a journey. *Teaching and Teacher Education*, 19, 45–56.

Bruffee, K. A. 1994. Making the most of knowledgeable peers. *Change*, 26(3), 38–45.

Bullough Jr., R. V. and Draper, R. J. 2004. Making sense of a failed triad: Mentors, university supervisors, and positioning theory. *Journal of Teacher Education*, 55, 407.

Coburn, C. E. 2005. The role of nonsystem actors in the relationship between policy and practice: The case of reading instruction in California. *Educational Evaluation and Policy Analysis*, 27(1), 23–52.

Cohen, D. K. and Hill, H. C. 2000. Instructional policy and classroom performance: The mathematics reform in California. *Teachers College Record*, 102, 294–343.

Colvin, J. W. 2007. *Peer Tutoring and the Social Dynamics of a Classroom*. Saarbrucken, Germany: VDM Verlag Publishing Company.

Colvin, J. W. and Ashman, M. 2010. Roles, risks, and benefits of peer mentoring relationships in higher education. *Mentoring and Tutoring: Partnership in Learning*, 18(2), 121–134.

Emmison, M. and Smith P. 2000. *Researching the Visual*. London: Sage Publications.

Hansford, B. C., Ehrich, L. C. and Tennent, L. 2004. Outcomes and perennial issues in preservice teacher education mentoring programs. *International Journal of Practical Experiences in Professional Education*, 8(2), 6–17.

Kemmis, S., and McTaggart, R. 1988. *The Action Research Planner*, Victoria: Deakin University Press.

Mallett, C. 2004. Reflective practices in teaching and coaching: Using reflective journals to enhance performance. In J. Wright, D. Macdonald and L. Burrows (Eds.) *Critical Inquiry and Problem-Solving in Physical Education*. London: Routledge, pp. 147–159.

Marks, M. J. 2007. Influences on preservice teacher socialization: A qualitative study. Paper presented at the American Educational Research Association Annual Meeting, Chicago, Illinois, April 9–13.

Smith, E. R. 2007. Negotiating power and pedagogy in student teaching: Expanding and shifting roles in expert-novice discourse. *Mentoring and Tutoring: Partnership in Learning*, 15(1), 87–106.

Stanulis, R. N. and Russell, D. 2000. "Jumping in": Trust and communication in mentoring student teachers. *Teaching and Teacher Education*, 16, 65–80.

TheFreeDictionary.com 2013. c.v. *Siren Song*. Retrieved from http://www.thefreedictionary. com/Siren's+Song accessed on 11th November 2013.

Resources

Mallett, C. 2004. Reflective practices in teaching and coaching: Using reflective journals to enhance performance. In J. Wright, D. Macdonald and L. Burrows (Eds.) *Critical Inquiry and Problem-Solving in Physical Education*. London: Routledge, pp. 147–159.

14

E-MENTORING IN PHYSICAL EDUCATION

A case study

Nate McCaughtry, Pamela Hodges Kulinna, Donetta Cothran, Michalis Stylianou and Ja Youn Kwon

Overview

Mentoring is important for new teachers, and even more so for new teachers entering challenging contexts like urban schools (McCaughtry *et al.* 2006a, b). New teachers are quickly confronted by the realities of unfamiliar roles and environments. Some succeed, but others struggle with reality shock, isolation and frustration, resulting in high attrition rates. The transition need not be so difficult, as effective mentoring can ease the transition and improve teacher attrition rates. Despite the positive potential of mentoring, roadblocks exist. For example, successful teacher pairings require commitment, interpersonal skills, and support from administrators. Access to discipline-specific mentors is also a challenge. While mentors from any content area can provide generalized guidance and emotional support, the optimal mentor is someone who understands the complexities of discipline-specific teaching.

Electronic mentoring, or e-mentoring, is a mechanism that can bridge challenges such as physical distance and incompatible schedules. Mueller (2004) suggests that e-mentoring helps solve four roadblocks to traditional mentoring: it provides independence from geography and time, interactions can improve with more regular correspondence, status hierarchies can lessen and logistical costs can be reduced. Initial evidence suggests that e-mentoring in physical education might improve both student teaching and new teacher experiences. For example, DeWert *et al.* (2003) found that peer mentors assisted new teachers to overcome reality shock; balance the coach-teacher role conflict; develop successful instructional and classroom management strategies; and cope with isolation and marginalization. Although a promising option, e-mentoring is also not without challenges. Mueller noted that e-mentoring requires some degree of participant technological sophistication, it may be difficult to cultivate trusting bonds through solely virtual interaction, and e-correspondence can lead to misinterpretation when the common visual and auditory cues of in-person communication are absent.

Vignette

Background

Five years prior to this study, a large urban school district in the USA adopted a common curriculum, the Exemplary Physical Education Curriculum (EPEC). They instituted a series of professional development seminars and launched its usage across the district. The year prior to this study, the district faced a new dilemma, specifically an influx of teachers who were new to elementary physical education (PE), the district, and/or using EPEC. Given that teacher professional development days are limited and expensive, and that one-day workshops have limited value in changing practice, the district wondered if a different professional development model would enhance teacher knowledge, skills and efficacy.

In response, our university partnered with the district to develop a mentoring program that paired fifteen successful EPEC teachers with fifteen protégés. Mentor teachers had more teaching experience ($m = 22.46$, $sd = 10.25$) than protégés ($m = 5.36$, $sd = 5.71$). There were twelve males and eighteen females and the teachers reported African-American ($n = 14$) or Caucasian ($n = 15$) ethnicities. Mentors participated in professional development to acquaint themselves with mentoring theories and strategies. New teachers participated in an initial EPEC training session. Next, mentors and protégés were paired and participated in a series of three in-person workshops as well as e-mentoring using asynchronous chat rooms supported by Blackboard. Each mentor-protégé pair was asked to use the chat rooms at least once per week.

Methods

To research the year-long program, multiple methodologies were used. We conducted regular surveys to learn how the mentoring program affected a variety of skills and attitudes. The frequency and content of the chat room conversations were recorded and analyzed. Those data were analyzed with traditional statistical approaches. We also interviewed participants and had formal workshop observations and those data were analyzed via a constant comparison process.

Collectively, the methodologies captured a rich understanding of how e-mentoring both succeeded and failed in supporting teachers in learning the new curriculum. Given that the research design also included three face-to-face all-day seminars, it is difficult to tease out the contributions of those days versus e-mentoring in the overall findings. Both were no doubt important, with different mentor pairs responding differently to various aspects of the intervention.

Findings

The surveys showed that mentoring and professional development contributed to a range of outcomes (Hodges Kulinna et al. 2008; Martin et al. 2009; Martin et al. 2008a; Martin et al. 2008b; McCaughtry et al. 2005). Some of the significant outcomes included the following:

1. Mentors' mentoring competency increased
2. Protégés felt increased psychological support
3. Protégés felt better about career success
4. Both groups increased technology efficacy
5. Both groups increased curricular efficacy
6. Both groups increased efficacy to overcome instructional barriers
7. Both groups increased locus of control in teaching
8. Both groups felt increased social support for teaching
9. Both groups felt more emotionally committed to curricular reform

Analysis

Beyond assessing impact using quantitative methodologies, we also employed a rigorous qualitative design to understand how the mentoring program impacted both sets of teachers from their viewpoints. For example, we often interviewed teachers to identify the mentor characteristics that protégés most wanted (Cothran *et al.* 2008; McCaughtry *et al.* 2005). We found that protégés appreciated mentors with strong knowledge of and experience with EPEC. Nina said, 'I'm just glad my mentor really knew the curriculum and had taught it before. If she didn't even really know the curriculum, I'm not sure how much help she would have been.' Each of the teachers also attested to the fact that curricular knowledge itself was not enough to serve as a mentor, rather knowledge also had to be accompanied by experience teaching it 'in their context.'

> Let's face it, we're teaching in really difficult schools. It's crazy the things we run into or the kinds of things we face daily. I don't want some guy who teaches this [EPEC] out in the cushy suburbs to be mentoring me. I needed somebody who's done this in the trenches. You know, out here in the real world where I teach. I'm so happy that's who I got.
>
> *Participant*

Second, protégés wanted mentors with the ability to listen and give advice:

> I was really worried at first because my mentor just talked the whole time when we first met. I was worried they didn't really want to hear about my struggles or what I face. But, that changed pretty quickly and she started to listen to what I was saying and what I needed before offering advice. I guess she was probably just nervous at first and wanted me to see her as credible or whatever. She really settled into someone I could share my troubles with and get really solid advice.
>
> *Participant*

The third characteristic that protégés wanted was a direct, solution-focused approach from their mentors. Most mentoring literature suggests that mentors follow adult learning theory and serve as a facilitator to help protégés solve their own challenges. Protégés in this study wanted the exact opposite. They wanted mentors to provide quick, specific solutions. Given the complexity of the new curriculum and setting, the opportunity to get targeted, rapid guidance from their mentor was most welcome:

> My world moves really fast. I can't tell you how many things I deal with in one day. You just wouldn't believe it. I don't have time for a big counseling session. I need advice pronto. I need him to tell me what they'd do if they were me. I'll decide whether to take it or not. Like, 'here's my problem, give me three solutions you'd try.' That's how I need to operate to keep pace around here.
>
> *Participant*

Last, every protégé mentioned the desire for their mentor to be available more often. Protégés often expressed frustration when mentors limited their hours of availability:

> I need her when I need her. It's really frustrating when she only communicates during her lunch hour. It's like pulling teeth to get her to engage like after school. I don't control when I encounter things I need help with. I need her when I need her.
>
> *Participant*

We also conducted archival analyses of the chat room use (Cothran *et al.* 2009; Faust *et al.* 2007). Overall, teachers demonstrated low rates of participation with limited exchanges. The chat room exchanges can be grouped into four categories:

1. Short postings with social content not focused on teaching ($N = 258$)
2. General and indirect comments about teaching ($N = 236$)
3. Short exchanges about general teaching issues and specific concerns ($N = 190$)
4. Longer, more involved, and detailed postings about understanding the EPEC and teaching it ($N = 83$)

Mentors posted more often and substantively than protégés, with 50 per cent more postings at category 3 (116 compared to 74) and 100 per cent more at category 4 (60 compared to 23).

Postings at levels 1 and 2 were not necessarily a negative trend as these short comments allowed mentors and protégés to 'check in' with one another and maintain an ongoing relationship. The relative lack of comments at levels 3 and 4 was problematic given that these exchanges were the most relevant to the new curriculum mentoring. Participant interviews explored these trends.

Lack of technology access and skills significantly limited the chat room involvement. Only sixteen teachers had office computers and, of those, only twelve had

Internet access. Six had smart phones with Internet capabilities and twenty-three used computers at home. Three teachers had never used the Internet prior to this project. Nick exemplified teachers who did not have computer access: 'I'm the only teacher that doesn't have a computer in their office. I have to go to somebody else's computer over in the office or something. I might have to go to the computer lab, and it's not always accessible.' Similarly, David voiced the dilemma of an office computer, with inconsistent or non-existent Internet access:

> My office is a storage room off the gym. I think the last thing they were thinking was to put internet in this room . . . It's not just my office. Half the time the entire computer lab isn't working. That's probably the biggest problem at this school, we're so behind when it comes to technology. . . . So then I work the after school tutoring program and go from there to coach my kid. Then I get home at 8:00 and the last thing I want to do is get on the internet and talk about my teaching day.

Brenda shared the perspectives of the five mentors who had virtually no computer experience:

> Yeah, yeah, yeah, I know they had us do those level one computer trainings. I'm doing my best, but to be honest, it takes me an hour just to get on there and post some simple message. It's hard because I think I have so much knowledge to help Julie but I can't get it across using this thing [computer].

Due to technology challenges and incompatible schedules, mentors and protégés reported the need for quicker and more substantive conversations than the chat rooms allowed. Every teacher talked about the constant challenges they faced in urban schools and the need for rapid solution-focused discussions, and the chat rooms simply did not offer a logistically friendly method of having time-sensitive interactions. Ben said:

> It's not that I don't want to use them [chat rooms], it's just that I'm flying a hundred miles an hour during the day and when I get home I want to focus on home. The last thing I want to do is sit on the computer for an hour chatting back and forth.

Most teacher pairs admitted to using telephones as their preferred communication because they could talk at any time since most teachers had cell phones and they could exchange far more information and have much deeper conversations in a shorter period of time. Julie summarized:

> Now if I have something pop up, I just give Brenda a call and we can discuss real quick and the problem's solved. Do you have any idea how long it would take if I had to use the chat room to get the same thing accomplished?

For many of the protégés, learning to teach in these urban schools represented, in their words, 'an emotional rollercoaster.' One minute, classes could be moving well, then the next minute a situation occurred that disrupted their teaching and led them to question their teaching abilities. Protégés felt chat rooms did not provide them with the emotional support they received when they met with their mentors in person. While they recognized that the online forum could help them solicit advice regarding minor, clear-cut issues, it did not provide them with the sense of support they needed to cope with the significant turmoil they experienced. Vanessa said:

> It's really hard to communicate and read someone in the chat rooms. Like, I know she cares and really wants to help me solve problems, but that doesn't really come across. I always feel better after we meet in person.

Mentors relayed similar perspectives and felt the chat rooms did not provide them with enough room to express their caring. Gloria explained:

> There's just so much I can't get across in those [chat rooms]. They're okay for staying in touch or dealing with little things, but when there's something major or important it takes too long and I can't express how much I care or want to help the way I want to. I'm a really caring person and I don't think that comes across as well here.
>
> *Participant*

Conclusions

Despite its promise, only eleven studies were found that related to e-mentoring in physical education (with five focused on broader technology issues). Of the six studies specific to e-mentoring, five of the papers studied pre-service teachers rather than in-service teachers. Due to both the rapid increase in the use of technology and the increasing demands on teachers and teacher educators, e-mentoring will likely become more common in the near future. We therefore need additional investigations in a variety of settings to understand and develop e-mentoring programs that meet the needs of participants in maximally effective ways.

Lessons learned . . . What could we add to the Mentor Pedagogy Toolbox?

This section of the chapter discusses lessons learned for e-mentoring from our study as well as the larger literature based on e-mentoring in physical education (eleven papers).

Teachers need access to and skills in technology.

Teacher access to and comfort level with technology is a significant factor in their ability and willingness to engage fully in e-mentoring. In this particular study, the school district assured the research team that all teachers had access to computers and the Internet; however, the reality was far from that. Given their already too-busy days and at least for some teachers, limited technology skills, teachers struggled to make time for and use the chat rooms.

The good news is that, in general, teachers acknowledge the importance of using technology and seem open to learning more about it. Both pre-service (Lockyer and Patterson 2007) and in-service (Thomas and Stratton 2006) teachers recognize the need to use technology in their teaching. Training can support technology use, as teachers in this study became more efficacious in using computers for a variety of tasks (e.g. e-mail, chat rooms etc.) over the control group teachers (Martin *et al.* 2008). Ince *et al.* (2006) reported similar positive findings, with technology training resulting in increased teacher competency and affinity. Technology skills may not always be an issue, as three-quarters of the pre-service physical educators in the Lockyer and Patterson (2007) study rated their technology knowledge as high or very high.

E-mentoring benefits protégés and mentors.

Across the studies related to e-mentoring in physical education, the trends are generally positive. The specifics vary by study, but in general, protégés feel more efficacious, supported, and committed to effective teaching (e.g. McDiarmid and Moosbrugger 2011). The benefits also extend to mentor teachers who often report positive professional and personal benefits such as increased leadership, communication and confidence in their own skills (e.g. Australian Council for Health, Physical Education and Recreation 2007).

To increase the benefits of e-mentoring, several challenges must be addressed. First, what is the optimal structure to prompt discussion and reflection? Lamb and Aldous (2014) found overall positive results of their e-mentoring program but suggested that too many rules can be restrictive. In contrast, we had almost no rules other than a request to post something at least once per week and our chat room use failed to address substantive issues on a regular basis. There seems to be a happy medium of structure without obstruction that is yet unknown. Second, beyond better technology access and skills, how can teacher needs for timely interactions be met? Perhaps other types of technology (e.g. Twitter, instant messaging) may be useful for e-mentoring. Our teachers preferred tele-mentoring, the use of telephones in mentoring, for quicker, more personal and deeper exchanges. One study showed success with a listserv group for physical education teachers who shared professional concerns and strategies (Pennington *et al.* 2004). Finally, whatever the medium, how can a personal connection with a partner be developed and enhanced? In our study, that was at least partially accomplished by a blended model of a few face-to-face days with e-mentoring. That is not always possible, however, so are there ways to structure e-mentoring exchanges that can meld the personal and the professional in ways that enhance both?

Key terms: e-mentoring, electronic mentoring, tele-mentoring.

References

Australian Council for Health, Physical Education and Recreation. 2007. A helping hand for beginning PDHPE teachers. *Active and Healthy Magazine,* 14(3/4), 11.

Cothran, D., McCaughtry, N., Faust, R., Garn, A., Hodges Kulinna, P. and Martin, J. 2009. E-mentoring in physical education: Promises and pitfalls. *Research Quarterly for Exercise and Sport,* 80, 552–562.

Cothran, D., McCaughtry, N., Smigell, S., Garn, A., Hodges Kulinna, P., Martin, J. and Faust, R. 2008. Teachers' preferences on the qualities and roles of a mentor teacher. *Journal of Teaching in Physical Education,* 27, 241–251.

DeWert, M. H., Babinski, L. M. and Jones, B. D. 2003. Safe passages: Providing online support to beginning teachers. *Journal of Teacher Education,* 54, 311–320.

Faust, R., Cothran, D. J., McCaughtry, N., Hodges Kulinna, P., Martin, J. and Smigell, S. 2007. Use of chat rooms as a mentoring tool. *Research Quarterly for Exercise and Sport,* 78, 56.

Hodges Kulinna, P., McCaughtry, N., Martin, J., Cothran, D. and Faust, R. 2008. The influence of professional development on teachers' psychosocial perceptions of teaching a health-related physical education curriculum. *Journal of Teaching in Physical Education,* 27, 292–307.

Ince, M. L., Goodway, J. D., Ward, P. and Lee, M. A. 2006. The effects of professional development on technological competency and the attitudes urban physical education teachers have toward using technology. *Journal of Teaching in Physical Education,* 25(4), 428–440.

Lamb, P. and Aldous, D. 2014. The role of e-mentoring in distinguishing pedagogic experiences of gifted and talented pupils in physical education. *Physical Education and Sport Pedagogy,* 19(3), 301–319.

Lockyer, L. and Patterson, J. 2007. Technology use, technology views: Anticipating professional use of ICT for beginning physical and health education teachers. *Issues in Informing Science and Information Technology,* 4, 261–267.

Martin, J., McCaughtry, N., Hodges Kulinna, P. and Cothran, D. 2008a. The influences of professional development on teachers' self-efficacy toward educational change. *Physical Education and Sport Pedagogy,* 13, 171–190.

Martin, J., McCaughtry, N., Hodges Kulinna, P. and Cothran, D. 2009. The impact of a social cognitive theory-based intervention on physical education teacher self-efficacy. *Professional Development in Education,* 35, 511–529.

Martin, J., McCaughtry, N., Hodges Kulinna, P., Cothran, D. and Faust, R. 2008b. The effectiveness of mentoring-based professional development on physical education teachers' pedometer and computer efficacy and anxiety. *Journal of Teaching in Physical Education,* 27, 68–82.

McCaughtry, N., Barnard, S., Martin, J., Shen, B. and Hodges Kulinna, P. 2006a. Teachers' perspectives on the challenges of teaching physical education in urban schools: The student emotional filter. *Research Quarterly for Exercise and Sport,* 77, 486–497.

McCaughtry, N., Hodges Kulinna, P., Cothran, D., Martin, J. and Faust, R. 2005. Teachers mentoring teachers: A view over time. *Journal of Teaching in Physical Education,* 24, 326–343.

McCaughtry, N., Martin, J., Hodges Kulinna, P. and Cothran, D. 2006b. The emotional dimensions of urban teacher change. *Journal of Teaching in Physical Education,* 25, 99–119.

McDiarmid, P. L. and Moosbrugger, M. E. 2011. E-mentoring and teaching efficacy in preservice physical educators. *Research Quarterly for Exercise and Sport,* 82, 48.

Mueller, S. 2004. Electronic mentoring as an example for the use of information and communication technology in engineering education. *European Journal of Engineering Education,* 29, 53–63.

Pennington, T., Wilkinson, C. and Vance, J. 2004. Physical educators online: What is on the minds of teachers in the trenches? *The Physical Educator*, 61(1), 45.

Thomas, A. and Stratton, G. 2006. What we are really doing with ICT in physical education: A national audit of equipment, use, teacher attitudes, support, and training. *British Journal of Educational Technology*, 37(4), 617–632.

Resources

Creating an E-Mentoring Community:
http://www.washington.edu/doit/Mentor/index_pdf.html
Overview of mentoring/e-mentoring/coaching including US-European differences:
http://www.versa.uk.com/apprenticeship/mentor_handbook.pdf

SECTION 4
Mentoring and sport coaching

15

NATIONAL GOVERNING BODIES

Sport policy, practice and mentoring

Tania Cassidy, Joan Merrilees and Sally Shaw

Overview

A range of interpretations of mentoring exists, varying from simple to complex. Despite the multiple perspectives, a common denominator in many analyses is that a mentoring relationship comprises a mentor and mentee, with the former providing support and guidance to the protégé/mentee (Merriam 1983). More recently, Bloom (2013) proposed that a successful mentor and mentee relationship requires the participating parties to have a degree of trust and respect for one another. These broad interpretations of mentoring guide the discussion in this chapter. In addition, our discussion is contextualised by primarily drawing on the findings of a study, conducted by the second author, who investigated how females 'become' elite performance coaches, how they learn their trade, whether they consider coaching to be 'work' and how they negotiated the associated power and gender relationships that occurred, and continue to occur, as they progress on their coaching journey (Merrilees in progress). The findings are represented in the form of vignettes in an effort to bring the findings 'alive' and make them resonate with a range of readers. The vignettes were constructed from data gathered via semi-structured interviews with two elite performance coaches involved in the track and field community in New Zealand and data gathered in semi-structured interviews with a Coach Manager employed by Athletics New Zealand who had designed, and had begun to implement, a Coach Mentor scheme. The subsequent analysis of the vignettes highlights the importance of coach developers recognising the relevance of the context in which the coach is working; the potential problems associated with viewing mentoring relationships along traditional lines; the fact that mentoring is only one strategy coaches employ in an effort to develop their practice; the value of theorising relationships as networks; and the role administrators play within coach development in a National Sporting Organisation, in this case, Athletics New Zealand.

Vignettes

Amy – Coach Manager employed by Athletics New Zealand

A few years ago, Athletics NZ had been involved in a SPARC[1]-funded trial of a coach mentor programme. This piloted project was the catalyst for the publication of a supporting manual, *Coach Mentor Programme* (SPARC 2010). Despite having been in the trial, Athletics NZ had not, until recently, incorporated a formal mentor scheme for its development coaches. After being appointed, the Coach Manager for Athletics NZ, Amy, talked with a number of community sport coaches in the performance community and identified 'a gap' in the developmental pathway to becoming a high-performance coach. In an attempt to rectify this, she began to design a Coach Mentor scheme, drawing on the experience she had previously gained whilst working with Netball NZ and becoming familiar with the content of the *Coach Mentor Programme* manual (SPARC 2010). Her aim for the Athletics NZ Coach Mentor scheme was to help targeted performance coaches gain the skill sets required to become high-performance coaches. That way, if and when the athletes the coaches worked with became high-performance athletes, the coaches could continue to work with them instead of the athletes having to change coaches and break up what had been, to that point, a successful partnership.

The Athletics NZ Coach Mentoring scheme was structured in a similar guise to that promoted by Sport New Zealand (formerly SPARC) in that there was a master coach, mentor coach and mentee coach. When choosing the mentor coach, Amy used her existing networks to identify, and then invite, people who already had mentoring experience within the broad sporting arena. In the trial programme, the coach mentors engaged with the mentee coaches in an eight- to ten-hour generic (i.e. not sport-specific) programme. Prior to identifying and inviting the master coaches, Amy asked the mentee coaches to identify if they had a preferred master coach, because she recognised that they may know of a potential master coach working within the same sport and discipline with which they could have, or already had, a relationship. Amy also asked the mentee coaches if they had a preferred gender for their mentor or master coach.

Jill – A performance coach affiliated with Athletics New Zealand

A few months ago, I was contacted by Amy, the Coach Manager for Athletics NZ, to see if I would be interested in being part of a Coach Mentoring Programme. Apparently I will have both a mentor coach and a master coach.

Today I met my mentor for the first time. We have previously communicated via email and it was through email that she told me about herself, her coaching philosophy and what she considers to be her strengths and skills. In contrast to this, I have known my master coach for some years now as a consequence of working together to organise events and train our athletes. I am really pleased he agreed to be my master coach because I know he is extremely busy with his job outside of coaching.

I think the Coach Mentor Programme is an excellent initiative by Athletics NZ. I see it as a great opportunity for coaches like me to further develop my skills and really improve as a coach. You always feel a little nervous or apprehensive when you have someone observing your coaching but I am hoping to get some positive feedback, as well as an indication of areas that the coaches think I need to improve on. The challenge of being on this programme will be trying to organise the practical sessions so they suit everyone as both my mentor and master coaches are busy people. I know the programme is just beginning, but I am really happy with how it is progressing so far because I feel as if assistance is there if I need it and I am looking forward to working with both the mentor and master coaches. This is a great opportunity for coaches like me to improve their skills and learn from more experienced coaches. Also it is a great opportunity to develop contacts and coaching networks around the country.

Wendy – A high-performance coach affiliated with Athletics NZ

Wendy has been coaching Tim for more than 15 years. Four years ago, after Tim had once again performed well in a major international competition, a top coach in their discipline had invited them to participate in a training camp in his country. Despite being a little anxious, they accepted the invitation because they already had a good relationship with him as a consequence of meeting up on a regular basis over the years at international competitions. For the two of them, the experience of attending the training camp was 'massive' because it enabled Tim to have a world-class athlete as his training partner and it gave Wendy the opportunity to coach alongside another world-class coach.

When reflecting on the experience, Wendy said, 'we just took everything, pretended we knew nothing, and re-learnt everything, reset out goals, reset our path, where we wanted to go, how we were gonna do it and just did it'. From what she had experienced in her national coaching community, Wendy wasn't used to the level of collegiality that this coach demonstrated, so one night she asked him why was he willing to share his ideas with her and Tim. She was astounded when the coach told her, 'don't think it's one way traffic, 'cause we're actually learning from you too'. He went on to say that he saw it as his responsibility to develop both coaches and athletes, regardless of where they resided, in order to create better world competitions because 'there are not that many of us world class coaches . . . so when we get together we must share ideas'.

Analysis

Analysing Amy's vignette

The rationale Amy gave for designing the Athletics NZ Coach Mentor scheme was that she had identified a gap in the developmental pathway of coaches, especially between the performance and high-performance coaches. The challenge for Amy and other coach development administrators who wish to design seamless developmental pathways for coaches, is to design something that is practicable, effective and informed by current research. In a recent article published in the *Olympic Coach*, a publication of the US Olympic Committee, Trudel and Gilbert (2013) made suggestions as to how coach development administrators like Amy can facilitate coach expertise development. In doing so they remind, and encourage, coach administrators to be cognisant of the various contexts in which the coaches are working when they design, deliver or select material for coach development. Many coaches who are on the cusp of becoming high-performance coaches are not paid full-time, rather they coach 'for the love of the sport'.

Mentoring is only one strategy coaches use to develop their coaching practices and it is acknowledged that it, as well as other strategies, can occur via formal, informal and non-formal means. In summarising recent literature on how coaches learn to coach, Trudel and Gilbert (2013, p. 16) noted that:

> [c]oaches indicate that most of their learning comes from books or videos, exploring Internet-based resources, interacting with others, including mentors and the observation of other coaches (Cushion and Nelson 2013). It is also clear that experience as an athlete directly influences the way in which coaches approach their craft (Chesterfield, Potrac and Jones 2010; Young 2013). Recent studies indicate that both primary socialization (family) and secondary socialization (school, sport) strongly influence one's coaching philosophy (Callary, Werthner and Trudel 2011; Nash and Sproule 2009). Generally, coaches attribute most of their learning to personal experience. Accepting that each coach's developmental path is shaped by their unique set of personal experiences – sometimes referred to as a personal biography – reinforces that there is no 'one best way' to develop coaching expertise (Gilbert, Côté and Mallett 2006; Mallett, Rynne and Dickens 2013; Werthner and Trudel 2009).

In an earlier review, Nelson *et al.* (2006, p. 247) explored 'how sports coaches acquire the knowledge that underpins their professional practice', and concluded, amongst other things, that 'formalized (i.e. formal and non-formal) learning episodes were found to be relatively low-impact endeavours when compared to informal, self-directed modes of learning'. More recently, in the *International Journal of Sports Science and Coaching*, Mallett *et al.* (2009) provided insights on 'Formal vs Informal Coach Education', to which five colleagues responded, and the original authors summarised. This collection of papers highlighted some of the issues that surround the modes of learning used in coach education and development initiatives.

As mentioned, traditional models of mentoring have been based on a two-person relationship: that of the mentor and the mentee/protégé. For this relationship to be successful, the challenge is to interpret and incorporate the unique learning history of both the mentor and protégé to their shared advantage (Walker *et al.* 2002). Amy appeared to recognise the importance of the biography and relationship in a mentor-mentee arrangement because once the mentee coaches were accepted into the Coach Mentor programme, she asked them if they had any preferences as to whom they would like to be their mentor and master coaches.

Analysing Jill's vignette

Jill appreciated Amy asking her to identify a preferred master coach because it provided an opportunity to identify a coach with whom she already had an existing, trusting and productive working relationship. It is praiseworthy that Amy recognised Jill's biography and the importance of building upon existing mentor-mentee relationships and reflects Cox's (2012, p. 427) findings that trust is a key component of a 'reciprocal peer coaching' relationship, a phrase which could be used to describe a mentoring relationship. Cox suggested that unless the members within the relationship have an ability to 'form a trusting bond based on values and respect' (p. 434), the relationship will not survive. She goes on to say that successful peer coaching, which could be described as mentoring, may be facilitated when the bonds between those in the relationship have been established prior to any attempt to formalise the relationship.

As a performance coach, Jill was coaching some athletes Athletics NZ had identified as having potential to qualify to compete at the 2016 Rio de Janeiro Olympic Games. A few years ago Jill, along with athletes who had been identified as potential Olympians, was invited to a 'Young Olympians Camp' where she had met various performance and high-performance coaches. Subsequently, Jill began informally working with the coach she had identified as her potential master coach. This experience, and Jill's closing comment in the vignette section that being part of the Athletics NZ Coach Mentoring programme was 'also a great opportunity to develop contacts and coaching networks around the country', highlights the blurred boundaries between what constitutes mentoring and networking and illustrates the difficulty associated with discussing the concepts as if they were mutually exclusive and static. When Mallett *et al.* (2008) conducted a study with Australian League Football coaches, they found these coaches preferred a 'dynamic and evolving informal coaching network'. They called this preference a dynamic social network (DSN), explaining that the network was social and dynamic because the coaches, in the process of developing their coaching practice, sought experienced coaches, amongst others, to help them resolve problems they were experiencing with their coaching. Another characteristic of the DSN is that it can take years to work out who is involved in the DSN, and for what purpose(s); what is more, its membership continually evolves throughout the coaches' careers (Occhino *et al.* 2013). Not surprisingly, given the investment the coaches had made in building a DSN, 'those involved in the coaches' DSN tended to be people (confidantes) with whom the coaches had established trust and respect over a long period of time' (p. 93).

Analysing Wendy's vignette

Wendy's experience, as illustrated in the vignette, highlights the importance of context specificity, trust and the value of relationships in the mentoring process, and supports Cushion's (2006) view that mentoring is more than a functional and unproblematic practice which has a focus on 'how to' coach. An alternative reading of Wendy's story is that what she experienced with the other coach is not mentoring. Instead, it illustrates her utilising existing social networks to support her development. According to Wenger *et al.* (2011, p. 9), networks refer to 'the set of relationships, personal interactions, and connections among participants who have personal reasons to connect'. While Wendy and the other coach already had an existing relationship, the network appeared to evolve and become more substantive when both parties had personal reasons to connect more significantly with each other. The relationship between Wendy and the other coach could be explained as being an outcome of a DSN (Mallett *et al.* 2008).

While it is generally accepted that coaches learn from others, Occhino *et al.* (2013, p. 91) noted that the 'subtle and textured understandings of these interactions and the role they play in developing coaching knowledge is still in its infancy', hence their investigation into the dynamic social networks in high-performance football coaching. In their study with high-performance coaches, Occhino *et al.* (2013) noted that these coaches reported 'coaches of influence' were their 'most important source of information' (p. 90). This appears to have been the case with how Wendy initially positioned herself in a mentee role. However, it is possible that the other coach's comment that the learning did not only occur in one direction and that he was also learning from her, was a potential catalyst for Wendy to reflect upon and re-evaluate her role and responsibilities in their relationship. An outcome of Wendy's reflection could be that she shifts from viewing their relationship as a traditional or classical mentor-mentee arrangement to considering it to be a DSN.

Lessons learned . . . What could we add to the Mentor Pedagogy Toolbox?

Emanating from the findings of the vignettes, these lessons may have more relevance for those working in national governing bodies designing mentoring initiatives than for individual mentors.

In most countries, coach education/development programmes do not have the same historical or institutional support as teacher education programmes. The findings of the study suggest that coach education/development mentoring initiatives are generative when they were designed in ways that reflected classical *as well as* instrumental perspectives, instead of adopting mentoring practices used in teacher education, which are typically informed by 'classical' *or* 'instrumental' perspectives (Chambers *et al.* 2013).

One specific area of tension that has arisen in teacher education, that could also be an issue in coach education/development, is the relationship between domain-specific expertise and the ability to be a good mentor. In the findings it was not clear what formal training in mentoring the mentor and master coaches received (or indeed if they received any) prior to being assigned to the mentee coach. In addition, the findings highlighted that having a mentor coach from outside the sport may provide the mentee coach with opportunities, and the safety, to critically reflect, not only on his or her practices, but also on the 'taken-for-granted' cultural practices of the sport.

The environment in which the mentor/master–mentee relationship occurs has been identified as being an important factor on the openness and willingness of a practitioner to critically reflect on practices with which they are familiar (Handcock and Cassidy 2014). Unlike teaching, which has been defined as a profession for years, coaching is increasingly being acknowledged as a 'blended profession' (Lara-Bercial and Duffy 2013) where coaches work in various capacities, from 'part-time volunteers, to part-time, and full-time paid employees', and so their degree of involvement is not limited to only 'vary by nation, organization and sport' (p. 30). This state of affairs was highlighted in the findings and demonstrates the challenges coach developers/educators have when designing initiatives to support the development of coaches. Therefore any mentoring initiative needs to recognise, and be sympathetic to, the environment in which the coaches are working.

Key terms: network, elite coaches, administrators, coaching learning, track and field, interactions, sport coaches.

Note

1 Sport and Recreation New Zealand (SPARC) was the government agency dedicated to fostering a sport and recreation environment. In 2012 SPARC was replaced by Sport New Zealand (SNZ).

References

Bloom, G. A. 2013. Mentoring for Sport Coaches. In P. Potrac, W. Gilbert and J. Denison (Eds.) *Routledge Handbook of Sports Coaching*. London: Routledge, pp. 476–485.

Chambers, F. C., Herold, F., McFlynn, P., Brennan, D. A. and Armour, K. 2013. *Developing Effective Mentor Pedagogies to Support Pre-service Teacher Learning on Teaching Practice (Mentor-Ped): A Capability Maturity Model for Mentor Teachers [CM'T]*. Report for the Standing Conference on Teacher Education North and South (SCoTENS).

Cox, E. 2012. Individual and Organizational Trust in a Reciprocal Peer Coaching Context. *Mentoring and Tutoring: Partnership in Learning*, 20(3), 427–443.

Cushion, C. 2006. Mentoring: Harnessing the power of experience. In R. L. Jones (Ed.) *The Sports Coach as Educator: Re-conceptualising Sports Coaching*. London: Routledge, pp. 128–144.

Handcock, P. and Cassidy, T. 2014. Reflective Practice for Rugby Union Strength and Conditioning Coaches. *Strength and Conditioning Journal*, 36(1), 41–45.

Lara-Bercial, S. and Duffy, P. 2013. A Glimpse at the New International Sport Coaching Framework. *Olympic Coach Publication*, 24(2), 29–36.

Mallett, C., Rossi, T. and Tinning, R. 2008. *Knowledge Networks and Australian Football League Coach Development: People of Influence*. Paper presented at the Association Internationale des Écoles Supérieures d'Éducation Physique Conférence, Sapporo, Japan, January.

Mallett, C. J., Trudel, P., Lyle, J. and Rynne, S. B. 2009. Formal vs. Informal Coach Education. *International Journal of Sports Science and Coaching*, 4(3), 325–334.

Merriam, S. 1983. Mentors and Protégés: A critical review of the literature. *Adult Education Quarterly*, 33, 161–173.

Merrilees, J. (in progress). Women Becoming Elite Track and Field Coaches in New Zealand. Unpublished MPhEd manuscript, University of Otago, New Zealand.

Nelson, L. J., Cushion, C. J. and Potrac, P. 2006. Formal, Nonformal and Informal Coach Learning: A holistic conceptualisation. *International Journal of Sport Science and Coaching*, 1(3), 247–258.

Occhino, J., Mallett, C. and Rynne, S. 2013. Dynamic Social Networks in High Performance Football Coaching. *Physical Education and Sport Pedagogy*, 18(1), 90–102.

SPARC. 2010. *Coach Mentor Programme*. SPARC, Wellington: New Zealand.

Trudel, P. and Gilbert, W. 2013. The Role of Deliberate Practice in Becoming an Expert Coach – Part 3 – Creating Optimal Setting. *Olympic Coach Publication*, 24(2), 15–28.

Walker, W. O., Kelly, P. C. and Hume, R. F. 2002. Mentoring for the New Millennium. *Medicine Education*, 7(15). Accessed at http://www.med-ed-online.org/f0000038.htm. Accessed on 14th October 2013.

Wenger, E., Trayner, B. and de Laat, M. 2011. *Promoting and Assessing Value Creation in Communities and Networks: A Conceptual Framework*. Ruud de Moor Centrum, Open Universiteit, The Netherlands. Accessed at http://www.open.ou.nl/rslmlt/Wenger_Trayner_DeLaat_Value_creation.pdf. Accessed on 20th October 2013.

Resources

http://www.coach.ca/resource-library-s15478
http://www.ausport.gov.au/participating/coaches/education/onlinecoach
http://www.youthmentoring.org.nz/content/docs/GYM.1.pdf

16

MENTORING FOR SUCCESS IN SPORT COACHING

Chris Cushion

Overview

Coaches' encounters with experienced coaches are fundamental in shaping coaching practice. Mentoring in coaching is 'just happening'. In its current form mentoring remains largely unstructured, uneven in terms of quality and outcome, and uncritical in style, and it serves to reproduce the existing culture, power relations, and importantly, existing coaching practice. The purpose of this chapter is to unpack some of these issues and consider how mentoring can be embraced as a positive pedagogical process to mentor for success in coaching.

Vignette

Background

In research published over a decade ago (Cushion *et al.* 2003), I argued that learning within coaching happens over time and is mediated by experiences both in and out of coaching sessions. Given the limitations and 'low-impact' of formal coach education, informal learning through practice and engaging with other coaches remains the dominant mode of learning by coaches. Therefore, learning is shaped by interaction between coaches and athletes, discussing with and observing others, trying different ways, reflecting on practice, and negotiating the rules and guidelines set by the sport. I sought to show that coaches serve an 'apprenticeship of observation', first, being observers and recipients of coaching as performers, and second, as neophyte coaches or assistants working with and observing experienced coaches (Cushion *et al.* 2003). Indeed, in coaching, the 'popular wisdom among practicing professionals is that the knowledge they acquire from practice is far more useful than what they acquire from more formal forms of education' (Cervero 1992, p. 91). In developing as practitioners, coaches therefore are 'initiated into the traditions, habits, rules, cultures and practices of the community they join' (Merriam 1983, p. 37). The key to this initiation is the process of mentoring, formal and informal (Cushion *et al.* 2003); mentoring in coaching is very much in operation.

Methods

The arguments are drawn from recent critical reviews (e.g. Cushion *et al.* 2003; Cushion 2006; Trudel and Gilbert 2006) and systematic reviews (Cushion *et al.* 2010; Jones *et al.* 2009) of coach learning and mentoring in coaching.

Findings

As research into coach learning has evolved, other research such as Trudel and Gilbert (2006) has demonstrated that experience and interaction with others are inevitable phenomena in coaching. However, this type of learning deals with knowing, not knowledge (Sfard 1998), and control of the learning content is therefore impossible. Therefore, to ensure an even development for coaches, these experiences and interactions should be facilitated in some way (Cushion 2006; Werthner and Trudel 2006). One method of facilitation is through the *formal* use of mentors to identify and develop learning opportunities. Indeed, I have more recently argued that it would seem logical for coach education to harness the obvious power and influence of experience and other influential coaches to work toward sound coach development objectives (Cushion 2006). These lines of argument present a strong case for formalised mentoring programmes, and increasingly these are part of sport governing body awards and on-going continuous professional development (CPD) and support for coaching. It would seem that the relevance and efficacy of formal mentoring programmes is readily apparent, and evidence from other practice fields (e.g. health care, education) lends weight to this.

However, mentoring, whether formal or informal, must contribute to the transformation of coaches' experience into knowledge and expertise. A recent review of coach development and learning (Cushion *et al.* 2010) argued that the existing mentoring literature, by and large, considers mentoring in a functional, positive and unproblematic way, with 'how-to' guides extolling the benefits of mentoring, of which there would seem to be many. Coaching, as a specific practice domain, has many challenges related to professional development; these are due to the limitations of current formal provision, the lack of an overarching coach education structure, and issues around volunteerism, which combine to encourage a negotiated and individualised learning curriculum for coaches (Cushion *et al.* 2010). This curriculum is problematic, often inclusive of underlying power relations whilst promoting and reinforcing certain ideological interpretations of knowledge and practice. It is against this backdrop that mentoring operates.

Analysis

Issues with mentoring – formalising the process

In coaching, practice leads theory. Informal mentoring is already pervasive, occurring on a daily basis and impacting practice (e.g. Bloom *et al.* 1998; Cushion *et al.*

2003). Therefore, in coaching, formalising the process has to be the first step. This will underpin the role of the mentor, the process of mentoring, and the development of mentoring relationships. Formalising develops consistency and interaction, and ultimately effectiveness, as well as defining the mentor's remit (Wright and Smith 2000). Mentoring is a type of learning practice where formal and informal learning meet (Colley et al. 2003). Therefore, increasing formalisation of mentoring addresses a practice in coaching that is inherently informal.

However, there are complex issues surrounding formalisation. 'Natural' mentoring (Colley et al. 2003) is where a mentor is sought within a community (e.g. Bloom et al. 1998; Jones et al. 2009). This process is often unplanned but intentional, with the mentee controlling the agenda and interactions. This mode of informal mentoring is currently dominant in coaching and is the rationale for the introduction of planned formal mentoring programmes (Cushion 2006; Jones et al. 2009). This type of formalised mentoring is known as 'engagement' mentoring (Colley 2001), and takes place within an institutional framework that is shaped by policy makers and professional practitioners, and has a more or less overt compulsion to participate, a narrow frame of outcomes and a high level of recording and monitoring. Importantly, mentors are often higher-status individuals. Engagement-mentoring relationships are marked by social distance, competing value systems and more intense power differentials than informal mentoring. Indeed, Colley et al. (2003) strike a cautionary note identifying problems with formalising as 'fervour without infrastructure'. This resonates in coaching as there remains a perception of mentoring as inherently informal, resulting in minimal training and support for mentors; mentoring will just 'happen' with unthinking assumptions that transference is straightforward. However, formalising mentoring in coaching has exposed its frailty and introduced external interests pursued by dominant groupings (Cushion et al. 2010; Jones et al. 2009). In reality, planned and formalised programmes change the mentoring process and this needs to be understood fully if coaching is to engage adequately and meaningfully with mentoring.

Does mentoring work?

The literature frequently offers theories and ideas 'for' mentoring, rather than evidence 'of' mentoring (cf. Cushion 2006). For example, Ehrich et al. (2004) reviewed 300 articles across business, education and medicine and found descriptive studies extolling the value of mentoring. Similarly, Jones et al. (2009), in considering mentoring in coaching, found that some mentoring programmes were evaluated while some were not. Very often evaluations consist simply of testimonials and opinions, or are cross-sectional and/or self-report studies. Mentoring is perceived as important but there seems little evidence to support this. Moreover, systematic reviews in nursing (Dorsey and Baker 2004) and business (Underhill 2006) reported a lack of valid evidence for the effectiveness of mentoring. Indeed, many of the positive claims about mentoring are largely unfounded. Colley et al. (2003, p. 1) concluded that 'existing research evidence scarcely justifies [mentoring's] use on such a massive scale, [while] the movement has not yet developed a sound theoretical base to underpin policy or practice'. Despite these shortcomings there remains overwhelming support for mentoring in coaching (e.g. Bloom *et al.* 1998; Cushion *et al.* 2003; Cushion 2006; Gilbert and Trudel 2004a, 2004b).

Developing practice

Meaningful learning and development for coaches will not occur simply by being involved. Consequently, mentoring must be part of a framework through which coaches construct knowledge. Because mentoring currently 'just happens', there must be conditions that make the process more or less successful. Understanding these conditions has obvious benefits to any mentoring programme and it is to these conditions that the chapter now turns.

Power

Coaching is a social structure involving power relations, and the way power is exercised can empower or disempower mentoring. Jones *et al.* (2009) identify 'toxic mentoring' with asymmetric power relationships shaping mentoring experiences and learning. Coaching is structured in ways that result in unequal access to, and major variations in, the quality and type of learning; the power the mentor may wield over a mentee is rarely discussed or recognised. Mentors may have too much control, thus stifling the creation and reflection upon knowledge. Mentors, either implicitly or explicitly, may be producing and passing on organisational and social norms without reflecting upon the appropriateness of the process. In coaching, mentors are instrumental in defining what is necessary knowledge, what counts as knowledge, tacit behaviours, attitudes and acceptable behaviour. Mentors 'choose' between different views of what knowledge is essential for practice. This is a form of social editing, where some approaches are eliminated and others promoted. The mentoring process becomes a political act, intimately linked with power and control over what constitutes legitimate knowledge and who holds that knowledge (Cushion *et al.* 2003).

Relationships

Given sport and coaching's traditions and cultures, there is a tension between continuity and displacement impacting mentoring relationships, and their success or failure. Process and role construct the nature of the mentoring relationship and success of learning within mentoring will be dependent upon the quality of the relationship. A strong co-operative relationship increases accountability for learning effectively, and seeking new knowledge. Matching mentor and mentee therefore is key. Relationships, carefully cultivated and constructed within the goals and objectives of the programme, ensure the success of the process. Importantly, this coming together cannot be assumed but must be developed. This ensures that mentors provide a 'safe' environment, where experiences are authenticated by links to real-world activities, ensuring that knowledge acquired is reinterpreted and developed through practice. Therefore, it is imperative that potential mentors and mentees are matched carefully, not simply thrown together. Mentors can be persons with more experience, or they may be peers. Regardless of who assumes the role, how this relationship is formed usually determines the nature of the relationship, and in coaching it is imperative for mentors to have established the appropriate position in the social field, and amount and mix of social, cultural and symbolic capital (Cushion *et al.* 2003). The mentor would also have to hold 'expert power' (French and Raven 1959) which is based not only on the knowledge of the mentor, but upon coach perceptions regarding that knowledge.

Effective mentors possess rich and sophisticated content, curricular and pedagogical knowledge and have strong listening and communication skills that can support, motivate and emotionally engage the mentee (Stroot *et al.* 1998). Most mentors, however, have not received formal training and there is often an inconsistency in preparatory courses (Podsen and Denmark 2000), increasing the likelihood that the relationship will not achieve its full promise. Chapters 10, 17 and 20 in this volume consider mentor training in more detail.

Lastly, Ehrich *et al.* (2004) pull together some common issues negatively impacting mentoring relationships and their effectiveness:

- Lack of time and training,
- Personal or professional compatibility,
- Undesirable attitudes or behaviours, and
- Additional unnoticed workloads.

Mentees were concerned with a lack of mentor interest and training, as well as problematic behaviour (e.g. overly critical, defensive). As a result, Ehrich *et al.* (2004, p. 533) state that 'mentoring is a highly complex dynamic and interpersonal relationship that requires at the very least, time, interest and commitment . . . and strong support from leaders responsible for overseeing programmes'.

Process

A common misconception of mentoring is to try and 'extract' the learning for the mentee post-practice, thus presenting it back in a helpful way with insights previously unrecognised (Loughran 2002). Instead, successful mentoring assists the mentee to become the focus, and to develop their abilities to analyse and develop meaning from key experiences. What is learned and how it is learned, as a result of mentoring, is as important as mentoring itself. Through the development of knowledge and understanding of the practice setting and the ability to recognise and respond to such knowledge, mentoring becomes responsive to the needs, issues and concerns that shape practice (ibid.). The knowledge developed may be the same, but the process is very different, as it has meaning for the mentee because they have ownership and links to their own experience. Mentoring processes should assist the mentee to recognise, develop and articulate knowledge about practice. This process is a powerful way of informing and challenging practice as it makes the tacit explicit, meaningful and useful. Therefore, the mentoring process has to have the ability to frame and re-frame the practice setting, to develop and respond to this framing through action so that practitioners' wisdom-in-action is enhanced, and to encourage an articulation of professional knowledge. Therefore, effective learning as a result of mentoring is situated in context, where new knowledge and skills are used and where individuals construct meaning for themselves but within a context of interaction with others. This understanding leads towards the evolution of a mentoring process and a clearer understanding of the role of the mentor.

Role

Simply copying the behaviours of the mentor results in imitation or cloning that is devoid of insight and initiative. By the same token, mentees have a perception of their needs and of the world around them and as such are not empty vessels waiting to be filled with professional dogma. However, the mentoring literature can be benign and simplistic, lacking in critical depth when it characterises the mentor as simply a supporter and provider of information, an articulator of practical knowledge. The role of the mentor is clearly greater than this. Mentors do model problem-solving strategies and provide guidance to approximate strategies but encourage learners to articulate *their* thought processes. Indeed, mentoring involves a 'capacity to foster an inquiring stance' (Field and Field 1994, p. 67), which has the potential to inform insightful learning, particularly in relation to understanding the holistic and complex nature of coaching.

Mentoring is crucial for coaches to explore personal dimensions and related anxieties and who have to deal with issues of marginality, isolation, role conflict, reality shock and the washout effect (Cushion *et al.* 2003). Mentoring is a personalised and relatively systematic way to be socialised into a culture, and cultural competence remains important in coaching settings (ibid.). However, this form of socialisation can be constraining if it involves a limited repertoire of practice views as well as expectations. Other aspects of the mentor's role relate directly to practice and can include providing guidance about coaching resources; assisting with the preparation and delivery of coaching sessions; guiding the coach's practical coaching; and indicating alternative appropriate strategies within a supportive framework. Mentors should also systematically challenge coaches with the intention of forcing them to constantly evaluate their whole understanding of the coaching role and their performance within it. A key part of the mentor's role is to de-mystify the coaching process and provide authentic, experiential learning opportunities, thus supplying coaches with the confidence that they can survive and thrive in a complex environment.

Conclusion

Coaching and learning to coach are complex practices in a social world. As a result, there is no such thing as one kind of learner, one learning goal, one way to learn or one setting in which learning takes place. While the 'principles of coaching' may remain the same, different contexts place different demands on the coach and athlete and, therefore, impact learning. Coaching still has unexamined assumptions about the existence and process of learning, and these implicit assumptions exist because the learning has its roots in practices that pre-date the establishment of structured learning. This is the backdrop against which mentoring sits in coaching where individual, ideological, institutional, cultural and social issues challenge the establishing of collaboration to the level required for effective and sustained mentoring practice. This chapter has gone some way to unpacking some of these issues and offered potential routes for understanding and supporting the sustained development of mentoring in coaching. As mentoring is developed in coaching, it is imperative that the literature does more than present arguments *for*, instead offering evidence *of*, as the current research falls short of robust evaluation, and there is limited literature explicitly addressing the impact of mentoring.

Lessons learned . . . What could we add to the Mentor Pedagogy Toolbox?

- **Impact.** While much literature extols the virtues of mentoring, little evidence exists connecting it to changes in practice. Impact and evaluation should be integral considerations to mentoring programmes.
- **Process.** Mentoring is assumed to be a benign and exclusively positive experience. Yet it exists in distinct cultures and contexts replete with power relationships. Ownership and purpose of the process need to be considered.
- **Relationships.** Relationships need to be cultivated and constructed, and should not be thrown together.
- **Role.** The mentor's role should be to provide and support authentic learning experiences.
- **Training.** Privileging technocratic rationality, providing 'tool boxes' or 'tricks of the trade' as professional knowledge is additive, grafting on new knowledge to existing understandings. It leaves contextual and cultural norms unexamined and unchallenged. Mentoring and its training should be critical and transformative.

Key terms: mentoring, coaching, mentoring process, mentoring relationships, role, relationships, training, impact.

References

Bloom, G. A., Durand-Bush, N., Schinke, R. and Salmela, J. H. 1998. The importance of mentoring in the development of coaches and athletes. *International Journal of Sport Psychology*, 29, 267–281.

Cervero, R. M. 1992. Professional practice, learning, and continuing education: an integrated perspective. *International Journal of Lifelong Education*, 11(2), 91–101.

Colley, H. 2001. *Unravelling myths of mentor: power dynamics of mentoring relationships with 'disaffected' young people.* Unpublished PhD thesis, Manchester Metropolitan University.

Colley, H., Hodkinson, P. and Malcolm, J. 2003. *Informality and formality in learning: a report for the learning skills research centre*. London: Learning and Skills Research Centre.

Cushion, C. J. 2006. Mentoring: harnessing the power of experience. In R. Jones (Ed.) *The sports coach as educator: re-conceptualising sports coaching*. London: Routledge, pp. 128–144.

Cushion, C. J., Nelson, L., Armour, K., Lyle, J., Jones R. L., Sandford, R. and O'Callaghan, C. 2010. *Coach learning and development: a review of literature*. Leeds: Sports Coach UK.

Cushion, C. J., Armour, K. M. and Jones, R. L. 2003. Coach education and continuing professional development: experience and learning to coach. *Quest*, 55, 215–230.

Dorsey, L. E. and Baker, C. M. 2004. Mentoring undergraduate nursing students: assessing the state of the science. *Nurse Educator*, 29(6), 260–265.

Ehrich, L., Hansford, B. and Tennent, L. 2004. Formal mentoring programs in education and other professions: a review of the literature. *Educational Administration Quarterly*, 40(4), 518–540.

Field, B. and Field, T. 1994. *Teachers as mentors: a practical guide*. London: The Palmer Press.

French Jr, J. R. P. and Raven, B. 1959. The bases of social power. In D. Cartwright (Ed.) *Studies in social power*. Ann Arbor: University of Michigan Press, pp. 150–167.

Gilbert, W. D. and Trudel, P. 2004a. Role of the coach: how model youth team sport coaches frame their roles. *The Sport Psychologist*, 18, 21–43.

Gilbert, W. D. and Trudel, P. 2004b. Analysis of coaching science research published from 1970–2001. *Research Quarterly for Exercise and Sport*, 75, 388–399.

Jones, R. L., Harris, R. A. and Miles, A. 2009. Mentoring in sports coaching: a review of the literature. *Physical Education and Sport Pedagogy*, 14(3), 267–284.

Loughran, J. J. 2002. Effective reflective practice: in search of meaning in learning about teaching. *Journal of Teacher Education*, 53(1), 33–43.

Merriam, S. 1983. Mentors and protégés: a critical review of the literature. *Adult Education Quarterly*, 33, 161–173.

Podsen, I. J. and Denmark, V. M. 2000. *Coaching and mentoring: first-year and student teachers*. Larchmont, NY: Eye on Education.

Sfard, A. 1998. On two metaphors for learning and the dangers of choosing just one. *Educational Researcher*, 27, 4–13.

Stroot, S., Keil, V., Stedman, P., Lohr, L., Faust, R., Schincariol-Randall, L., Sullivan, A., Czerniak, G., Kuchcinski, J., Orel, N. and Richter, M. 1998. *Peer assistance and review guidebook: developmental stages of teachers*. Columbus, OH: Ohio Department of Education.

Trudel, P. and Gilbert, W. 2006. Coaching and coach education. In D. Kirk, D. Macdonald and M. O'Sullivan (Eds.) *The handbook of physical education*. London: Sage Publications, pp. 516–539.

Underhill C. M. 2006. The effectiveness of mentoring programs in corporate settings: a meta-analytical review of the literature. *Journal of Vocational Behavior*, 68, 292–307.

Werthner, P. and Trudel, P. 2006. A new theoretical perspective for understanding how coaches learn to coach. *The Sport Psychologist*, 20, 198–212.

Wright, S. C. and Smith, D. E. 2000. A case for formalised mentoring. *Quest*, 52, 200–213.

Resources

Cushion, C. J., Nelson, L., Armour, K., Lyle, J., Jones R. L., Sandford, R. and O'Callaghan, C. 2010. *Coach learning and development: a review of literature*. Leeds: Sports Coach UK.

Jones, R. L., Harris, R. A. and Miles, A. 2009. Mentoring in sports coaching: a review of the literature. *Physical Education and Sport Pedagogy*, 14(3), 267–284.

17

TRAINING COACHES AS MENTORS

Mark Griffiths

Overview

Educational systems in many countries have embraced the concept of learning communities because of their systematic and constructive effect on learning (Talbert 2009). The foundations of such a collaborative approach to learning are located in the belief that participants construct new knowledge through learning conversations with colleagues (Lieberman and Miller 2008). It is in this context that many sports organisations conceive the mentoring role. In learning communities, mentors are transfer agents charged with maintaining and transmitting organisational cohesiveness and continuity, particularly through periods of change (Kerka 1998). Mentors are learning facilitators who create challenging, collaborative and transforming environments by supporting and assisting the learning process. In both function and process, such descriptions point to the pedagogical (teaching and learning) competencies of effective mentors beyond the accumulation of just experience. Yet despite this demanding pedagogical role, coach mentors are often given little guidance beyond an initial introductory 'workshop'. As Karcher *et al.* (2010) astutely observe: 'mentors often find themselves responding to their mentee's requests for activity ideas with something like, "I dunno, what do you wanna do?"' (p. 52).

Vignette

Background

This chapter reports on a study that examined how a large sports organisation in the UK attempted to construct a learning community in order to influence the learning culture of the coaching workforce. The organisation set out to move the structure of their professional development efforts towards a culture of collaborative work that promised a more sustainable, authentic and relevant continuous professional development (CPD) provision. Mentoring (and mentors) was identified as the agent of change. In the proceeding sections, the skills required for the mentoring role are examined and the implications for training addressed. It is argued that generating a better understanding of *how* mentors are prepared in meeting the challenges of the mentoring process is an important step in the design of effective professional development provision for the wider coaching workforce.

The research question which underpinned this study was:

> What skills and competencies do mentors need to facilitate coach learning, and how should sports organisations recruit and train coaches for this role?

In this study, mentors were recruited from the existing coaching workforce and employed in a full-time capacity based on criteria which included experience, depth of knowledge and an ability to work in a collaborative environment. The aim of the programme, and the work of mentors, was to create a sustainable network of professional learning that supported coaches' growth.

Methods

Drawing on a mixed-methods research design (i.e. qualitative data was used to help explain quantitative results), the study was divided into two phases and conducted over a twelve-month period. Phase one involved the use of an electronic survey ($n = 225$) in order to gain a broad understanding of how participating coaches conceived the programme. One hundred and ten coaches (48.8 per cent response rate) completed the survey. Phase two involved individual interviews and focus groups with mentors ($n = 8$) and mentees ($n = 26$). Participants were identified using purposeful and snowballing sampling. Interviews were conducted using a semi-structured interview schedule which allowed for some flexibility based on the different roles held by participants. Interviews were then transcribed verbatim and data analysed thematically drawing on the procedures described in Charmaz's (2006) constructivist grounded theory method.

Findings

Data suggested that the programme had created a dynamic and supportive learning environment. The construction of a network of coach mentors was particularly valued because these relationships offered accessibility to relevant sport-specific knowledge. The main findings from the study were that

- mentoring was primarily valued as a way of accessing professional knowledge;
- observational feedback was highly valued by coaches;
- mentoring outcomes included an increase in coaches' self-efficacy; and
- the programme engendered a coaching identity and developed a sense of shared ownership and commitment from the group.

There was an overwhelming positive response from coaches concerning the impact of the programme on their coaching (e.g. changes in practice in terms of content). In the survey, 94 per cent of coaches reported that their coaching had improved as a consequence of the programme. There was consensus that mentors would act as a central resource and would provide knowledge about drills, technical skills, organisation, and performance analysis. As one coach observed:

> I don't see how a mentor can improve my coaching unless he has a greater knowledge of the event than me. I'm an experienced coach, involved for many years.
>
> *Coach*

Mentors also acknowledged subject knowledge as an important component of a mentor's skill set. Subject knowledge gave the mentor credibility. In the majority of interviews, knowledge exchange was the most referenced benefit of the programme:

> I think subject knowledge is absolutely vital . . . for credibility you must have the ability to exchange knowledge, therefore you must have subject knowledge; I think the majority [of mentors] have been chosen because of their raised knowledge and definitely for their competence.
>
> *Mentor*

It became evident that the programme was primarily valued as an opportunity to access and exchange sport-specific knowledge. Yet, at the same time, participation had created a powerful group identity that had fostered a sense of collegiality and reciprocity in supporting coach learning:

> The culture of coaching has always been insular and protective with coaches being reluctant to share knowledge with each other. These barriers are being broken down as a result of the programme. I've seen it. It's flourishing . . . the camaraderie.
>
> *Coach*

It was interesting to gather how mentors conceived their role in the context of the organisation. It was evident that mentors were challenged with an entrenched and sometimes suspicious learning culture:

> I just thought it was a wonderful way to proceed [mentoring] . . . . the culture a few years ago was not good. And coaches were very isolated from each other and very antagonistic towards each other, they were resentful.
>
> *Mentor*

Adult learners bring with them an established learning biography to all learning situations. An individual's learning biography is an accumulation of their learning experiences, and has to be challenged if change is to be a realistic outcome of any educational activity, such as mentoring (Trudel *et al.* 2010). Evidence from this study suggested that a significant number of coaches were rethinking how they approached their practices (in terms of content and delivery), and in some cases, had coaching beliefs challenged. That said, the overwhelming approach to mentoring in this programme is perhaps best summed up in the following extract:

> I'm not sure I know what mentoring is, all I know is that he knows more than me and I want that knowledge.
>
> *Coach*

Conclusion

Participants valued the social and interactional opportunities afforded by the programme, and particularly coaching conversations with mentors and other practitioners, which were enthusiastically consumed. Such conversations were viewed both as professional learning and, at the same time, as a form of social modelling. Nonetheless, and despite the perceived impact of the programme on coaches' subject knowledge, it was difficult to establish causality between the mentoring role and any form of generative change. Rather, reported changes appeared to be the outcome of increased collaborative networking opportunities rather than the direct instructional role of mentors. An understanding of *how* mentors facilitate behavioural change through the interplay of the mentoring process was not clearly evident.

Analysis

Mentoring, as a source of learning, continues to challenge both researchers and organisations, particularly in the context of complex and shifting organisational structures where mentoring is sometimes regarded as a solution to all professional development needs (Browne-Ferrigno and Muth 2004). Coaches learn some things from experience, but the ability to give meaning to an experience in a planned and systematic way can create a vital link between tacit knowledge and the professional knowledge that is embedded in sports organisations. However, reflection is limited by a coach's own knowledge, suggesting that an opportunity to share experiences would offer opportunities to develop a more effective knowledge base. In the coaching literature, the ability of the coach to integrate and transform knowledge and skills from existing formal continuous professional development (CPD) programmes to the context of practice has been questioned (Cassidy *et al.* 2004). The place of practice-specific conversations with a skilled mentor, or mentors, in a supportive community of like-minded coaches may go some way towards bridging this perceived limitation. With this in mind, the mentor's role, as a learning facilitator, is to make 'thinking visible' (Collins *et al.* 1991, p. 1) in promoting coach learning.

Mentor: A learning facilitator

Although mentoring as a learning strategy has been criticised for being intrinsically ambiguous and open to interpretation (Cushion 2006), there appears to be a consensus that mentoring interactions should facilitate some form of change (Gilles and Wilson 2004). Mentoring as a co-learning activity involves mentors and mentees exchanging ideas and information and, in so doing, constructing new knowledge (e.g. organisational knowledge and personal knowledge). Mentors, as facilitators of change, assist the novice in navigating the complexities of practice (Parsloe and Wray 2000). It is interesting, therefore, to consider how mentor training historically has been dominated by a focus on phases, behaviour and structures (Schunk and Mullen 2013). Examples include (but are not limited to) building effective relationships, resolving difficulties, goal planning, effective communication and role construction. As Cushion (2006) has pointed out, despite the enthusiastic application of mentoring as a learning strategy, coach mentoring remains a highly descriptive concept and is often treated in a functional and highly unproblematic way.

This chapter doesn't offer a prescriptive account of mentor training *per se*. Different organisational views, with different situational requirements, mean mentoring will be contested in terms of function and process (Billett 2003). Indeed, how an occupation conceives the mentoring role will influence the aims and content of training opportunities. It might be more appropriate to consider a mentoring paradigm (i.e. a belief system that identifies what is significant, legitimate and tenable) from which stakeholders might then construct a mentoring programme for a particular cultural setting.

A mentoring paradigm for coaching

There is a consensus in the literature about the complex nature of coaching, the interpersonal relationship between coach and athlete, and the coach's pivotal role in the development of talent (Gilbert and Trudel 2005). Moreover, an emerging body of work, drawn from sociological and pedagogical theories, has described how coaches operate in a socially dynamic and educational environment (Cassidy *et al.* 2004; Jones 2006). Alongside these descriptions of coaching function, role and context, Lyle (2002) described coaching as a process-driven activity: one in which rather than representing coaching as the aggregation of isolated training activities, coaching should be understood as a series of integrated activities and interventions designed to improve performance. These selected descriptions of coaching are significant in their marked contrast to traditional approaches where coaches were portrayed as 'technicians' who transferred coaching knowledge in an unproblematic way (Potrac *et al.* 2002). Unsurprisingly, coach mentoring programmes (historically) have reflected these conceptions of coaching, conceiving the mentoring relationship in terms of information transmission (Griffiths and Armour 2012). Put another way, and reflecting the findings from the study described in this chapter, the currency of mentoring was the exchange of sport-specific knowledge (e.g. drills). The implications of this work in the context of mentor training are threefold:

1. Mentoring should be conceived as a learning strategy, which is socially constructed (mentoring is a two-way process), experiential and grounded in the practices of coaches' context. Beyond the accumulation of sport-specific

knowledge, mentors should support coaches' function in challenging, collaborative and transformative learning environments.

2. Mentors should consider the coach/mentor relationship (individual), mentoring process (activity) and coaching context (environment). The value of using a situated framework in this way is that mentors are presented with a triad of relationships in examining the mentoring processes relevant to the coaching context.

3. Coach mentor training should be cautious in 'borrowing' from occupations such as business and education, where the occupational workforce is full time and remunerated. Such an approach is problematic with the coaching workforce in most countries, which is heavily reliant on volunteerism.

Abraham and Collins' (1998) work on the nature of coaching knowledge, and its implications for the development of coaching expertise, is helpful in considering a mentoring paradigm for coaching. Adopting a cognitive psychological perspective (the study of mental processes – learning), Abraham and Collins (ibid.) suggested that expert coaches are characterised by their declarative and procedural knowledge, and their capacity to organize this knowledge. The expert coach, they argue, is faced with a number of constraints to which solutions must be provided through a combination of deductive reasoning and the cognitive organisation of knowledge. Implications for coach mentoring programmes are clear:

> Expertise is the knowledge of making correct decisions within the constraints of the session. Thus coaching is not a behaviour to be copied but a cognitive skill to be taught.
>
> *Abraham and Collins 1998, p. 68*

It is clear from Abraham and Collins' account (ibid.) that expert coaches, alongside expert practitioners in other fields, search for new knowledge, which they apply creatively to unique and novel situations. Moreover, they share knowledge, make better use of knowledge, and have extensive pedagogical content knowledge, including deep representations of subject matter knowledge (Bereiter and Scardamalia 1993; Housner and French 1994). Expert coaches, therefore, have better problem-solving strategies, better adaptation and modification goals for diverse learners, better skills for improvisation, better decision-making and greater sensitivity to context.

From these descriptions of expert coaches, it is essential that mentor training should be clear about the assumptions around learning that inform it, and what the objectives of any formalised programme might be. For instance, an indication of a healthy and productive mentoring relationship is one in which learning progression is palpable, impact on practice is evident, and the novice moves from high dependence to autonomy and self-reliance (Gilles and Wilson 2004). It could be argued that a key function of mentoring in coach development is to help coaches develop their cognitive skills in progressing towards an increasingly autonomous/ expert position. For instance, they should support and develop the novice coach's ability to contextualise problems, underpin their actions by reference to theoretical concepts and professional knowledge, and have rich and well-organised mental networks. It might be more valuable, therefore, to conceptualise the mentor as a 'cognitive coach' (Barnett 1995), where the mentor is a catalyst for developing knowledge in reflective thinking, cognitive development and problem-solving. The implications of such a conceptual position is that the mentor is a reflective practitioner who is an expert problem-solver capable of helping novices to develop the same capacities, and, in so doing, helps them to become autonomous and independent problem-solvers.

This section has attempted to highlight the requisite skills needed by both mentor and coach in optimising the learning potential of mentoring. Actions, such as managing transitions (i.e. using knowledge from an occupational workplace in the coaching environment) and decision making, which may be familiar to the mentor, will need to be made explicit to the coach (Gilles and Wilson 2004). Such lucidity and transparency in communicating a reflexive account (a form of social knowledge production) of personal practice may not come easily to the mentor. At the very least, it would seem that such aptitude requires practice because as Knowles *et al.* (2006) have argued, 'the quality of the mentor will often determine the quality of the experience' (p. 175). Moreover, if mentoring is a co-learning activity, then both mentors and mentees must be part of the planning process. Typically, each group is prepared and supported initially in separate preparation programmes; it might be suggested that when appropriate, both groups are combined to negotiate and support mentoring, thereby creating an emerging 'learning community' (Wenger 1998).

Lessons learned . . . What could we add to the Mentor Pedagogy Toolbox?

- The purpose of mentoring should be to help the coach develop their cognitive skills in progressing towards an increasingly autonomous and expert position.
- Mentors (and organisations) should conceive the role in terms of developing coaches' knowledge in reflective thinking, cognitive development, and problem-solving (Schunk and Mullen 2013).
- In translating these ideas into design, a cognitive approach to mentor training would integrate the following:

  o **Content.** Mentors need support in constructing a mentoring knowledge base, for example, learning strategies (e.g. interactions between mentor and coach might be active, social and creative); domain knowledge (e.g. building relationships, resolving difficulties, encouraging critical reflection); heuristics strategies ('tricks of the trade').

  o **Pedagogy.** Mentors need to understand factors that will facilitate coach learning, for example, the use of scaffolding (e.g. direction); conversations that are relevant and authentic to practice; reasoning/problem solving; critical reflection.

○ **Sequencing.** Mentors should be mindful in matching coaches' competencies and skills with mentoring tasks, for example, identifying a mentoring model that would underpin the mentoring process (e.g. apprenticeship model, competency model, reflective practitioner model).

- It is important to consider how the impact of the mentoring relationship might be captured. For example, Costa and Garmston (1994), suggested the following 'checklist' in capturing how participants proceed to use their new knowledge:

  ○ Increased self-efficacy
  ○ Addressing a multiplicity of challenges
  ○ Identifying gaps in domains of knowledge
  ○ Re-visiting beliefs, values and actions
  ○ Adopting an interdependent approach in working with others in seeking solutions

- Training strategies should support mentors in creating effective relationships, underpinned by contemporary learning theories. Evidence suggests this would secure the cognitive, behavioural, motivational and affective processes that impact the outcomes claimed on behalf of mentoring.

Key terms: learning community, pedagogy, paradigm, cognitive.

References

Abraham, A. and Collins, D. 1998. Examining and extending research in coach development. *Quest*, 50, 59–79.

Barnett, B. 1995. Developing reflection and expertise: can mentors make the difference? *Journal of Educational Administration*, 33(5), 45–59.

Bereiter, C. and Scardamalia, M. 1993. *Surpassing Ourselves: An inquiry into the nature and implications of expertise*. Chicago: Open Court Publishing Company.

Billett, S. 2003. Workplace mentors: demands and benefits. *Journal of Workplace Learning*, 15(3), 105–113.

Browne-Ferrigno, T. and Muth, R. 2004. Leadership mentoring in clinical practice: role socialization, professional development, and capacity building. *Educational Administration Quarterly*, 40(4), 468–494.

Cassidy, T., Jones, R. and Potrac, P. 2004. *Understanding Sports Coaching: The social, cultural and pedagogical foundations of coaching practice*. Abingdon: Routledge.

Charmaz, K. 2006. *Constructing Grounded Theory: A practical guide through qualitative analysis*. Thousand Oaks: Sage Publications.

Collins, A., Brown, J. S. and Holum, A. 1991. Cognitive apprenticeship: making thinking visible. *American Educator*, 6(11), 38–46.

Costa, A. L. and Garmston, R. J. 1994. *Cognitive Coaching: A foundation for Renaissance schools*. Second edition. Norwood, MA: Christopher-Gordon Publishers, Inc.

Cushion, C. 2006. Mentoring: harnessing the power of experience. In R. L. Jones (Ed.) *The Sports Coach as Educator: Re-conceptualising sports coaching*. Routledge.

Gilbert, W. D. and Trudel, P. 2005. Learning to coach through experience: conditions that influence reflection. *Physical Educator*, 62(1), 32–43.

Griffiths, M. and Armour, K. 2012. Mentoring as a formalized learning strategy with community sports volunteers. *Mentoring and Tutoring: Partnership in Learning*, 20(1), 151–173.

Gilles, C. and Wilson, J. 2004. Receiving as well as giving: mentors' perceptions of their professional development in one teacher induction program. *Mentoring and Tutoring*, 12(1), 87–106.

Housner, L. D. and French, K. E. 1994. Future directions for research on expertise in learning, performance, and instruction in sport and physical activity. *Quest*, 46(2), 241–246.

Jones, R. L. 2006. *The Sports Coach as Educator: Re-conceptualising sports coaching*. London: Routledge.

Karcher, M. J., Herrera, C. and Hansen, K. 2010. "I dunno, what do you wanna do?" Testing a framework to guide mentor training and activity selection. *New Directions for Youth Development*, 126, 51–69.

Kerka, S. 1998. *New perspectives on mentoring*. Eric Digest No 194.

Knowles, Z., Tyler, G., Gilbourne, D. and Eubank. M. 2006. Reflecting on reflection: exploring the practice of sports coaching graduates. *Reflective Practice*, 7(2), 163–179.

Lieberman, A. and Miller, L. 2008. *Teachers in Professional Communities*. New York: Teachers College Press.

Lyle J. 2002. *Sports Coaching Concepts: A framework for coaches' behaviour*. London: Routledge.

Parsloe, E. and Wray, M. 2000. *Coaching and Mentoring: Practical methods to improve learning*. London: Kogan Page.

Potrac, P., Jones, R. and Armour, K. 2002. 'It's all about getting respect': the coaching behaviours of an expert English soccer coach. *Sport, Education and Society*, 7(2), 183–202.

Schunk, D. H. and Mullen, C. A. 2013. Toward a conceptual model of mentoring research: integration with self-regulated learning. *Educational Psychology Review*, 25(3), 361–389.

Talbert, J. E. 2009. Professional learning communities at the crossroads: how systems hinder or engender change. In A. Hargreaves, A. Lieberman, M. Fullan and D. Hopkins (Eds.) *Second International Handbook of Educational Change*. Springer Netherland, pp. 555–571.

Trudel, P., Gilbert, W. and Werthner, P. 2010. Coach education effectiveness. In Lyle and Cushion (Eds.) *Sport coaching: Professionalisation and practice*. Elsevier Health Sciences, pp. 135–152.

Wenger, E. 1998. *Communities of Practice: Learning, meaning, and identity*. Cambridge, UK: Cambridge University Press.

Resources

Center for Evidence-Based Mentoring: http://www.umbmentoring.org/

American Psychological Association – Responsible Mentoring: https://apa.org/research/responsible/mentoring/index.aspx

Oxford Learning Institute: http://www.learning.ox.ac.uk/resources/mentoring/

18

MENTORING HIGH-PERFORMANCE ATHLETES

Clifford J. Mallett, Matthew Emmett and Steven B. Rynne

Overview

The concept of mentor is an oft-used term but it probably means different things to different people. In comparison with the conception of 'mentor' in Ancient Greek times, contemporary notions of the term might be considered somewhat different in relation to their nature, focus, and outcomes (Ehrich *et al.* 2004). Moreover, in recent times, academic discourses using the term *mentoring* have not addressed a key issue – the lack of conceptual and practical clarity of the term (Jones *et al.* 2009). Despite this lack of clarity, an element common to most conceptions is 'guidance by a trusted other' (Cassidy *et al.* 2004; Jones *et al.* 2009).

It is a reasonable proposition that sport coaching could be viewed as a form of (in)formal mentoring (informal in the sense that there is generally no agreed curriculum; formal in the sense that coaches and athletes are generally partnered in highly structured, sometimes contractually obligated ways). Reade (2013) makes the point that 'coaching (at least at the higher levels) involves mentorship, and mentorship certainly involves coaching' (p. 238). Of course, guidance is an element inherent in sport coaching practice and indeed previous work has noted the presence of 'mentoring functions' within coaching work (e.g. Miller *et al.* 2002). Indeed, more recently the relationship between mentoring and coaching has been examined (Jenkins 2013), and while some argue strongly regarding the distinctions between the two, this has primarily been with respect to the notion of mentoring and coaching in business. In a similar way, much of the debate about mentoring in sports coaching has related to the mentoring *of* sports coaches as opposed to the mentoring of athletes *by* sports coaches (Jones *et al.* 2009). This chapter is focused on the latter.

Within the context of high-performance sports coaching, the conceptual links between the terms *coach* and *mentor* are somewhat muddied, which may be linked to how coaches view the scope of their work; for example, some might conceive sport coaching as primarily performance-related and therefore the scope of their work is about the development of 'skills, drills, and tactics'. However, this 'narrow conception of coaching' is not consistent with Côté and Gilbert's (2009) definition of effective sport coaching: 'The consistent application of integrated professional, interpersonal, and intrapersonal knowledge to improve athletes' competence, confidence, connection, and character in specific coaching contexts' (p. 316). Similar to the notion of mentoring, the aforementioned definition of effective coaching suggests a more holistic approach to development that extends beyond the sporting arena. Côté and Gilbert's definition of effective coaching is based on the 4 Cs (competence, confidence, connectedness, character) of positive youth development (Larson 2000; Lerner 2003), in which the focus is on developing young people's capacity for growth (Larson 2006) through sport. This focus on people's strengths to promote adaptive development is consistent with the positive psychology movement (Peterson and Seligman 2004). Self-determination theory (SDT; Deci and Ryan 1985), which is a social-cognitive and organismic theory of human motivation and personality development, purports the centrality of significant others (e.g. adults) in creating adaptive learning environments that foster psychological need satisfaction (competence, autonomy, belonging) to subsequently contribute to personal growth. This notion of learning and development, which is guided by another, is a key feature of coaching and mentoring. So, it is proposed that coaching in its broader sense is linked strongly with the key elements of mentoring; in other words, the terms *sports coaching* and *mentoring* might be considered synonymous. Nevertheless, it is proposed that how coaches understand and enact their role will influence the degree to which the two terms might be considered synonymous. For the purpose of this chapter, we consider that (high-performance) coaches and those they influence (athletes) are often in a long-term coach–athlete relationship both in terms of weekly contact and usually over several months annually, and in many instances for several years. Hence, functional coach-athlete relationships, which are enduring, are likely to be characterised by learning, development, mutual trust and respect, similar to the notion of mentoring (Occhino *et al.* 2013).

Vignette[1]

Background

The coach featured in this vignette is a National Collegiate Athletic Association (NCAA) Division 1 Head Coach of a team sport. University sport in the United States of America (USA), especially in the highly competitive NCAA Division 1 competitions, is considered to be a key transition period from elite youth to elite senior; therefore, the coach featured is considered a high-performance coach. Coach Smith was thought to be a fitting example as his profile is consistent with how coaching effectiveness has been recently defined: the consistent application of coaching knowledge to continually improve well-defined athlete outcomes within specific coaching contexts (Côté and Gilbert 2009). The primary outcomes of the collegiate sport setting are (i) winning games and (ii) graduating student-athletes. During Coach Smith's tenure, the team won multiple consecutive conference championships and entry into national championships. In the classroom, Coach Smith taught numerous student-athletes who earned all conference academic honours. These successful outcomes demonstrate that Coach Smith has consistently produced championship-winning teams and successfully graduated high-achieving student-athletes.

Methods

The case of Coach Smith (Head Coach) was part of an extensive multi-year study conducted by a group of researchers at the same NCAA Division 1 University in the USA. The study comprised multiple methods to systematically document coaching effectiveness in action over the course of a full season. As part of the study, fourteen interviews were undertaken with Coach Smith, and at the end of the season two separate sixty-minute student-athlete focus groups were conducted: one group consisting of five senior student-athletes and the other focus group containing five non-senior student-athletes. The purpose of the coach interviews was to capture insights into coaching effectiveness at various stages of the season – prior to, during and after. Interviews with Coach Smith revealed insights into the coach's philosophy, expectations for the season, and the nature of his relationship with the student-athletes. The purpose of the student-athlete focus group interviews was to examine if the perceptions of the coach concurred with how the student-athletes viewed their experience under the coach's leadership. The questions were designed to uncover the student-athletes' perceptions of the coach's style and the degree of satisfaction felt within the coach-athlete relationship.

Findings

The senior athletes reported the three key themes of connection, caring and trust, in a positive light:

> We used to go in to the [coach's] office randomly, sit there and just chat. The group after us, I don't think that would ever cross their mind, to go in and just chat with one of the coaches. I feel like they are a bit scared, they avoid it, and you shouldn't. It makes for a better connection, and then they [Coach Smith] can actually learn their personality. [*Connection – from personal relationships with others*]

> Coach Smith will tear you down in practice but will be the first to bring you back up. Coach Smith will rip your head off but you best believe a couple of hours later you are going to get a phone call or a text saying I think you're the best player I have got. [*Caring and showing some empathy for others*]

> We had to learn the system and to trust the system before we could actually buy in to what Coach Smith was actually talking about. We were new to the program, we didn't know anybody, we didn't trust anybody. So in order for us to trust in Coach Smith it took time, about a year for us to trust and buy in. [*Trust*]

In contrast, the non-senior athletes reported less connection, caring and trust with Coach Smith:

> I don't feel like I have ever gone to speak to coach about a problem because they wouldn't care enough. I don't feel like I could ever open up to Coach Smith. It's definitely easier for some to approach Coach Smith and talk about their problems, their needs and their feelings. [*Lack of connection*]

> Coach Smith is so mean at practice and I've felt really overlooked. Coach Smith never really talked to me or called me and I felt like I really wasn't part of the team. [*Lack of caring*]

> The first day of school the seniors sit us down and say this is what we do and this is how we do it, get with the program. The seniors have the power because they have been here the longest, they pretty much know what Coach Smith expects. [*Lack of trust and respect*]

Coach Smith interview data:

> What I learned is that I think I paid too little attention to the freshmen; probably isolated them a little too much. They felt a little vulnerable, a little underappreciated and that's not the type of environment I want to have. The number one thing is that we didn't spend any time with them outside of our sport. I feel like correcting it . . . just means spending a little more time with them. I think that's the key to dealing with teams and with young people. Show them you care. So that's what I am working on this year, breaking the team down in to little life groups, to where each coach is responsible for a player. They don't really care how much I know about the game until they know how much I care about them.

Analysis

A hierarchical content analysis of the student-athlete focus group data showed discrepancies between the two groups – senior student-athletes and non-senior student-athletes. The senior student-athletes felt a very strong personal bond with the coach but perceived an apparent disconnect between the non-senior student-athletes and the coach. The feedback from both focus groups highlighted that the student-athletes reported differential experiences of coach connection, trust and caring.

The differing perceptions of connection, trust, and caring can be traced to the degree of personal investment each student-athlete received from the coach. The data, from both the coach and the athletes, supports the view that the coach invested more of his time and emotion in the senior student-athlete group. The coach explained that the senior student-athletes were his first recruiting class and deliberately held weekly 'life lesson' meetings in their freshmen year. These meetings were specifically designed to not only establish a vision for each student-athlete (within the team structure) but also to earn their trust and demonstrate a deep level of care for them as people first – consistent with an autonomy-supportive motivational climate (Mageau and Vallerand 2003). The coach admitted that he failed to continue this process with incoming freshmen (non-senior student-athletes). Attending to the student-athlete perceptions illustrates the coach's openness to adapting his behaviours to meet the needs of the student-athletes and in particular consideration of the whole person rather than an exclusive focus on performance. This recognition to respond to the needs of the student-athletes is consistent with Côté and Gilbert's (2009) definition of effective sport coaching and SDT, especially in supporting the student-athletes' sense of connectedness (4 Cs) and belonging (SDT; Deci and Ryan 1985). Demonstrating coaching effectiveness is not a state (in which one arrives) but a target condition (a quest of becoming), which is characterized by the dynamic, reciprocal and fluid nature of coach-athlete relationships (Lorimer and Jowett 2009).

It is assumed that a mentor typically focuses on the person (being mentored), their career and support for their individual growth and maturity, whilst coaches have tended to be more job focused and performance-oriented (Starcevich 1998). However, the case of Coach Smith illustrates that mentoring is not necessarily a separate aspect of coaching work, but is considered to be an essential part of what we might term 'quality coaching', that is, a broad understanding of coaching effectiveness as defined by Côté and Gilbert (2009). Coach Smith successfully created a persona in which the senior student-athlete group viewed him not only as their basketball coach but also as their mentor – someone who nurtured them, whom they trusted and who showed he cared. Coach Smith was able to consistently produce championship-winning teams and also establish a strong personal bond with the senior student-athletes through the coaching process. This was possible as Coach Smith focused on creating an environment conducive to student-athlete learning and involvement. The notion of mentoring and Coach Smith's intention to show the student-athletes he cared and to seek their active engagement in the coaching process is consistent with the creation of an autonomy-supportive motivational climate (Mageau and Vallerand 2003; Mallett 2005) and adopting an athlete-centred coaching approach (Kidman et al. 2005).

Coaches' behaviours influence athletes' self-determined motivation through their impact on athletes' perceptions of autonomy, competence and relatedness/belonging (SDT; Deci and Ryan 1985; Mageau and Vallerand 2003; Mallett 2005). Being autonomy supportive (Deci and Ryan 1985) means that 'an individual in a position of authority (e.g. a coach or mentor) takes the other's (e.g. an athlete's or mentee's) perspective, acknowledges the other's feelings, and provides the other with pertinent information and opportunities for choice, while minimizing the use of pressures and demands' (Black and Deci 2000). Behaving in these ways shows that coaches/mentors care about the person, which in turn, nurtures peoples' adaptive personality development (Mageau and Vallerand 2003).

Coaches possess their own unique interpersonal style but effective (high-performance) coaches all share one common trait: they recognize the importance of gaining the trust of their athletes (Côté and Gilbert 2009). Effective coaches understand that developing relationships grounded in showing an interest in the welfare of athletes as well as mutual trust and respect will greatly increase the probability of the athlete experiencing enjoyment and satisfaction in their sporting experiences and contribute to personal growth (Emmett *et al.*, in prep.). Hence, coaching and mentoring can be considered somewhat synonymous but contingent upon how coaches consider and enact their role in the coach-athlete relationship. In conclusion, it is considered pertinent to reiterate Coach Smith's approach to cultivating positive coach-athlete relations: 'People will never care how much you know until they know how much you care'.

Lessons learned . . . What could we add to the Mentor Pedagogy Toolbox?

There are a couple of important lessons to consider from this study:

- **It is important to *show* you care.** The centrality of showing you care seems important to athletes and is consistent with the literature associated with adaptive coach-athlete relationships (e.g. Deci and Ryan 1985; Mageau and Vallerand 2003) and notions of 'effective' and 'quality' coaching (e.g. Côté and Gilbert 2009; Occhino *et al.* 2013). Furthermore, caring for others is central to a functional mentor-mentee relationship (e.g. Miller *et al.* 2002; Reade 2013).
- **Coaches may underestimate or be unaware of their impact.** Coaches might not be cognisant of their impact on others and their differential guidance and care for athletes within the same team or squad. Indeed, coaches are likely to differentially impact on those they guide, and when the primary focus is on winning, perhaps reflection on the individual as a person is marginalised. It is proposed that in the main, coaches unintentionally/unconsciously show preference to some athletes over others. Perhaps some coaches don't reflect beyond the performance itself and how one's behaviours impact on individuals in a more holistic way. Coaches who see themselves as mentors and therefore consider the whole person should consider individual athletes within the team/squad; in other words, there is some argument for an 'I' in 'Team'.
- **Coaches could benefit from adopting a pedagogical approach that considers the 'person' not just the 'performer' (Cassidy *et al.* 2009).** To be effective in their work, coaches should move beyond a focus on skills and drills to consider the 'person' rather than their performance. It is the 'person' who underpins the performance, and showing that you care enables coaches to develop sufficient rapport with athletes to enable coaches to get the best from athletes. It is possible that the time to build trust between the freshmen and Coach Smith took longer than necessary because of the lack of involvement and showing that he cared for his players. In terms of the pedagogical approach to developing adaptive coach-athlete relationships, the following reiterated quote from Coach Smith is highlighted:

> The number one thing is that we didn't spend any time with them outside of our sport. I feel like correcting it . . . just means spending a little more time with them. I think that's the key to dealing with teams and with young people. Show them you care . . . They don't really care how much I know about the game until they know how much I care about them.

- **Coach reflexivity on the coach–athletes' relationships** would benefit from discussing their holistic coaching relationship with the athlete as well as another knowledgeable person.
- **An analysis of the data (trust, caring, connection) supports several aspects of the CM³T model of mentor competencies,** including (a) *Affective* (trust, empathy, support); (b) *Cognitive* (leadership, facilitator); and (c) *Hybrid* (building rapport, approachable, co-existence of professional and personal relationships).

Note

1 The coach featured in this vignette has been assigned a pseudonym to protect his anonymity.

Key terms: coaching effectiveness, quality coaching, psychological growth, learning, development, trust, caring, connection.

References

Black, A. E. and Deci, E. L. 2000. The Effects of Instructors' Autonomy Support and Students' Autonomous Motivation on Learning Organic Chemistry: A self-determination theory perspective. *Science Education,* 84, 740–756.

Cassidy, T., Jones, R. L. and Potrac, P. 2004. *Understanding Sports Coaching: The social, cultural and pedagogical foundations of coaching practice.* New York: Routledge.

Cassidy, T., Jones, R. L. and Potrac, P. 2009. *Understanding Sports Coaching: The social, cultural and pedagogical foundations of coaching practice* (2nd edition). London: Routledge.

Côté, J. and Gilbert, W. 2009. An Integrative Definition of Coaching Effectiveness and Expertise. *International Journal of Sports Science and Coaching,* 4, 307–323.

Deci, E. L. and Ryan, R. M. 1985. *Intrinsic Motivation and Self-determination in Human Behavior.* New York: Plenum.

Ehrich, L. C, Hansford, B. and Tennant, L. 2004. Formal Mentoring Programs in Education and other Professions: A review of the literature. *Educational Administration Quarterly,* 40, 518–540.

Emmett, M., Gilbert, W. and Hamel, T. (in preparation). Teaching Behavior Profile of an Effective Elite Team Sport Coach.

Jenkins, S. 2013. David Clutterbuck, Mentoring and Coaching. *International Journal of Sports Science and Coaching,* 8, 139–254.

Jones, R. L., Harris, R. and Miles, A. 2009. Mentoring in Sports Coaching: A review of the literature. *Physical Education and Sport Pedagogy,* 14, 267–284.

Kidman, L., Thorpe, R. and Hadfield, D. 2005. *Athlete-centred Coaching: Developing inspired and inspiring people.* Christchurch: Innovative Print Communications.

Larson, R.W. 2000. Toward a Psychology of Positive Youth Development. *American Psychologist*, 55, 170–183.

Larson, R. 2006. Positive Youth Development, Willful Adolescents, and Mentoring. *Journal of Community Psychology*, 34(6), 677–689.

Lerner, R. M. 2003. Developmental Assets and Asset-building Communities: A view of the issues. In R. M. Lerner and P. L. Benson (Eds.) *Developmental Assets and Asset-building Communities: Implications for Research, Policy, and Practice*. New York: Kluwer Academic/Plenum, pp. 3–18.

Lorimer, R. and Jowett, S. 2009. Empathetic Accuracy in Coach-Athlete Dyads Who Participate in Team and Individual Sports. *Psychology of Sport and Exercise Science*, 10, 152–158.

Mageau, G. A. and Vallerand, R. J. 2003. The Coach-athlete Relationship: A motivational model. *Journal of Sports Sciences*, 21, 883–904.

Mallett, C. J. 2005. Self-determination Theory: A case study of evidence-based coaching. *The Sport Psychologist*, 19, 417–429.

Miller, P. S., Salmela, J. H. and Kerr, G. 2002. Coaches' Perceived Role in Mentoring Athletes. *International Journal of Sport Psychology*, 33, 410–430.

Occhino, J., Mallett, C. J. and Rynne, S. B. 2013. Dynamic Social Networks in High Performance Football Coaching. *Physical Education and Sport Pedagogy*, 18, 90–102.

Petersen, C. and Seligman, M. E. P. 2004. *Character Strengths and Virtues: A handbook and classification*. American Psychological Association, Washington, DC.

Reade, I. 2013. David Clutterbuck, Mentoring and Coaching: A commentary. *International Journal of Sports Science and Coaching*, 8, 237–239.

Starcevich, M. 1998. *Coach, Mentor: Is there a difference?* Centre for coaching and mentoring. Accessed at http://www.coachingandmentoring.com/Articles/mentoring.html, on 15th May 2013.

Resources

http://www.ausport.gov.au/participating/coachofficial/presenter/Mentor

http://www.ausport.gov.au/participating/aasc/community_coaches/ongoing_development/communtiy_coach_mentoring_program

http://www.ausport.gov.au/participating/coaches/videos/mentor_training/mentoring_-_in_action

http://www.ausport.gov.au/participating/women/resources/issues/mentor

http://shop.ausport.gov.au/epages/ais.sf/en_AU/?ObjectPath=/Shops/ais/Products/12-038

19

DESIGNING SUSTAINABLE MODELS OF MENTORING FOR SPORTS CLUBS

Julia Walsh and Fiona C. Chambers

Overview

> The structure of practice is emergent, both highly perturbable and highly resilient, always reconstituting itself in the face of new events . . . In a world that is not predictable, improvisation and innovation are more than desirable, they are essential.
>
> *Wenger 1998, p. 233*

The 'new event' (ibid.), i.e. the European Education and Training 2020 strategy (ET 2020), advocates a 'knowledge triangle' encompassing education, research and innovation and encourages partnerships between education and business, partnerships which foster advanced pedagogies that improve the wellbeing of citizens (European Commission 2010). In response to this 'new event' (Wenger 1998, p. 233), a partnership was formed between a university specializing in sport and physical education and a local sports club to design and deliver a mentor education initiative to support novice coach development. The Coaching the Coaches programme was innovated in order 'to do something new that created value' (Online Etymology Dictionary 2010) within coach education and the local community.

> We started the mentoring project as equal partners, the university and ourselves. It was unknown territory for both organisations and we had to listen and be patient with each other. We all had to learn, I could organize logistics but mentoring was new to me. The club executive really embraced the programme and got involved, some even worked as mentors. The programme grew each year and more of us developed mentoring skills to the point it is now common practice at the club.

Vignette

Background

The reason for this initiative was to create a new model of professional development for novice coaches that were self-sustaining at the local club level. The partnership between the university and the sports club created a space for sharing, reflecting and developing expertise in mentoring and coach professional development. Mentoring was positioned as the hub for learning, and learning was situated and distributed within and across both organisations. This research traces the emergence of principles in the establishment of mentoring programmes to support professional development in education and sports organisations. The foundational theories which inform the development of the Coaching the Coaches programme are (i) the Principles of Innovation (Drucker 2009) and (ii) an advanced 'pedagogy of mentor education' (Webb *et al.* 2007).

The Principles of Innovation

When creating the Coaching the Coaches programme, the researchers built upon Drucker's (2009) 'Principles of Innovation' to guide the design process:

1. Analysis of opportunities
2. Using the conceptual and the perceptual
3. Keeping it simple and focused
4. Starting small
5. Aiming at leadership (p. 123).

These principles aligned each initiative around the central concept of an 'advanced pedagogy of mentor education' (Webb *et al.* 2007, p. 172).

An advanced pedagogy of mentor education

The 'advanced pedagogy of mentor education' (ibid., p. 172) reflects theories that emphasise the situatedness of learning, i.e. Wenger's (1998) Communities of Practice, and recognises the formal, non-formal and informal qualities of learning processes. The advanced pedagogy is based on the view that preparation for mentoring is not a technical issue that can be enabled by a simple training programme, but rather is 'an interpretative process that is enabled through collaboration, challenge and reflection' (Webb *et al.* 2007, p. 184).

Methodology

Several qualitative data collection methods (open profile questionnaires, coach and mentor reflective journals, coach observation sheets) were employed to investigate the programme. Sixteen coaches and two mentors participated in the study over a two-year period. Data were collected using a constructivist framework and analysed using grounded theory (Strauss and Corbin 1998).

Findings

The impact of the mentoring project was multi-layered and positively influenced participant (athletes, coaches, mentors and both the organisations) learning. The major outcome was the creation of a learning environment that was collaborative, where knowledge, skills, experience and problems were shared. This is in contrast to many coach development programmes that privilege an individual formalized approach to coach development (Trudel and Gilbert 2004).

Working collaboratively was a challenge for all participants. The novice coaches took time to develop trust in the mentoring process. This is understandable as previous education experience had been structured and formal. The time to establish a mentoring relationship varied; however, all mentors and mentees were working collaboratively within 4–5 weeks.

The mentors had to learn to be mentors and reframe their assumptions about the role and needs of novice coaches. It required the mentor to be actively engaged in problem-solving with the mentee before, during and after coaching practice. The programme structure encouraged mentors to work closely together enabling the distribution and propagation of mentoring knowledge. The reflection in and on action was powerful as the mentee and mentor could test solutions and receive feedback in context and at the conclusion of the practice.

Both organisations enriched their programmes and positioned themselves as learning organisations. The local sports organisation developed competence and confidence in their ability to conduct an internal Coaching the Coaches programme. The benefits for the university included building its mentoring knowledge base and establishing strong collaborative community links.

There were four principles that emerged from the project: (1) local problem, local solution, (2) all members are learners, (3) context is central to planning and (4) engagement in reflection and reflexive practice by novice coaches and mentors. The LACE principles promote working and learning together to achieve a solution, being aware and considerate of context when problem-solving, and developing metacognitive skills and the use of reflection as a communication bridge between the mentor and mentee to engage in learning.

Analysis

Through the 'advanced pedagogy of mentor education' (Webb et al. 2007, p. 172), the mentor initiative became a professional development hub that embraced formal, non-formal and informal sites of learning. The following section charts the development of the enterprise.

Coaching the Coaches

Coaches learn from a number of sources (Lemyre *et al.* 2007). While the dominant educational framework is based on individual learning, coaches engage in collaborative learning through networking and mentoring. Many mentoring programmes reinforce an individual approach to coach development and do not promote a distributed model of knowledge (Trudel and Gilbert 2004) or assist with entry into the coaching subculture (Cushion *et al.* 2003). An 'advanced pedagogy of mentor education' (Webb *et al.* 2007, p. 172) that supports learners in all aspects of coaching lays the foundation for life-long engagement in physical activity and sport.

When innovating the Coaching the Coaches programme, Drucker's (2009) 'Principles of Innovation' guided the design process, and the practice responded to the design (Wenger 1998). Two additional principles of innovation evolved: accountability and individual agency. The framework used was called the LACE model and has four stages: **L**ocal problem, local solution; **A**ll members are learners; **C**ontext is central to planning and engagement; **E**ngagement in reflective and reflexive practice by coaches and mentors.

Local problem, local solution

Two local organisations had a problem and were seeking an innovative solution to address their needs. The local sports organisation required coaches for the academy programme. The university needed student placements in coaching.

All members are learners

Initial discussions between organisations focused on understanding each other's needs, developing trust, and actively working to build a shared vision underpinned by learning and supported by a community of practice. Members of the learning community were the athletes, novice coaches, mentors and both organisations.

Context is central to planning and engagement

There were multiple contexts that varied according to role (i.e. participant, coach, mentor). For the novice coach, context was shaped by participant characteristics and needs, soccer expertise and experience, personal competence and confidence to perform the coaching role, and academic requirements. In the mentor's case their context was further expanded to include novice coach development, health and safety, and organisational outcomes.

Engagement in reflective and reflexive practice by coaches and mentors

Reflective practice was the communication bridge for learning and took several forms, e.g. reflective discussion in action and a six-week reflective journal with reflections submitted twenty-four hours after the coaching session. The classroom became a problem-solving space that responded to current issues where all participants experienced autonomy and agency.

There are several places where innovation can gain a footing and one of these is 'process', i.e. changing the way people engage in practice (Drucker 2009). The Coaching the Coaches programme innovated across three processes: (a) partnership, (b) equality and (c) creating a safe, inclusive learning environment.

Conclusion

The 'advanced pedagogy of mentor education' (Webb *et al.* 2007) is used to encourage coaches to think differently about how they package Physical Activity (PA) and sport in the gym and on the playing field. For the mentor and organisation the cultural shift was situating all participants as learners and moving to a model of distributed knowledge. The sites for mentor training became a safe space in which to challenge and provoke coaches' and mentor thinking in a collaborative setting and to initiate creative practice that might encourage life-long engagement in physical activity and sport for all participants.

Creating sustainable mentoring programmes in sports clubs helps them to educate their volunteer workforce, create better learning environments for participants, and distribute knowledge throughout the organisation. There are good professional development programmes available for volunteers (i.e. coach accreditation, specialist seminars, mentor programmes); however, making a programme sustainable is the real challenge. To be sustainable a project must meet the needs of the current population, endure, and not have a negative impact on future generations (United Nations 1987). The Coaching the Coaches programme was a three-year project that evolved over time. It required people in both organisations to listen, be patient, reflect on and in action, and have a willingness to work in a dynamic environment that was continually adapting to its context. Through this process the programme created a strong, flexible foundation to serve current and future coaches at the local community level.

The two theories that underpinned the project, the Principles of Innovation (Drucker 2009) and the advanced 'pedagogy of mentor education' (Webb *et al.* 2007), played out in interesting ways. The Principles of Innovation (Drucker 2009) were demonstrated as the LACE framework developed. The principles that emerged from the LACE framework provide valuable guidelines for any club considering a mentoring programme as an alternative professional development programme for coaches.

The Coaching the Coaches programme was initially driven by the needs of the local sports organisation. The sports club was unable to attract enough club coaches to coach youth athletes in the annual six-week academy. There was no internal solution so the club conducted an external analysis to identify possible solutions to ensure the youth academy survived and prospered. In his 'Principles of Innovation', Drucker (2009) notes the need for an 'analysis of opportunities' as the first stage of any innovation. The analysis should be systematic and have internal and external foci. The local sports club, having conducted an internal and external analysis, approached the local university because they offered an education degree with a coaching minor that required students to participate in a coaching placement. In the early stages of discussion there was no mention of mentoring, what was on offer was coaching placements in football. The club would provide athletes, facilities and resources and the university students would coach the participants. It was only at the next stage when discussion continued that a mentoring programme emerged.

Implementing any form of professional development programme and ensuring its sustainability requires a deep understanding of the current and future context. This requires the allocation of time and resources, which can be a challenge in an organisation manned by volunteers (Walsh *et al.* 2010). A first step is to identify the club's professional development needs, available expertise and resources within the club, and ensure there is buy-in from the management team to pursue the project. The results from an internal analysis guide the direction of the external analysis. If the club is considering a mentoring programme, the external analysis should include looking at a variety of mentor programmes, models of best practice, and talking to people with expertise in the development and/or implementation of mentoring programmes. This background information provides a foundation for matching and adapting a mentor programme or selecting a partner to assist that matches the club's needs, context, and culture. The analysis stage does take time and resources but this investment helps clarify the problem and set clear and realistic expectations.

Drucker's (2009) second principle of innovation states 'innovation is both conceptual and perceptual'. This means not only giving time and consideration to the mentoring process but also listening to people and how they feel about a professional development model based on collaboration through a mentoring programme. In the local sports club it is people who provide impetus and make a programme sustainable by ensuring the goals of the programme continue to be met (J. Cripps Clarke, personal communication, February 20, 2014). The Coaching the Coaches programme moved away from traditional models of professional development based on individual learning (Lemyre *et al.* 2007) to a mentoring model built on collaboration. Like the analysis stage there was much discussion, listening and prototyping of ideas. The two organisations were new partners and needed to understand each other, and develop trust and a shared language in order to build a sustainable mentoring programme. The conceptual idea of mentoring was well accepted; however, the perceptual issues about responsibility for mentoring challenged both organisations.

Introducing mentoring as the focal learning pathway required shifts in thinking and systemic change within both organisations. Sports club members were not confident to perform the mentoring role, and the university was not interested in a service model and wanted shared responsibility for mentoring novice coaches. By partner organisations listening to each other and then positioning everyone as learners rather than experts or non-experts, people were given permission to learn and develop mentoring skills as part of an ongoing process. The perceptual and conceptual are responsive to each other; with perceptual clarity the conceptual work is continually refined. The context of sports clubs is continually changing; for a mentoring programme to become sustainable, engagement in the conceptual and perceptual must be ongoing so that timely adjustments can be made to meet the needs of the organisation.

'Keeping the program simple and focused', Drucker's (2009) third principle of innovation provided opportunity for the programme to pilot new ideas without large investments in time or resources. The focus was on building a sustainable mentoring programme to support the development of novice coaches; over three years this focus remained unchanged but the knowledge base grew and was distributed within and between organisations. Mentoring practice and engagement between mentors changed over time; not only was there better understanding of mentoring but in practice identification of cues and temporal response improved. Mentors knew why, when and how to solve problems, not just what to solve.

The fourth principle of innovation, 'keeping it small' (Drucker 2009) was achieved through programme structure and independence from other club programmes. The Coaching the Coaches programme was a discrete six-week programme. By maintaining distance from other organisational programmes and traditions, it allows for the innovation to develop new life and escape the thicket of detractors. When the programme is successful it can return to the organizational fold and the success can be shared (Devos and Hampden-Turner 2002). Small changes were occurring all the time as people learnt and reflected on the experience. It was kept small by limiting numbers of participants and the length of the programme, and by using a core group of people to mentor within the programme. Sometimes good ideas become big ideas before the foundation is in place. Keeping it small and working through several cycles provided time for reflection, action and evaluation without taxing resources.

According to Drucker's fifth principle, a successful innovation 'aims at leadership' (Drucker 2009). Leading the field was a by-product of the LACE framework. The defining moments were small and were about taking time to ask the right question and continuing to test solutions. Spending time refining the mentoring programme through the conceptual and perceptual process meant small changes were actively taking place and shaping the programme to its context. Actively working towards an equal partnership and valuing people's skills and knowledge brought unexpected resources to the project and improved the richness of the mentoring experience for novice coaches. For example, sports club coaches presented guest lectures at the university, and the university worked closely with the club in other aspects of the programme. Positioning all participants as learners and creating an inclusive community of practice changed how people negotiated identity, and developed agency and autonomy. It was safe to learn and safe to fail.

Both organisations entered the project with different intentions and measurements of success. The sports club wanted to maintain its youth academy and provide high-quality football coaching that attracted and maintained young athletes at the club. The university was responsible for delivering coach education that included a placement component. Good-quality placements and mentoring enabled students to put theory into practice. The outcome of the project was a shared objective, a mentoring programme that improved coaching performance and hence the athlete experience. But it did more than this. A community of practice (COP) (Wenger 1998) emerged, and within this community there were mentors, novice coaches, and club administrators; at times it expanded to include interested club coaches. On academy nights, there was interaction between mentors, novice coaches and athletes and it was a mutual engagement; the expectation was all participants helped each other to learn. It was a collective process of negotiation and meaning making, competence sharing, and competence development. Reflection was the communication bridge: there was reflection in action (during coaching), on action at the end of the training session, and submission of coach and mentor reflections twenty-four hours after the training session. This reflective information was fed back into theoretical classes for further discussion and problem-solving. Sustainability of the mentoring programme was established through mutual engagement in the project, sharing of significant learning and a history embedded in the cultural roots of both organisations that is situated and contextualized.

Lessons learned . . . What could we add to the Mentor Pedagogy Toolbox?

- Building a sustainable mentoring programme takes time. It is important to spend time in the initial stages analyzing the professional development needs of the sports club carefully using well-chosen and pertinent questions.
- The core objective for organisations is to develop shared professional practice.
- It is vital to provide space for the new programme to develop and establish a solid foundation before embedding it in organizational core practice.
- If in a partnership, look for multiple ways to connect and contribute to each other's learning community.
- When everyone is positioned as a learner, there is joint responsibility by the community to solve problems. There is not a 'blame culture'; it is about working together for a solution and learning from the process. The community also shares success at any level. For example, if the novice coach has finally learned how to manage a group of young, excitable athletes, that is success for the athletes, coach, mentor and the partner organisations.
- Reflection in action provides immediate feedback and enables the novice coach to test other strategies in a similar context and reflect on practice.
- Submission of reflections from mentors and novice coaches within twenty-four hours to capture critical learning incidents that may be lost or reconstructed incorrectly with time.
- The early stages of learning require large amounts of cognitive space. It is imperative to find ways of distributing knowledge, for example, by having

novice coaches working in pairs, so that they have time to reflect in action and make considered adjustments and to be proactive in their practice rather than responsive to the current situation.

Key terms: mentoring, innovation, sustainability, sports clubs, partnerships.

References

Cushion, C., Armour, K. and Jones, R. 2003. Coaching education and continuing professional development: Experience and learning to coach. *Quest,* 55, 215–230.

Devos D. and Hampden-Turner C. 2002. Recapturing the true mission: Christian Majgaard, LEGO. In A. Trompenaars and C. Hampden-Turner (Eds.) *21 Leaders for the 21st Century: How Innovative Leaders Manage in the Digital Age.* NY: McGraw-Hill.

Drucker, P. F. 2009. *Innovation and Entrepreneurship.* Oxford: Butterworth-Heinemann.

European Commission. 2010. ERA in the Knowledge Triangle. Accessed at http://ec.europa.eu/research/era/understanding/what/era_in_the_knowledge_triangle_en.htm. Accessed on 24 August 2010.

Lemyre, F., Trudel, P. and Durand-Bush, N. 2007. How youth-sport coaches learn to coach. *The Sport Psychologist, 21,* 191–209.

Online Etymology Dictionary. 2010. *c.v.* 'Innovate'. Accessed on 19 August 2010.

Strauss, A. and Corbin, J. 1998. *Basics of Qualitative Research: Techniques and Procedures for Developing Grounded Theory* (2nd edition). Thousand Oaks, CA: Sage.

Trudel, P. and Gilbert, W. 2004. Communities of practice as an approach to foster ice hockey coach development. In D. Pearsall and A. Ashare (Eds.) *Safety in Ice Hockey: Fourth Volume, STP 1446.* Philadelphia: American Society for Testing and Materials, pp. 167–179.

United Nations. 1987. Our common future: The Brundtland report, the Netherlands.

Walsh, J., Tannehill, D. and Woods, C. B. 2010. The Children's Sport Participation and Physical Activity Study (CSPPA): Volunteer Study. Dublin: Dublin City University.

Webb, M. E., Pachler, N., Mitchell, H. and Herrington, N. 2007. Towards a pedagogy of mentor education. *Professional Development in Education,* 33(2), 171–188.

Wenger, E. 1998. *Communities of Practice: Learning, Meaning and Identity.* Cambridge, UK: Cambridge University Press.

Resources

Cushion, C., Armour, K. and Jones, R. 2003. Coaching education and continuing professional development: Experience and learning to coach. *Quest,* 55, 215–230.

The Mentor Pedagogy Toolbox

An ecological systems perspective

20

THE MENTOR PEDAGOGY TOOLBOX

An ecological systems perspective

Fiona C. Chambers

Introduction

In the literature, and often in practice, those designing mentor systems opt for an economic or 'one size fits all' model (Chambers *et al.* 2014). A progression from this is the adoption of the continuum approach (see Figure 3.1. 'Continuum of factors influencing quality of mentor pedagogy' [Chambers *et al.* 2012]). While this represents a more nuanced strategy than a 'one size fits all' model, it is clearly a linear model as it is guided by Huberman's (1989) 'Professional Life Cycle of Teachers'. This is neither ideal nor realistic.

Appropriating Handy's (1994) comparative metaphor of Western *and* Eastern society may help to explicate the two opposing approaches to mentor system design, which can be either:

> [c]rystalline; clearly defined, facets that have their own shape with obvious joints between them [or] more amorphous (like mud) . . . it is easily shaped and changed and is flexible and responsive to external forces and circumstances.
>
> *Handy 1994, p. 172*

The latter view, according to Dewey (2004), emphasises social process rather than educational subject matter and presents problems for those interested in conceiving programmes that can be easily replicated and widely disseminated. Cavanagh (2006) opines that clean-cut, linear mentor systems do not capture the messy and multifarious nature of learning. If we view all systems as being holistic, there is an imperative to step back and focus on the mentoring system as a whole and see what is created when the parts interact (ibid.). For many, this is not a comfortable process as it is unpredictable and chaotic.

The Gestalt approach is helpful in accenting the social process of mentoring, shining a spotlight on the intricacy of individuals as part of their environment. According to The Gestalt Centre London (2013), *gestalt* is a German word meaning 'whole, pattern or form' (p. 1). It embraces a holistic view of the person/team within the context of their current milieu. It acknowledges past and present cultural issues to fully incorporate the kaleidoscope of experiences, which comprise the person in context. Gestalt celebrates the impact of the individual on others and their environment, which is quite a complex and ecological view. This perspective helps the individual to appreciate cultural diversity and difference. Therefore, mentoring programmes which use this approach, first of all consider the mentor as individual within his or her context. It is envisioned that the mentor may in turn use this approach when working with individual mentees in the amorphous and 'real' context of schools and sports clubs. The task of the mentor therefore is to help the mentee to navigate through the paradoxes of their context (Handy 1994), e.g. school/sports club life.

In trying to tease out the convolutions of the mentoring process on this journey, we turn to Lave and Wenger's (1991) 'situated' perspective on learning, which is at the core of mentoring. Embracing this 'situated and grounded' perspective on mentoring leads to the all-encompassing concept of *terroir*, a term unique to the French language and French winemaking which may help us to understand the spirit of mentoring.

Terroir captures the intricacies and the amorphous character of winemaking. In the main, *terroir* refers to the sum of all the external influences on grape growing, often translated as a 'sense of place'. The chemistry of soil, bedrock, sun and wind exposure, water table, climate and farming techniques come together in a unique expression in the wine, which is specific to a particular region. The theory of *terroir* encompasses the almost metaphysical circle of soil, nature, appellation and human activity. Culture is etymologically related to *terroir*, as it has at its root the Latin *colere,* meaning 'to till'. Culture, therefore, is akin to *terroir*. In applying this very compelling metaphor to mentoring, the contention is that just as the characteristics of wine are influenced by the *terroir* which they, in turn, influence, so too are the mentor/mentee by the culture in which they are located. I have referenced this elsewhere as 'The Terroir of Mentoring' (Chambers 2012).

The 'Terroir of Mentoring' (ibid.), using the words of Resnick (1994), 'incorporates a number of linked theories that centre on the whole person and on the relationship between that person and the context and culture in which they learn' (p. 16). Understanding the nature of learning within the 'Terroir of Mentoring' (Chambers 2012) demands

> [an] integrated framework of developmental, learning, and social theories . . . Whether conceptualized as traditional dyadic relationships or as developmental networks situated within communities of practice, researchers may draw on this framework to analyze, critique, design, and redesign mentoring programs.
>
> *Dominguez and Hager 2013, p. 184*

Perhaps, Bronfenbrenner's (1979) multilevel ecological systems perspective is helpful here when probing the 'Terroir of Mentoring' further (Chambers 2012). Such a perspective moves our thinking of mentoring as collaboration between individuals to a richer and more nuanced view of mentoring as a component of whole systems (Chandler *et al.* 2011). It considers how the mentoring is enacted and shaped by systems at Bronfenbrenner's (1979) multiple levels: (a) the ontogenic system/level (psychological and demographic individual characteristics [Tinbergen 1951]), (b) the microsystem/level (the immediate social context), and (c) the macro level/system (broader societal influences). Chandler *et al.* (2011, p. 526) describe why such a view of the mentoring system might be useful:

> Although the ecological model was originally used to understand how the environment interacts with individual processes of change, it is applicable to mentoring. Thus . . . an ecological systems perspective acknowledge(s) the composite of individual and environmental forces that mutually influence and constitute the phenomenon of mentoring at work.

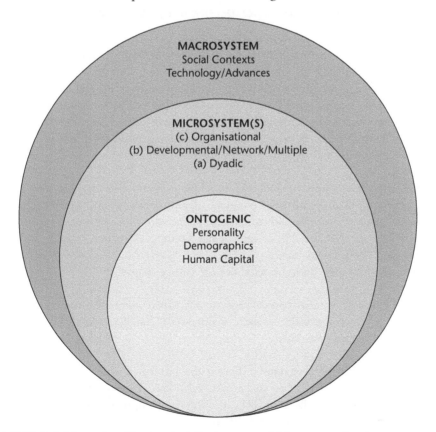

FIGURE 20.1 Mentoring: Ontogenic, Microsystem and Macrosystem levels

Adapted from 'Figure 1: Mentoring: Ontogenic, Microsystem and Macrosystem Levels of Analysis', Chandler *et al.* (2011, p. 523)

It is important to consider how the 'parts of the system interact' (p. 521):

> An ecological systems perspective requires us to consider how person and environmental systems are not independent from each other, but rather reciprocal and interdependent. This suggests that we consider patterns of relationships between systems and what happens at their interface.

In fact, often the most exciting learning occurs at the interfaces of these levels (see Figure 20.1). In the words of Heaney (1995): 'the dynamic and at times chaotic energy . . . is experienced "on the edge", where the frenzy of transformative learning is more likely to occur' (p. 3). Transformative learning occurs when learners change their 'meaning schemes (specific beliefs, attitudes and emotional reactions) and engage in critical reflection on their experiences, which in turn leads to a perspective transformation' (Mezirow 1991, p. 167) and to a progressive change in personal and pedagogic identity (Zukas 2001).

Using an ecological systems perspective to design the Mentor Pedagogy Toolbox

The 'Terroir of Mentoring' (Chambers 2012) represents an ecological systems perspective of mentoring. It comprises a synthesis of the 'Lessons learned . . . what could be added to the Mentor Pedagogy Toolbox' entries at the end of each chapter which are categorized within a Model of Ecological Mentoring (ontogenic system, microsystem and macrosystem) (Bronfenbrenner 1979; Chandler *et al.* 2011).

The 'Terroir of Mentoring' schematic captures a multi-level and ecological view of mentoring and all of its component parts. There are three levels:

Level One: The Ontogenic System (psychological and demographic individual characteristics). This comprises 'ontogenic development factors (e.g. personality, race, and gender) that offer individual-level explanations for mentoring outcomes' (Chandler *et al.* 2011, p. 526). To capture the Ontogenic System, Table 20.1 comprises the CM³T competences (see Chapter 10) and *Lessons learned* from other chapters in this book (these are referenced to source chapters).

Level Two: The Microsystem. Microsystem factors represent the immediate context within which a protégé or mentor interacts (Chandler *et al.* 2011, p. 526). There are three microsystems:

1. **The Dyadic Microsystem.** This is the immediate social context, which includes 'mentor-protégé agreement, relational characteristics, quality of a relationship' (Chandler *et al.* 2011, p. 526); this comprises *Lessons learned* across chapters in this book (see Table 20.2).
2. **The Developmental/Network/Multiple Microsystem.** This is the immediate social context, which includes the diversity of social spheres represented in a person's developmental network (Chandler *et al.* 2011, p. 526) (see Table 20.3).

3. **The Organisational Microsystem.** This is the immediate social context, which includes organizational influences (e.g. formal mentoring programme attributes) (Chandler *et al.* 2011, p. 526) (see Table 20.4).

Level Three: The Macrosystem. (Broader societal influences.) At this level, we discuss cultural, technological, and societal factors that exert influence on mentoring outcomes through their effect on ontogenic development and all three microsystems (see Table 20.5).

TABLE 20.1 Mentor Pedagogy Toolbox – Ontogenic system components

ONTOGENIC SYSTEM: Psychological and demographic individual characteristics of mentor (Chandler 2011, p. 256)

Affective Domain [Feeling]	Cognitive Domain [Thinking]	Hybrid [Feeling and Thinking]
Caring for mentees [C18]	Advisor [C10]	Application of mentoring styles [C10]
Defining mentee expectations [C10]	Collaborative [C10]	Approachable [C10]
Emotional maturity [C5]	Context knowledge [C10]	Building rapport [C10]
Empathy [C6]	Critical reflection [C13]	Coexistence of professional and personal relationships [C10]
Fostering positivity [C10]	Cross-fertilisation of mentoring skills from one subject to another [C10]	Conflict management [C10]
Interpersonal skills [C10]	Decision making [C10]	Delivering criticism [C10]
Protective [C10]	Delegating [C10]	Developing the mentee [C10]
Support [C10]	Discerning [C10]	Holistic approach 'person and performer' [C18]
Trust [C10]	Empowering the mentee [C10]	Interacting with triad partners [C10]
	Facilitating appropriate progression [C12]	Issuing feedback and corrective action [C10]
	Flexibility [C10]	Mentee focused [C10]
	Fostering teamwork [C10]	Negotiation [C10]
	Guided discovery [C10]	Non-directive [C10]
	Leadership [C10]	Objective [C10]
	Multi-tasking [C10]	Recognising success [C10]
	Observation [C10]	Self-confidence [C6]
	Organisation [C10]	Sensitive listener [C10]
	Planning [C10]	Unthreatened [C10]
	Recognising excellent performance [C10]	Understanding group dynamics [C12]
	Resourceful [C10]	Understanding boundaries [C12]
	Role model [C10]	Teacher/role model/resource [C1]
	Expert subject knowledge [C6/C10/C12]	Motivator/communicator/counsellor/confidant [C1]
	Team teaching [C10]	Evaluator [C1]
	Technology expertise for e-mentoring [C14]	Collaborator/colleague [C1]
	Accountable [C1]	Negotiator/boundary setter [C1]
		Liberator [C1]

TABLE 20.2 Mentor Pedagogy Toolbox – Dyadic Microsystem components

DYADIC MICROSYSTEM: The immediate social context which includes mentor-mentee agreement, relational characteristics and quality of the relationship (Chandler 2011, p. 256)

Multiple perspectives

In mentoring programmes, all parties are likely to interpret the activity differently [C2]

In mentoring dyads, both parties will seek to recontextualise the mentoring activity and simultaneously reconstruct themselves. [C2]

The learner-centred model outlined in this chapter recognises that mentor pedagogy is 'essentially idiosyncratic' because 'each instance of mentoring is based on a unique relationship involving an extremely complex interplay of cognitive, affective and interpersonal factors' (Hawkey 1997, p. 326). [C9]

The role of mentor evolves and is inextricably linked to the specific needs of each student teacher and their relative stage of teacher development. 'Mentoring support is most effective when it is adjusted to the needs of student or beginning teachers' (Krull 2005, p. 147). [C9]

The environment in which the mentor/master–mentee relationship occurs has been identified as being an important factor on the openness and willingness of a practitioner to critically reflect on practices with which they are familiar (Handcock and Cassidy, in press). [C15 TC]

Quality of the mentoring process

It's not just about the relationships, it's about the quality of the conversations (Cavanagh 2006, p. 318) across the three reflective spaces [mentor, mentee and mentor-mentee]. [C3]

If we do not engage in the correct mentor training, we are just 'well meaning amateurs' (Cavanagh 2006). [C3]

Coach reflexivity on the coach-athletes' relationships would benefit from discussing their holistic coaching relationship with the athlete as well as another knowledgeable person. [C18]

Accessible – being available to the mentee for on-going development. There are no time gaps in the relationship, but a continuous partnership. [C1]

The power of mentoring

Transformative learning: Effective mentor pedagogies promote transformative learning through Daloz's (1986) model of supporting and challenging the mentee which advances the holistic development of the adult learner as both person and professional. This is done through the dyad actively examining dilemmas (Dominguez and Hager, p. 176). [C3]

It is important to consider how the impact of the mentoring relationship might be captured. For example, Costa and Garmston (1994) suggested the following 'checklist' in capturing how participants proceed to use their new knowledge:

- Increased self-efficacy
- Addressing a multiplicity of challenges
- Identifying gaps in domains of knowledge
- Re-visiting beliefs, values and actions
- Adopting an interdependent approach in working with others in seeking solutions [C17]

Mutual benefits

Enabling teachers to continue to grow, learn and be excited about their work depends on both on-going, high-quality learning opportunities and career opportunities that enable them to share their expertise in a variety of ways (Darling-Hammond and Lieberman 2012, p. 164). [C9]

Mentoring may be viewed as a reciprocal relationship, mutually beneficial for both mentor and mentee. Mentors engage in a process of self-reflection as they articulate and model best practice for student teachers that they mentor. 'Serving as a mentor pushes one not only to model but also to be accountable for that modelling' (Weasmer and Woods 2003, p. 69). [C9]

Given a shared vision for the mentoring process, both mentors and mentees can have a valuable educational experience. It is highly rewarding for mentors to feel that their learning and experience are esteemed by mentees and it can be empowering for mentees to have the opportunity to express and explore opinions in a supportive atmosphere. [C12]

Fine-tuning the process

Tele-mentoring: the use of telephones in mentoring, for quicker, more personal, and deeper exchanges. [C14]

TABLE 20.3 Mentor Pedagogy Toolbox – Developmental/Network/Multiple Microsystem components

---

DEVELOPMENTAL/NETWORK/MULTIPLE MICROSYSTEM: The immediate social context which includes the diversity of social spheres represented in a person's developmental network (Chandler 2011, p. 256)

Partnership approach to mentoring [multiple sites]

Developing networks of mentors [C4] to support professional learning.

The success of the Telemachus Project was due of the development of a strong school-university partnership. [C11]

This school-university partnership imbued mutual trust (Trubowitz 1986), reciprocal learning (Callahan and Martin 2007), reflective practice (Schon 1987) and ultimately, a shared, logical idea of teacher education (McIntyre et al. 1996; Hardy 1999). Therefore, this school-university partnership was ideally placed to provide a strong platform to support the transition of cooperating teachers to their new role as PE teacher mentors. [C11]

If in a partnership, it is beneficial to look for multiple ways to connect and contribute to each other's learning community. [C19]

When everyone is positioned as a learner, there is joint responsibility by the community to solve problems. There is a no-blame culture. It is about working together toward a solution and learning from the process. Success at any level is also shared by the community, for example, if the novice coach has finally learned how to manage a group of young excitable athletes, that is success for the athletes, coach, mentor and the partner organisations. [C19]

Mentoring programmes are an investment in volunteer and club development. This is an attractive incentive for local sports clubs as it encourages people to volunteer and helps to retain them in that role. [C8]

The majority of people who volunteer commit 3–6 years to the organization (Cuskelly 2008). Learning needs for those new to volunteering or to a specialist role (i.e. coaches, managers, club secretary) require a combination of knowledge, skills, and social connection. Volunteers want personal contact when learning and their preference is that it is locally available. [C8]

The challenge for any local sport club is to build an environment where learning is central and knowledge is distributed across all members. It is a long-term investment requiring cultural change and buy-in from all participants. It should be seen as a long-term project. [C8]

TABLE 20.4 Mentor Pedagogy Toolbox – Organisational Microsystem components

ORGANISATIONAL MICROSYSTEM: The immediate social context which includes organizational influences (e.g. formal mentoring program attributes (Chandler 2011, p. 256)

Finding the 'right' mentor

'Assigning' effective formal mentors is a challenging task. [C2]

Purposeful matching of mentor and mentee would be appropriate. By implementing this, empathy and understanding within the dyad can potentially be established. [C5]

Informal/found mentors are likely to be very powerful and may act to support a mentee by reinforcing current beliefs and prior assumptions. [C2]

Mentoring programmes and relationships designed to satisfy mentees' needs and goals increase their probability of success by providing the right type of mentoring at the right time, by matching mentees with appropriate mentors, and by helping mentees to learn with a method that best suits them. [C3]

Cross-cultural mentoring in the Physical Education context requires considerable interpersonal skills, emotional maturity and empathy on the part of the mentor. [C5]

Mentoring relationships need to be cultivated and constructed, and should not be thrown together. [C16]

Having a mentor coach from outside the sport may provide the mentee coach with opportunities, and the safety, to critically reflect, not only on his/her practices but also on the 'taken-for-granted' cultural practices of the sport. [C15]

The role of the mentor

The mentor needs to be *both* suitable, i.e. possess the right disposition for the role, *and* 'participate in appropriate and informed mentor training and development opportunities' (Chambers *et al.* 2012; Hobson and Malderez 2013, p. 13). [C3]

Long-Term Strategy: Thought should be given to how youth mentoring relationships are set up, supported and sustained, in order to ensure the process is effective, constructive and meaningful for all involved (Rappaport 2002). Included within this should be some element of planning for the end of structured mentor relationships, with the identification of clear pathways to additional/alternative/follow-on support. [C4]

The mentor's role should be to provide and support authentic learning experiences. [C16]

The purpose of mentoring should be to help the coach develop their cognitive skills in progressing towards an increasingly autonomous and expert position. [C17]

Mentors (and organisations) should conceive the role in terms of developing coaches' knowledge in reflective thinking, cognitive development and problem-solving (Schunk and Mullen 2013). [C17]

Peer mentor training for HPETE practicum programs engages all parties in an exploration and clarification of the roles, expectations and teaching philosophies circulating within the HPETE practicum. [C13]

One specific area of tension that has arisen in teacher education, which could also be an issue in coach education/development, is the relationship between domain-specific expertise and the ability to be a good mentor. [C15]

Components of effective mentor training programmes

Mentors as 'Informal Educators' training strategy. [C4]

Provide space for the new programme to develop and establish a solid foundation before embedding it in organizational core practice. [C19]

Mentor training is advocated as a form of continuing professional development within the Continuum of Teacher Education (Teaching Council of Ireland 2011); 'mentors should view the development of these knowledge and skills as opportunities to strengthen their professional practice as lifelong learners' (Kajs 2002, p. 62). [C9]

Privileging technocratic rationality, providing 'tool boxes' or 'tricks of the trade' as professional knowledge is additive, grafting on new knowledge to existing understandings. It leaves contextual and cultural norms unexamined and unchallenged. Mentoring and its training should be critical and transformative. [C16]

A cognitive approach to mentor training would integrate the following:

Content. Support mentors in constructing a mentoring knowledge base: learning strategies (e.g. interactions between mentor and coach might be active, social and creative); domain knowledge (e.g. building relationships, resolving difficulties, encouraging critical reflection); heuristics strategies ('tricks of the trade'). [C17]

Pedagogy. Mentors need to understand factors that will facilitate coach learning, for example, the use of scaffolding (e.g. direction), conversations that are relevant and authentic to practice, reasoning/problem-solving, critical reflection. [C17]

Sequencing. Mentors should be mindful in matching coaches' competencies and skills with mentoring tasks; they should identify a mentoring model that would underpin the mentoring process (e.g. Apprenticeship Model, Competency Model, Reflective Practitioner Model). [C17]

Training strategies should support mentors in creating effective relationships, underpinned by contemporary learning theories. Evidence suggests this would secure the cognitive, behavioural, motivational and affective processes that impact the outcomes claimed on behalf of mentoring. [C17]

The early stages of learning require large amounts of cognitive space. Organisations should find ways of distributing knowledge, for example, they may have novice coaches working in pairs, so that they have time to reflect in action and make considered adjustments and be proactive in their practice rather than responsive to the current situation. [C19]

Reflection in action provides immediate feedback and enables the novice coach to test other strategies in a similar context and reflect on practice. [C19]

Reflections from mentors and novice coaches should be submitted within 24 hours to capture critical learning incidents that may be lost or reconstructed incorrectly with time. [C19]

Creating opportunities for critical reflection should not be considered a mere luxury, but an essential pre-requisite to enhance, where possible, the congruency of messages within the triadic relationship and to ensure peer mentors have the best possible opportunity to enact their role according to mutuality, collaboration and equality (Awaya et al. 2003; Stanulis and Russell 2000). [C13]

Mentoring experience can be shared by using a 'feedback loop' in training. [C4]

Mentor training needs to have a strong reflexive component which challenges the mentor to develop a mature awareness of their own racial assumptions. [C5]

A more gender-inclusive pedagogy in Physical Education needs to be inculcated. For this broad aim to be achieved, the schools-based mentor, as a conduit between old and new generations of PE teachers, is in a position to interrupt the downward transmission of pedagogies centred on hegemonic masculinity. [C6]

(continued)

TABLE 20.4 *(continued)*

An awareness of the socially constructed nature of gender in society needs to be embedded in mentor training. [C6]

Pedagogies that de-emphasise physical confrontation and muscularity need to be encouraged and promoted by the mentor. As Gorely and her colleagues (2003) have argued, if PE has physical empowerment as its goal, it should not promote activities that favour physical prowess, strength and the causing of physical harm to young people. [C6]

Physical education curricula need to encompass a broad range of activities that mentors and trainees, irrespective of gender, are competent in delivering. Problematically, it has been shown that in single-sex schools, the choice of PE activity is likely to be determined by gender and can, therefore, reinforce gender stereotypes (Stidder and Hayes 2006, p. 330). [C6]

Inclusion of 'alternative movement forms' that prioritise aesthetic above competitive components could reduce the potential alienating effects of the existing system (Rich 2004, p. 236). Activities that minimise competitive elements such as dance and gymnastics, if accorded equal priority to competitive sports, can challenge dominant male behaviours. [C6]

Developing a pedagogy that tackles gender inequality requires a personal commitment to social justice on the part of the mentor and a desire to challenge the prevailing Gender Order. [C6]

A pedagogy that challenges racialised thinking needs to be developed (Dowling and Flintoff 2011). [C5]

Training should be incorporated in use of technology to enable mentors to engage fully in e-mentoring. [C14]

To increase the benefits of e-mentoring, several challenges must be addressed. First, what is the optimal structure to prompt discussion and reflection? [C14]

Finally, whatever the medium, how can a personal connection with a partner be developed and enhanced? In our study, that was at least partially accomplished by a blended model of a few face-to-face days with e-mentoring. [C14]

TABLE 20.5 Mentor Pedagogy Toolbox – Macrosystem components

MACROSYSTEM: Broader societal influences, i.e. cultural, technological and societal factors that exert influence on mentoring outcomes through their effect on ontogenic development and the microsystems. (Chandler 2011, p. 256)

Highly performative cultures influence the potential range and impact of mentoring programmes. [C2]

If learning is *the* business of teaching (and coaching), it could be argued that mentoring framed around deep understandings of both the theory and practice of learning could offer valuable and professionally challenging CPD possibilities. [C2]

Mentoring as a panacea? [C4]

Mentoring is assumed to be a benign and exclusively positive experience. Yet it exists in distinct cultures and contexts replete with power relationships. Ownership and purpose of the process need to be considered [C16]

Schools are now obliged to take the issue of 'race' and ethnicity seriously. Yet more effort needs to be made to ensure that teachers from ethnic minorities can operate in a productive, non-hostile environment. [C5]

In most countries, coach education/development programmes do not have the same historical or institutional support as teacher education programmes. [C15]

Conclusion

In this book, chapter authors have critically analysed a range of research on mentoring (and related studies) to reveal clear 'Lessons learned' for the mentor system. In this chapter, these 'Lessons learned' have been coded by the author and inserted into Chandler *et al.*'s (2011) multi-layer ecological system of mentoring. Readers can turn to the Ontogenic System to reveal the optimum characteristics of effective mentors. They can move to the Dyadic Microsystem to understand the nuances of the successful mentor-mentee relationship. If interested in how the partnership (e.g. school-university, national governing body–club) impacts on mentoring, they can turn to the Development/Network/Multiple Microsystem. If a reader is interested in what must be taken into consideration when designing the mentoring programme, the Organisation Microsystem will yield insights. Finally, if a more 'helicopter view' of the process is required, the Macrosystem will provide a clear oversight of societal factors impacting on mentoring. The Ontogenic, Microsystem and Macrosystem layers combine to form the 'Terroir of Mentoring' schematic, an ecological view of mentoring. This is the Mentor Pedagogy Toolbox.

Future directions

Chandler *et al.* (2011) purport that the majority of research to date has been within the Ontogenic System level and the Dyadic Microsystem level with a dearth of research at the Developmental Microsystem, Organisational Microsystem and Macrosystem levels. In addition, there appears to be a scarcity of multilevel research, with research focusing on one layer and not across layers or at the intersections between layers, which might capture the frenzy of transformative learning (Heaney 1995) for both mentor and mentee and the mentoring ecosystem as a whole. Perhaps this book has encouraged readers to construe mentoring a little differently, taking all aspects of the mentoring ecosystem into account.

Key terms: ontogenic, dyadic, organisation, microsystem, macrosystem, ecological system of mentoring.

References

Awaya, A., McEwan, H., Heyler, D., Linsky, S., Lum, D. and Wakukawa, P. 2003. Mentoring as a journey. *Teaching and Teacher Education,* 19, 45–56.

Bronfenbrenner, U. 1979. *The Ecology of Human Development: Experiments by Nature and Design.* Cambridge, MA: Harvard University Press.

Callahan, J. L. and Martin, D. 2007. The spectrum of school–university partnerships: A typology of organizational learning systems. *Teaching and Teacher Education,* 23, 136–145.

Cavanagh, M. 2006. Coaching from a systemic perspective: A complex adaptive conversation. In D. R. Stober and A. M. Grant (Eds.) *Evidence Based Coaching Handbook.* Hoboken, New Jersey: John Wiley & Sons.

Chambers, F. C. 2012. Storying the terroir of mentoring. *Australian Association of Research in Education.* University of Sydney, Australia.

Chambers, F. C. and Armour, K. 2012. School-university partnerships and physical education teacher education student learning: A fruitful division of labour? *European Physical Education Review*, 18(2), 159–181.

Chambers, F. C., Armour, K., Herold, F. A., McFlynn, P., Brennan, D. A. and Bleakley, E. W. 2014. Designing sustainable models of mentoring for sports clubs. *AIESEP World Congress*, University of Auckland, New Zealand.

Chambers, F. C., Armour, K., Luttrell, S., Bleakley, E. W., Brennan, D. A. and Herold, F. A. 2012. Mentoring as a profession-building process in physical education teacher education. *Irish Educational Studies*, 31, 345–362.

Chandler, D. E., Kram, K. E. and Yip, J. 2011. An ecological systems perspective on mentoring at work: A review and future prospects. *The Academy of Management Annals*, 5, 519–570.

Cuskelly, G. 2008. Volunteering in community sport organizations: Implications for social capital. In M. Nicholson and R. Hoye (Eds.) *Sport and Social Capital*, Oxford, United Kingdom: Elsevier, pp. 187–203.

Costa, A. and Garmston, R. 1994. *Cognitive Coaching: A Foundation for Renaissance Schools*. Norwood, Mass.: Christopher-Gordon.

Darling-Hammond, L. and Lieberman, A. 2012. *Teacher Education around the World*. London and New York: Routledge.

Dewey, J. 2004. *Democracy and Education*. New York: Courier Dover Publications.

Dominguez, N. and Hager, M. 2013. Mentoring frameworks: Synthesis and critique. *International Journal of Mentoring and Coaching in Education*, 2(3), 171–188.

Dowling, F. and Flintoff, A. 2011. Getting beyond the dilemmas of normative interview talk of sameness and celebrating difference. *Qualitative Research in Sport and Exercise*, 3(1), 63–79.

Gorely, T., Holroyd, R. and Kirk, D. 2003. Muscularity, the habitus and the social construction of gender: Towards a gender-relevant physical education. *British Journal of Sociology of Education*, 24, 429–448.

Handcock, P. and Cassidy, T. 2014. Reflective practice for rugby union strength and conditioning coaches. *Strength and Conditioning Journal*, 36(1), 44–45.

Handy, C. 1994. *The Empty Raincoat: Making Sense of the Future*. London: Hutchinson.

Hardy, C. A. 1999. Pre-service teachers' perceptions of learning to teach in a predominantly school-based teacher education program. *Journal of Teaching in Physical Education*, 18, 175–198.

Hawkey, K. 1997. Roles, responsibilities and relationships in mentoring: A literature review and agenda for research. *Journal of Teacher Education*, 48(5), 325–335.

Heaney, T. 1995. Learning to control democratically: Ethical questions in situated adult education. Proceedings of the 36th Annual Adult Education Research Conference, May 19–21 1995. Edmonton, Alberta: University of Alberta, pp. 147–152.

Hobson, J. P. A., Malderez, A. and Tomlinson, P. 2009. Mentoring beginning teachers: What we know and what we don't. *Teaching and Teacher Education*, 25, 207–216.

Huberman, M. 1989. The professional life cycle of teachers. *Teachers College Record*, 91, 31–57.

Kajs, L. T. 2002. Framework for designing a mentoring program for novice teachers. *Mentoring and Tutoring: Partnership in Learning*, 10(1), 57–69.

Krull, E. 2005. Mentoring as a means for supporting student and beginning teachers' practice-based learning. *TRAMES: A Journal of the Humanities & Social Sciences*, 9(59), 143–158.

Lave, J. and Wenger, E. 1991. *Situated Learning and Legitimate Peripheral Participation*. Cambridge: Cambridge Press.

McIntyre, D. and Hagger, H. 1996. *Mentors in Schools: Developing the Profession of Teaching*. London: David Fulton.

Mezirow, J. 1991. *Transformative Dimensions of Adult Learning.* San Francisco, CA: Jossey-Bass.

Rappaport, N. 2002. Can advising lead to meaningful relationships? In J. Rhodes (Ed.) *A Critical View of Youth Mentoring: New Directions for Youth Development.* San Francisco, CA: Jossey-Bass.

Resnick, L. 1994. Situated rationalism: Biological and social preparation for learning. In L. A. Hirschfeld and S. A. Gelman (Eds.) *Mapping the Mind: Domain Specificity in Cognition and Culture.* Cambridge: Cambridge University Press.

Rich, E. 2004. Exploring teachers' biographies and perceptions of girls' participation in Physical Education. *European Physical Education Review,* 10(2), 220–245.

Schon, D. 1987. *Educating the Reflective Practitioner: Toward a New Design for Teaching and Learning in the Professions.* San Francisco, CA: Jossey-Bass.

Schunk, D. H. and Mullen, C. A. 2013. Motivation. In J. Hattie and E. M. Anderman (Eds.), *International Guide to Student Achievement.* New York: Routledge, pp. 67–69.

Stanulis, R. N. and Russell, D. 2000. 'Jumping in': Trust and communication in mentoring student teachers. *Teaching and Teacher Education,* 16(1), pp. 65–80.

Stidder, G. and Hayes, S. 2006. A longitudinal study of physical education trainee teachers' experiences on school placements in the south-east of England (1994-2004). *European Physical Education Review,* 12, 317–338.

Teaching Council of Ireland 2011. Policy on the continuum of teacher education. maynooth: Teaching Council of Ireland.

The Gestalt Centre London. 2013. *What is Gestalt?* [Online]. [Accessed 9th May 2014].

Tinbergen, N. 1951. *The Study of Instinct.* Oxford, England: Clarendon Press.

Trubowitz, S. 1986. *When a College Works With a Public School: A Case Study of School-College Collaboration.* Boston: Institute of Responsive Education.

Weasmer, J. and Woods, A. M. 2003. Mentoring: Professional development through reflection. *The Teacher Educator,* 39, 64–77.

INDEX